Historic Preservation

Historic Preservation

An Introduction to Its History, Principles, and Practice

Norman Tyler

W. W. Norton & Company
New York · London

Unless otherwise noted, the original sketches used throughout the book are by the author.

Copyright © 2000, 1994 by Norman Tyler

Previous edition published as *Issues in Historic Preservation*

The text of this book is set in Bembo with the display set in Bernhard Tango
Composition by Ken Gross
Manufacturing by Edwards Brothers
Book design by Charlotte Staub

ISBN 0-393-73039-5 (pbk)

W. W. Norton & Company, Inc., 500 Fifth Avenue, New York, NY 10110
www.wwnorton.com

W. W. Norton & Company Ltd., 10 Coptic Street, London WC1A 1PU

7 8 9 0

Contents

Therefore, when we build, let us think that we build for ever. Let it not be for present delight, nor for present use alone; let it be such work as our descendants will thank us for, and let us think, as we lay stone on stone, that a time is to come when those stones will be held sacred because our hands have touched them, and that men will say as they look upon the labor and wrought substance of them, "See! this our fathers did for us." For, indeed, the greatest glory of a building is not in its stones, or in its gold. Its glory is in its Age."

John Ruskin

Preface

The interest of the American public in historic preservation has grown tremendously since the nation's bicentennial year. There is now a wealth of preservation activity across the United States and publications concerned with these issues are abundant. This book, however, fills a void in the preservation literature. This single text presents the full range of preservation topics, from a look at basic preservation philosophies to presenting techniques of rehabilitation economic analysis. Although other authors—many listed in the bibliography—explore these and other subjects in greater detail, this book serves as a primer on historic preservation issues. In layman's language, it serves as a reference for students, home-owners, local officials, and community leaders.

Originally written to serve as a text for my course in historic preservation at Eastern Michigan University, this much-revised book benefited greatly from the comments of Dorothy Miner, a lawyer and consultant in historic preservation, who clarified many of the legal issues associated with historic preservation, and Thomas Jester of the National Park Service, who reviewed the many references to federal programs and made substantive suggestions for improvement. I am grateful for the time and energy they devoted to making this a better and more accurate text; any inaccuracies that remain are my own.

Finally, I thank Ilene Tyler, my wife, who provided counsel throughout, made available the considerable resources of her firm, Quinn Evans/Architects, and wrote the chapter on preservation technology.

Chapter 1

Introduction

This book introduces readers to the many facets of historic preservation. As a society, we have always had some appreciation of our cultural and architectural heritage, but in the last few decades Americans have become increasingly aware of the significance of our historic structures and sites and have recognized how fast we have been losing many of them. They are irreplaceable. It is our duty, as a society and as a community, to protect and preserve our heritage, which is deep and rich. Preservationists in every state of the union have been campaigning to preserve the best of it, and with the help of organizations ranging from the National Trust for Historic Preservation to local historical associations and historic district and landmark commissions, the preservation movement has established itself as both powerful and integral to virtually every community.

Readers might consider their potential role in preservation by developing an awareness of preservation's role in their own communities. Are the activities described in the following pages appropriate? Are the communities doing enough to protect their heritage? Are they doing too much, imposing their will too aggressively and infringing the property rights of others? The following chapters are intended to present issues from a variety of perspectives so readers can draw their own conclusions about the role of historic preservation in our everyday lives.

What role is historic preservation meant to play in our society? This question is being debated by numerous organizations, agencies, and individuals across the country. Among property owners and developers, in city council chambers, even during historic district commission meetings, questions arise: Does preservation stand in the way of progress? Is it appropriate to establish new restrictions on property owners? Who should determine what is historically significant?

Is Historic Preservation Un-American?

Since the bicentennial year of 1976, the American public has developed deeper interest in the preservation of the country's architectural heritage. Individuals and organizations have supported historic preservation activities for over a century, but in the last two or three decades interest on the part of the general public has increased markedly. Preservation receives significant consideration at the federal and state levels, but is especially dynamic at the local level in communities of all sizes and in all parts of the United States.

Yet the role of historic preservation is still being defined, and many perspectives remain to be explored. Clem Labine, publisher of the magazine *Traditional Building*, considered the role of the preservationist in a 1979 article titled "Preservationists Are Un-American":

And then it hit me. The more I inquired into the forces that make preservationists do the things we do, the more I realized that preservation is really un-American. . . . the fact is that preservation goes against the basic historical thrust that built America into a world power. America was built on the concept of the frontier. Land was limitless. Resources were never-ending. The pioneer way was to use it up, throw it away and move west.

. . . So where do preservationists fit into this scheme of things? Are we merely folks who think that the apex of civilization was reached in the 19th century and are vainly trying to recreate that vanished world? No, we are not making futile, reactionary gestures. Rather, we represent the cutting edge of a true cultural revolution, a revolution generating new perceptions that will have a dramatic impact on America's way of thinking in the next 50 years.

That is why we are un-American. Preservationists oppose the conventional American idea of consuming ever more. We are actually the new wave of pioneer. We are struggling to reverse the "use it up and move on" mentality. We are moving in and picking up the pieces. We are taking individual buildings and whole neighborhoods that have been discarded and trying to make them live again. We are cleaning up after society's litterbugs.[1]

These are strong words with which to challenge the American psyche. American tradition does not focus on preservation but rather on opportunism. Even the founding fathers can be seen as opportunistic. The new Americans strove to leave their old-world traditions behind and to strike forth on an adventure in the uncharted wilderness of the frontier. Such growth was long ago recognized as this country's "manifest destiny."

Why, then, do preservationists counter this thrust and feel so strongly committed to preserving the past, when America's challenge is in its

Crossroads Village, Flint, Michigan

future? To answer that question, it is important to recognize that preservationists are not against growth and development. Rather, they see growth as built on the past. "The past is prologue," a phrase commonly used to represent this perspective, challenges us as a society to base our plans for growth on our past—to look at how our society has evolved historically, and to have that past serve as a guide for the future. The word *preserve*, when broken into its root forms "pre-serve," includes the concept of contributing to the future. As stated by John Lawrence, dean of Tulane's school of architecture, "The basic purpose of preservation is not to arrest time, but to mediate sensitively with the forces of change. It is to understand the present as a product of the past and a modifier of the future."[2]

The twentieth century has been an era of unprecedented change. As a people, we realized we could accomplish virtually anything—and in shorter and shorter periods of time. The process of change is now so rapid it is almost impossible to observe. That is why historic preservation has taken on such significance in recent decades. Adele Chatfield-Taylor discussed this perspective in a presentation celebrating Columbia University's program in historic preservation.

So it is no wonder that an interest in historic preservation (a puny term to describe a gigantically important moment in this progression) surfaces in earnest in the early part of the twentieth century, in the swirling midst of these other developments.

. . . It is our increasing lack of access to a familiar world that has generated a hunger for the sight and touch of a gritty reality that old buildings provide—and not impenetrably preserved, bionic old buildings—but buildings that have registered the imprint of the passage of time. Old buildings that are a time line, old buildings that are real.

. . . [T]he technological ability to build 100-story buildings on every square inch of the face of the earth—whether it be Madison Avenue, Times Square, or the plains of Kansas—is not necessarily a mandate to do so. . . . In a sense, then, historic preservation represents a desire to reduce this power to a possibility rather than an inevitability.[3]

The momentum of the historic preservation movement has increased because, as a society, we recognize the importance of not just making new and better but of preserving reminders of the past as well. In the past, we needed to tame the vast landscape of the United States. Eighteenth- and nineteenth-century Americans saw themselves as conquerors of nature and as builders of cities. But now nature is conquered and most of the American landscape is either cultivated or built upon. This allows us, for the first time, to address the issues of quality of life and to recognize elements worthy of preservation, even if they no longer serve a primary economic function. A society is matured when its primary focus shifts from the quantitative to the qualitative. This maturation is evident when we recognize that we must preserve our built heritage because it is part of what we are as a people and as a community.

More and more, we recognize that our past is integral to our future. Peter Eisenmann, the architect and theorist, gives a graphic example to consider. Imagine, he suggests, a picture of an arrow:

Eisenmann arrow

An object (the arrow) is represented in this picture. Whether the arrow is static or in flight cannot be perceived. And yet the situation is entirely different depending on what is understood. An arrow at rest is simply an object, but an arrow in motion is part of a much richer story, for it has both a shooter and a target. How can we understand the arrow without understanding where it began and where it is going? Its current position, as portrayed in the drawing, is but a small part of that story, and much of the meaning is lost without knowing the larger context of time and place.

Similarly with our cities. An older district in an American city is often seen only in terms of its current condition. It can be viewed as a collection of neglected structures and businesses with little to offer. However, this perspective overlooks too much. To fully appreciate such an older historic district, we must consider its current status within the context of time and look at both its past and its future. As we recognize its richness by looking back in time, we are able to better understand its potential as we look forward.

The role of historic preservation is to ensure that such critical perspectives are not ignored and to insist that our society looks carefully both at where it has been and where it is going. As the writer I. L. Peretz said, "Not only an individual, but a people, too, must possess a memory. A people's memory is called history. What is true of an individual without memory is also true of a people without history: they cannot become wiser or better."[4]

NOUNS AND VERBS

Historic preservation can be understood in many ways. One useful analogy is to think of the preservation of buildings in terms of nouns and verbs. When buildings are viewed as objects, they are nouns. They make up a part of the physical presence of a space. Thinking of historic landmarks in terms of their physical structure is the most prevalent viewpoint. But they should be seen as more than that. If they also are seen as places of involvement—where historic events took place—then we can see them also as verbs. In other words, buildings can be seen as part of history and not only as static structures.

Just as nouns and verbs are both needed to make a complete sentence, both the noun and verb aspects of historic buildings are needed to describe their full significance. Preservationists need to recognize that the preservation of historic buildings should include not only the physical structure but also the history of the place. Only in this way does a historic building maintain its full meaning. To consider the spaces within and around buildings as part of their living history allows historic structures a more active and significant role within the community.

Therefore, preservation should be seen as more than the protection of older buildings. Preserving buildings only as inanimate structures makes them period set pieces—objects of curiosity, but not much more. This can lead, in the absurd, to the kind of protection represented by the text on a sign found in a South Carolina gas station:[5]

> *In order to preserve the architectural traditions of Charleston, the brickwork and woodwork of the demolished Gabriel Manigault house 1800 AD were used in this station.*

The preservation represented in this sign is little more than tokenism and serves little real purpose. Surely we can do better than that.

The grammatical analogy can be applied to the exhibits in historical museums. Conventionally, such museums are places where historical items are collected, archived, and displayed. The basic function is to display artifacts in a gallery for the public to view.

Curators have become aware, however, that visitors' interest in historical artifacts increases significantly if objects are displayed in their actual environment rather than in museum display cases, which gives the artifacts a richer context.

The impression on a visitor can be enhanced through live recreations of historical events by actors in period costumes. Sometimes this format is carried even further, and visitors are drawn in, to become active participants. A good example of this type of "living history museum" is Plimoth Plantation in Massachusetts.

In 1969, a living village replaced the conventional static exhibits at Plimoth Plantation with a daily ongoing reenactment of seventeenth-

Recreation of Plimoth Plantation

Settler at
Plimoth Plantation

century life in the original Plimoth colony. By 1978, a personal approach was adopted: everyday village activities are performed by staff dressed in period costumes. Plimoth Plantation is now inhabited, at least during museum hours, by these "residents." The public is invited to walk through the re-created 1620s settlement and strike up neighborly conversations with whomever they wish. The actors, who have thoroughly studied the dossiers of the individuals they portray, pretend to know only seventeenth-century life, so visitors must adapt to that historical perspective in order to talk with them. The Plantation's residents often question visitors on their strange dialect and look askance at their "heathen" manner of dress. However, they are a friendly group and willing to share information about their activities.

The ability to go beyond static representation of artifacts (history as nouns) and to present history as a complete environment (history as verbs) is the source of the success of Plimoth Plantation and other such museums.

With this in mind, local historians can keep alive their community's history by preserving its structures. For example, a community's courthouse square can not only be saved but *used* as a point of congregation for community events. Similarly, older residences can be protected from demolition while the spirit of the neighborhood is encouraged through organizations and events. In these ways, a town can preserve its cultural heritage in the process of preserving its buildings.

PRESERVATION PHILOSOPHIES

The underlying philosophy of the historic preservation movement in the United States is defined more through activities than through theory. One could conclude "Preservation is as preservation does," for preservationists bring many perspectives to the field. Some see their role primarily as saving old buildings, some as preserving a cultural heritage, some as urban revitalization, and some as an alternative approach to current development practices.

Preservationists bring a diversity of approaches even to so basic an activity as saving old buildings. Some individuals feel historic structures should be kept in their original state or, if they have been altered, that they should be returned to the original state. Others feel they should protect the overall historic character but that change can and should be accommodated. The pendulum swings with the times and the circumstances. What is considered an appropriate response in one instance may be seen quite differently in another. Indeed, as a society, Americans have changed considerably in their views. In the 1950s and 1960s, the prevailing attitude was that little that was old was good. In an age of space travel, new technologies, and the revolutions in transportation and communications, the new was considered far superior to the old. Attitudes have shifted considerably since then. Some now see new development as the cause of a significant deterioration of our communities and the environment. They look on older, "simpler" times as superior. The debate will continue, as it has for generations.

The issue of old versus new was also part of the debate among nineteenth-century "preservationists." The contrast in opinions was nowhere greater than the differences found in the writings of the French architect Eugène Emmanuel Viollet-le-Duc and the English art historian and essayist John Ruskin.

EUGÈNE EMMANUEL VIOLLET-LE-DUC

Viollet-le-Duc (vee'-o-lay leh dewk) was one of the first master builders concerned with the restoration of landmarks. Previously, buildings either followed a natural course of deterioration or were informally maintained by local craftsmen. Viollet-le-Duc changed this attitude. He not only devoted his career to restoration work (and is considered the first restoration architect) but also presented his methods, technology, and philosophy in a series of books, including a ten-volume dictionary of architecture. Although much of his philosophy of restoration is now discounted by historic preservation professionals, the knowledge of historical and technical information that he cataloged is invaluable. His work had no precedent and was highly influential.

Church of La Madeleine de Vézelay, restored by Eugène Emmanuel Viollet-le-Duc

Viollet-le-Duc's restoration philosophy was that important monuments should be rebuilt not necessarily as they originally were but as they "should have been." "To restore a building is not only to preserve it, to repair it, or to rebuild, but to bring it back to a state of completion such as may never have existed at any given moment."[6]

For his first major project, the church called La Madeleine de Vézelay in France, new stone elements were sculpted to duplicate the old and new statuary—not of original design but which Viollet-le-Duc deemed compatible—installed.

After Viollet-le-Duc's death, one critic, Paul Léon, disagreed with his approach, saying, "A monument to be a testimony to the past must stay as the past has bequeathed it. To pretend to restore it to its original state is dangerous and deceitful; we must preserve buildings as they are, respecting the contribution of successive generations."[7] Because he

*Third Santa Barbara
County Courthouse, 1927*

added new elements and embellished without appropriate historical basis, Viollet-le-Duc's restoration methods are now discredited.

Contemporary examples based more or less on his philosophy do exist. The city of Santa Barbara, California, was largely destroyed by an earthquake in 1925. The downtown had to be rebuilt almost from scratch. City authorities saw this as an opportunity to establish new, firm design controls. They determined that newly constructed buildings would be in the Spanish mission style and established a board of architectural review to ensure the city was rebuilt thus uniformly. Much of the new construction since then has been in this style, giving an almost unparalleled uniformity to the streetscape. The guiding philosophy adopted by Santa Barbara was that the image of the city would be better than before, just as Viollet-le-Duc advocated.

In contrast to Viollet-le-Duc, nineteenth-century writer and critic John Ruskin felt that older buildings should not be restored but should remain untouched. He argued that a society has no right to improve, or even restore, the craftsmanship of another era. As he explained in *The Seven Lamps of Architecture*, "It is impossible, as impossible as to raise the dead, to restore anything that has ever been great or beautiful in architecture." Old buildings should be left to look old, he argued. They gain their beauty only after four or five centuries, and the richness of their beauty is enhanced when seen as ruins. "The greatest glory of a building is not in its stones, or in its gold. Its glory is in its Age." Ruskin felt that buildings should be built to last: "When we build, let us think that we build forever."[8]

Who are we to try to restore a former glory? Ruskin asked. In his mind, restoration was comparable to erasing the character evident in the face of an older person through plastic surgery, trying to make that person look young again. The beauty in age lines should be respected rather than artificially changed. We often want to make older buildings look too perfect, to restore them to a state where they look more like museum pieces than buildings used daily. "We have a tendency to clean old buildings too much, to strip them of their age and character, to make them look too new, and to turn them into spectacles, rather than allow them to look old and merely befriended."[9]

Ruskin saw restoration as that same type of artificiality, which he termed an "indiscreet zeal for restoration."

> Restoration may possibly . . . produce good imitation of an ancient work of art; but the original is then falsified, and in its restored state it is no longer an example of the art of the period to which it belonged. [In fact,] the more exact the imitation the more it is adapted to mislead posterity.
>
> No restoration should ever be attempted, otherwise than . . . in the sense of preservation from further injuries. . . . Anything beyond this is untrue in art, unjustifiable in taste, destructive in practice, and wholly opposed to the judgment of the best Archaeologists.
>
> Do not let us talk then of restoration. The thing is a Lie from beginning to end.[10]

ANOTHER PERSPECTIVE: THE CHINESE VIEW

Not all cultures see preservation as saving older structures. For example, the Chinese see it as the saving of images through art or writings. Perhaps because theirs is an ancient culture in a crowded country whose thousands of historic sites each bear many layers of history, the Chinese do not consider the preservation of structures as critical. As described by David Lowenthal, professor emeritus of geography at University College, London:

> The Chinese endorse tradition in language and ideas but discard material remains or let them decay. Mao's orders to demolish ancient monuments were easy to carry out; few old structures had survived recurrent iconoclasm. Revering ancestral memory, the Chinese disdain the past's purely physical traces. Old works must perish for new ones to take their place. And Confucian precepts judge material possession a burdensome vice. In the traditional Chinese view, preserving objects and buildings reduces creation to commodity; it demeans both object and owner.[11]

TYPES OF INTERVENTION

Viollet-le-Duc and Ruskin, and others who followed them, presented divergent approaches to restoration and historic preservation. Over time, consideration of the more extreme viewpoints was tempered and refined and a general consensus formed as to the appropriate strategy for "intervention"—that is, what is done to the building.

In the United States, the National Park Service, within the Department of the Interior, administers preservation programs at the national level. The definitions of treatment standards and guidelines formulated by the department are now generally accepted. Each strategy has a special meaning and represents an intervention that may be appropriate for a particular situation. A review of these definitions, with examples of their application, points out differences as well as similarities.

PRESERVATION

The term *preservation* refers to the maintenance of a property without significant alteration to its current condition. This approach should be taken when it is appropriate to maintain a building or structure as is. A structure changes over its lifetime and each change represents a part of its history and integrity. The preservation of a historic building accepts those changes but maintains its historic integrity and as much original fabric or features as possible. According to the Secretary of the Interior's *Guidelines*, the definitive sourcebook for appropriate building intervention techniques, "Changes which may have taken place in the course of time are evidence of the history and development of a building, structure, or site and its environment. These changes may have acquired significance in their own right, and this significance shall be recognized and respected.[12]

Pike Place Market, Seattle, Washington

When preservation is the appropriate strategy, the only intervention is normal maintenance or special work needed to protect the structure against further damage.

Seattle's Pike Place Market applies preservation techniques in an innovative way.[13] This old city market was threatened with demolition to make way for an urban renewal project. However, the residents of Seattle considered the market an important part of their city's life and culture and wanted to preserve it. A citywide ballot proposal provided clear evidence that most people wanted the market saved.

Soon city planners perceived a new problem. They recognized that the market might be so successful that its character would change into that of a boutique center and lose its original character as a somewhat scruffy everyday market run by local farmers and small entrepreneurs. To prevent this, the city developed an ordinance that not only protected the structure from demolition but also from becoming trendy in its appearance and operation.

The protective ordinance deals with two primary considerations. The first part states that the structure must remain common, or ordinary, in its construction materials. If any structural material deteriorates, it should be repaired, if possible. If it must be replaced, the replacement material may not be of a quality different from the original. In other words, a solid wood beam cannot be replaced by a wood box beam or steel beam—only by another solid wood beam. Similarly, the ordinance provides protection via the market's management techniques by specifying that all vendors either make or grow their own products. This prevents upscale franchisees from becoming the primary market tenants.

The city also tries to maintain the ambience of the market's neighborhood, which consists largely of low-income, single-room occupancy (SRO) housing inhabited by transients. Rather than pushing this segment of society out to another area of the city to allow for gentrification (see Chapter 6), the city insists the neighborhood buildings retain their SRO function.

The Pike Place Market area uses these unusual preservation measures to retain, at many levels, the character that residents first recognized and loved and then protected.

RESTORATION

Restoration refers to the process of returning a building to its condition at a specific time period, often to its original condition. Restoration of a building is appropriate when portions of a structure's historic integrity are lost or where its importance at one time was particularly significant. A decision made to restore to a defined time period recognizes that importance. This decision must be made carefully, for it means ignoring the natural evolution of the building and creating, essentially, a contrived picture of its survival. However, if a building has a past of great significance, then restoration may be justified.

Frank Lloyd Wright's home and studio in Oak Park, Illinois, is an example. Over the decades, the structure was modified many times and eventually split into apartments. A foundation established to preserve the Wright home and studio purchased the property. A program of restoration was begun, but restoration architects and conservationists faced a problem. Wright had lived in the home for many years and had continually added to and modified the structure. Beginning as a small, modest home, the property gradually became an elaborate complex of wings and additions. Thus, the decision to restore made it necessary to choose a specific period of its construction for restoration. Restoring it to one period meant excluding elements from other periods.

After intensive study and discussion, the decision was made to restore the property to the year 1913, Wright's last year there. The foundation then undertook an extensive study of the original plans, photographs, and other archival material to determine what elements remained from

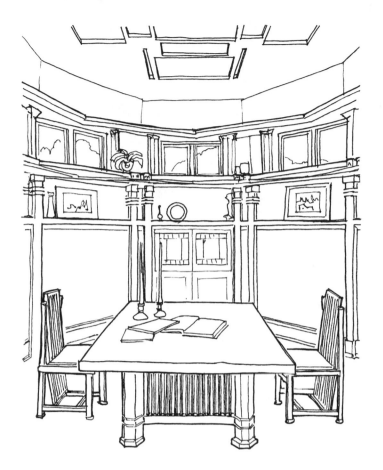

Restoration of interior, Frank Lloyd Wright Home and Studio, Oak Park, Illinois

that period and which had to be reconstructed. Changes made after 1913 were removed.

A guiding principle of good restoration practice is that an original element, even if in poor condition, is preferable to a replicated element. Historical conjecture is especially discouraged. If documentation does not show an original element, then it is generally better to leave it out or, if necessary, replace it with a compatible contemporary element. Restoration work should not be based on guesses about what a historical element might have been (as Viollet-le-Duc did) but should work from actual evidence, even if limited. As stated in the Secretary of the Interior's *Guidelines*, "Repair or replacement of missing architectural features should be based on accurate duplications of features, substantiated by historic, physical, or pictorial evidence rather than on conjectural designs or the availability of different architectural elements from other buildings or structures."[14]

House and barn, Cobblestone Farm, Ann Arbor, Michigan

Cobblestone Farm, a historic homestead in Ann Arbor, Michigan, is a property that includes an original farmhouse constructed with a cobblestone veneer exterior. The Cobblestone Farm Association, a group of volunteers, was formed to preserve this unique construction, restore the structure, and open it as a house museum to represent farm life in the nineteenth century.

The original farm included a barn, sheds, and other structures. Although the layout of the original farmstead was well documented in photographs, association members decided to relocate structures to better accommodate visitors and the frequent festivals and outdoor activities held at the site. Much of the farm's character was already altered because of its location in what is now a developed portion of the city, along a busy thoroughfare and surrounded by a large city park, so these revisions were considered acceptable.

A large barn was needed to complete the group of buildings and to serve as an assembly and office facility. As the farm's original barn no longer existed, the association had three options: (1) to reconstruct or replicate the original barn based on available photographs, (2) to find an existing barn from that era at another location and move it to the site, and (3) to design a contemporary barnlike structure. They selected the third option as as the best way to accommodate the space needs for new uses. A new barn could also meet modern building code requirements, including universal access, and yield rental income that could be applied to the restoration costs of the house.

From a preservationist viewpoint, however, this choice was the least desirable. The barnlike design was neither an authentic replication of an existing structure nor a compatible contemporary design. Instead, it tried to be both, and failed. Visitors to the historic farm complex may be confused as to whether or not this structure was part of the grouping of otherwise authentic historic structures. Some elements (e.g., post-and-beam framing, barn wood siding) make it appear to be, yet other elements (e.g., window treatment, elevator) are clearly out of place. This kind of confusion, unfortunately, can cast doubt on the authenticity of restored structures in the complex as well.

The creation of history can be a problem for preservationists. Garrison Keillor, writer, performer, and observer of American lifestyles and traditions, put it succinctly when he noted, "The past was copied, quoted, and constantly looked at until one day, the country looked more like it used to than it ever had before."[15]

RECONSTRUCTION

The term *reconstruction* means the building of a historic structure using replicated design and/or materials. This approach is taken when a historic structure no longer exists but needs to be physically in place for contextual reasons. For example, when the Rockefeller family sponsored the restoration of historic Williamsburg, Virginia, many of the historic buildings remained and various intervention techniques were used on them. However, nothing remained of the Governor's Palace, which was the focus of the town's original layout until it was destroyed by fire in 1781.

Governor's Palace, Williamsburg, Virginia

Planners decided to reconstruct this building according to a design based on plans and descriptions that were still available, even though none of the original building remained. The original building plans were sketchy, so some aspects of the reconstruction were necessarily conjectural, but the discovery of some documentation provided information used to make the reconstruction as authentic as possible.

A different decision was made with respect to reconstruction of the Benjamin Franklin house in Philadelphia. The location of the house was known, but no documentation at all existed about the appearance of the structure. Any reconstruction would be based completely on conjecture. So the architects designed a metal framework to represent the outline of a typical house of the period and constructed it on the site of the original home. It spatially represents the location of the house and its adjunct coach house but leaves no confusion over whether or not the structure is original.

REHABILITATION (ADAPTIVE USE)

Many historic buildings are no longer viable in their original function and use but retain their architectural integrity. For these structures, a common type of intervention is rehabilitation, also referred to as *adaptive use*. Rehabilitation describes a suitable approach when existing historic features are damaged or deteriorated but modifications can be made to update portions of the structure, even adapting the building for a new purpose. Generally, the changes are most radical on the interior, where more latitude may be taken in making changes. To maintain the building's historic integrity, however, exterior changes are generally minimal.

When adaptive use is chosen as the appropriate intervention technique, alterations or additions may be made, but they should not be confused with original historic elements. New construction is typically contemporary in design and may be either compatible with or contrasting to the historic structure. Compatible design is new design that maintains some existing elements, such as scale, color, massing, proportions, and materials. It makes some ties to the older elements, if not fully matching them. Typically, the newer portion is architecturally expressed as supportive in design to the original building rather than in competition with it.

Contrasting design tries to respect the older structure by emphasizing differences rather than similarities. For instance, a sleek, dark glass office addition to an older brick structure may emphasize the distinctiveness of each rather than present one as subservient to the other. (See chapter 6 for more discussion of contextual design issues.)

Each design approach has its place, and owners and architects should carefully consider the appropriateness of the approach on a case-by-case basis.

PRESERVATION AND CONTEMPORARY ARCHITECTURE

Many contemporary writers and critics address issues of preservation. Their viewpoints vary widely, from those who see the need for greater sensitivity to historic context to those who feel it is largely irrelevant.

The architectural critic Vincent Scully has long been an advocate of preservation. He spoke unambiguously of the important role it has played in the rebuilding of older cities when he said to a group of architecture and planning students, "This rebuilding has been supported and helped in every way by the most important mass movement that I know of in modern history to affect architecture: historic preservation."[16]

Philip Johnson, one of the most quoted and controversial of today's architects, has also long been a preservation advocate, but qualifies his support. He feels much of current preservation is a sham. In a 1986 interview, he expressed clearly feelings at that time about preservation and the preservation movement. Johnson remarked that preservation is "rather a phony movement," for it tries to restrict change rather than encourage it. "Preservation can always be used as an argument to kill something," even if a proposed project is well planned, needed, and in the community's best interests. Challenging preservationists, he is hard on those who cannot distinguish what is old and significant from what is simply old. "Today, preservationists are trying to save everything, but there is no criterion for how important a building is.... Sentiment overlaps architecture and history.... It gets too broad, and every lady in tennis shoes feels that everything should be preserved. There is no judgment."[17]

Architect Robert Venturi is an iconoclast who brought a new way of thinking to architecture during the 1960s. He encouraged architects to break away from their immediate past and the decades of blind adherence to the unidimensional approach of the modernist movement, an architectural period best represented by Mies van der Rohe's famous dictum, "Less is more." Venturi reflected on the sterile designs of this Modernist period and saw value in reestablishing "a conscious sense of the past." He encouraged architects to see the past in a broad context and time frame. The past should again become part of the present, for, as he suggested, "Tradition is a matter of much wider significance." To see oneself only in one's own time period, and as a product of that time period, is to deny the richness of history and the meaning of that history to one's own time.

Venturi urged architects to see buildings and their designs not in terms of modernist simplicity but of "complexity and contradiction." In his landmark book of that name, Venturi defined the need for incorporating many aspects of architecture, both in time and in place. Architecture should be inclusive, with room for improvisation, for fragments, and for the tensions these produce.[18] This book opened the door for architects and their critics to accept historical architecture as an influence on contemporary design. Venturi loosened the straightjacket the profession had put on and showed how historic "references" could be reinterpreted and incorporated in new design. His influence was seminal to the 1970s postmodern period of architecture.

Robert A. M. Stern, an influential architect and educator, has been a leader of the postmodern movement in architecture, which represents a blending of the old and new and attempts to counter the sterility found in architecture from the 1950s and 1960s. Postmodernism brings historical references back to architectural design. It is inspired primarily by classical styles, but with classical elements reinterpreted in contemporary terms. According to Stern:

There is a desire to return to the larger tradition of architecture—not to revive it, because no one can ever really revive anything. But we want to look again at the work of the past, classicism in particular, but also various vernacular styles, to see them afresh, to recombine them in new programs, new situations, new techniques. We want to forge a synthesis that bespeaks our time, but also make connections to the past, so that it does not seem strident or iconoclastic.[19]

Stern observed that postmodernists share an interest in three aspects of architectural design: (1) *contextualism*: the possibility for the future expansion of a given building and the desire to relate it to the immediate surroundings; (2) *allusionism*: references to the history of architecture that somehow go beyond "eclecticism" to a somewhat vague category called "the relationship between form and shape and the meanings that particular shapes have assumed over the course of time"; (3) *ornamentalism*: the simple pleasure in decorating architecture.[20] This merging of modern technology with historical richness has created an architecture full of possibilities.

But what kind of critiques do preservation professionals give about the preservation movement? Peter Neill, president of the South Street Seaport Museum in New York City, spoke of the need for a fuller understanding of the role of preservation in his speech to the 1991 National Preservation Conference:

What is historic preservation? Preservation is uncommon-place. It is a face-to-face confrontation with the past. It is an epiphany as enthralling as a new metaphor. It is an equation between self and history so powerful that it makes us lie down in front of bulldozers, raise toppled statues, salvage old boats.[21]

As shown throughout this chapter, many perspectives are brought to the field of historic preservation. Historic preservation does not have set rules to follow. Rather, its supporters constructively argue over how to preserve all types of historic properties in all types of situations. The four types of intervention presented here represent simply a departure point for these discussions, rather than a culmination.

People bring various interests and perspectives to their involvement in preservation. Some individuals want to take a hands-off approach to historic structures, and their tendency is to protect each historic property from change. Other individuals feel the historic significance of properties evolves over time, and a strict protectionist approach removes preservation too much from the mainstream of our culture and our communities. Whether the viewpoints are represented by Viollet-le-Duc versus Ruskin, or Johnson versus Venturi, such dialogs are important in keeping the preservation movement alive.

Chapter 2

The Preservation Movement in the United States

Historic preservation in the United States followed two distinct paths—in the private and the public sectors—from the earliest periods in the eighteenth century until the mid-twentieth century. Private-sector activities tended to revolve around important historical figures and associated landmark structures, while government involvement was limited to preserving natural features and establishing national parks. This chapter describes these parallel paths and how they finally merged with the establishment of the National Trust for Historic Preservation in 1949 and passage of the National Historic Preservation Act in 1966.

Preservation up to 1966

EARLY ACTIVITIES

The successful effort, in 1816, to save Independence Hall (then known as the Old State House) from demolition was one of the first acts of preservation. This Philadelphia building had tremendous historical significance, as every student of American history recognizes. Nevertheless, the site had been offered for subdivision into smaller parcels. Fortunately, a number of historical associations made strong appeals and the city of Philadelphia purchased it for preservation.

The Mount Vernon Ladies' Association of the Union is generally considered the first preservation group organized in the United States. It was founded in 1853 to save the deteriorating Mount Vernon, George Washington's homestead. A petition was presented to Congress for "The Proposed Purchase of Mount Vernon by the Citizens of the United States, in Order that They May at All Times Have a Legal and Indisputable Right to Visit the Grounds, Mansion, and Tomb of Washington." The petition failed, and the federal government showed no interest in taking care of the property. As a result, in 1856 Ann Pamela Cunningham chartered the Ladies' Association. Motivated primarily by patriotism, she offered the challenge, "Those who go to the Home in which

Mount Vernon

he lived and died, wish to see in what he lived and died! Let one spot in this grand country of ours be saved from change!"[1]

Through this private organization, Cunningham raised the money to acquire Mount Vernon. She found other women of means who had both the time and the inclination to help. Located in each state of the Union, the Association's members spearheaded the bold and successful campaign that saved and allowed for restoration of the structure.

The Association served as a model for historic associations involved in saving landmark structures threatened by growth or by time. This significant effort to save Mount Vernon also helped form the early trends of the preservation movement in the United States:

1. Preservation activities were largely supported by private individuals.
2. Women had a prominent role in these activities.
3. The goal of most efforts was to save individual landmark buildings.

With the emphasis on saving landmarks, there was little interest in preservation for preservation's sake. Nineteenth- and early twentieth-century organizations, including historical or patriotic societies, family organizations, and government agencies, saved landmark buildings more for patriotic reasons than because of their architectural significance. The historical associations of structures—to great men and important events, the earlier the better—were the only criteria worth considering for preservation of a structure. It was not until the mid-twentieth century, when our society began to realize what was being lost to demolition and neglect, that buildings were considered for preservation based on their architectural significance.

ACTIVITIES OF THE FEDERAL GOVERNMENT

Through the nineteenth century, the federal government took virtually no active role in preservation and showed no inclination to recognize or protect buildings of potential historical significance. Instead, the government's interest was in protecting natural features.

The federal government established Yellowstone National Park, comprising land in three states, as a protected area in 1872. It also began a program of acquiring Civil War battlefield sites to protect them from development. In the Southwest, government showed interest in preserving adobe dwellings, some of which dated to the fourteenth century. Settlers exploring this new territory often looted and destroyed these dwellings to get artifacts for sale. In 1889, Congress designated the Casa Grande ruin in Arizona as the nation's first National Monument and appropriated $2,000 to protect it—the first funding ever allocated for preservation.

In 1888, two cowboys looking for cattle in Arizona came across a spectacular site, the Cliff Palace dwellings of Mesa Verde. For the next eighteen years, word of the site spread and scavengers came to take well-preserved artifacts to sell on the international market. Recognizing the loss, Congress established the Mesa Verde National Park with the intention of preserving the dwellings and remaining artifacts. The Antiquities Act of 1906 established stiff penalties for destroying federally owned sites. Giving the President authority to designate "historic landmarks, historic and prehistoric structures, and other objects of historic or scientific interest" situated on federal lands, the Act was the first historic

Casa Grande ruin with
protective cover, Arizona

preservation legislation and prompted the surveying and identification of historic sites throughout the country. It transferred the authority for administering preservation activities at the federal level from Congress to the executive branch of government, allowing for more efficient management. The Act further established the administration of preservation efforts through the office of the secretary of the interior, where it remains today.

THE NATIONAL PARK SERVICE

The National Park Service was established in 1916 within the U.S. Department of the Interior as the administrative agency for national parks. The goal was to establish an apparatus to handle sites too large for private protection or preservation, such as the Jamestown and Yorktown sites in Virginia, which were combined to form the Colonial National Historical Park. Starting with its early involvement with the protection of natural sites, the National Park Service since its inception has played an integral role in preservation at the federal level. Today it is the sponsoring agency for most federal preservation programs.

CULTURAL RESOURCE PROGRAMS OF THE NATIONAL PARK SERVICE

PROGRAM	RESPONSIBILITY
American Indian Liaison Office	Advisory services to Native Americans
Archeology and Ethnography Program	Protect archeological and traditional cultural and natural resources
Heritage Preservation Services	Assist states and local communities in identifying and protecting historic sites
Historic American Buildings Survey/Historic American Engineering Record (HABS/HAER)	Documentation of architectural, engineering, and industrial sites
Museum Management Program	Preservation of museum collections in parks
National Center for Preservation Techology and Training	Promotes preservation technology and training
National Center for Recreation and Conservation	Assist communities in developing local cultural and natural resources through citizen-based planning
National Register, History and Education Program	Identification, recognition, and listing of significant historic properties
Park Historic Structures and Cultural Landscapes	Preservation of historic and prehistoric sites in national parks

OTHER EARLY PRESERVATION ACTIVITIES

Williamsburg was first settled in 1633 and became the colonial capital of Virginia in 1699. Even at that early date it was a carefully planned town, with provisions in the "Act directing the Building the Capitoll and the City of Williamsburg" laying out lot sizes (half-acre), setbacks (six feet), roof slopes ("less than tenn Foot Pitch"), as well as the location of the large central square, the capitol building, the Bruton Parish Church, and William and Mary College. During the War of Independence, Williamsburg was shown to be in a vulnerable location, and in 1778 Virginia's governor, Thomas Jefferson, wanted to have the capital moved to a more safe and central location. The next year the capital was moved to Richmond, and Williamsburg began a long period of stagnation.

In 1923 Dr. William Goodwin returned to Williamsburg as rector of the local parish church. He recognized the historical importance of the town, which had been overlooked for a century, and began a campaign for the town's reconstruction. Most of the original buildings were still standing, although they had accumulated many additions and alterations. Goodwin appealed to major philanthropists on the grounds that "Williamsburg is the one remaining colonial village any man could buy."[2] John D. Rockefeller found the opportunity to restore an entire

Williamsburg street

colonial town irresistible, and Williamsburg's restoration became the first attempt anywhere to restore an entire city.

The project presented many problems of preservation not previously encountered elsewhere. The primary problem was that much of the original town had been lost over the centuries and had to be rebuilt. Yet lost historic buildings cannot be fully replaced by reconstruction or replication. As John Ruskin argued (see chapter 1), the true beauty of a building can only be realized through the passage of time; it cannot be replicated by later reconstruction ("The thing is a Lie from beginning to end"). The first efforts to reconstruct Williamsburg are now perceived as misguided in some respects, but the importance of the early and significant restoration effort should not be overlooked.

Preservationists today see many of the early efforts at Williamsburg as inappropriate, but recognize that more recent work has been done with greater sensitivity to the historic significance of the original structures. Williamsburg's curators have understood that sometimes a secondary building that is original is more significant historically than an important structure that has been reconstructed, because the reconstruction cannot fully replace the original, no matter how well done. They have also recognized that structures age over time, and the staff no longer keeps every building in perfect condition; they let time do its part. Thus, on some structures the paint has been allowed to weather and lawns that had been carefully manicured are now home to grazing sheep, as would have been common in the seventeenth century. Such approaches allow a patina to develop and emphasize the "age value" of sites.

Williamsburg remains one of the most significant and visited historic districts in the United States, for it represents more than its buildings. As Rockefeller saw, it is valuable for "the lesson it teaches of the patriotism, high purpose, and unselfish devotion of our forefathers to the common good."[3]

Another great twentieth-century preservation project sponsored by a wealthy individual is Greenfield Village, established in 1929 with funding from Henry Ford. At this site in Dearborn, Michigan, Ford rebuilt an entire community of structures gathered from his travels across the United States. Although recognized as a significant historical museum, Greenfield Village is consistently criticized as too much a product of Ford's personal tastes. Indeed, it is a mixture of structures, many of which relate to the collector's great love of inventions and inventors. Restoration of the structures was often done according to Ford's taste without regard for historical accuracy so the structures lost the contextual significance of their original sites. Preservationists prefer that buildings be

Thomas Edison's workshop,
Greenfield Village, Dearborn,
Michigan

maintained in their historic context, but for educational purposes such changes can be acceptable.

Greenfield Village should be evaluated on other terms, however. Ford intended that the museum be an "animated textbook" and act as an accessible teaching laboratory for students. Seen in this light, it serves its purpose well.

The first city to establish a historic district with regulatory control was Charleston, South Carolina. To counter a threat from outsiders, who were dismantling many of the beautiful Charleston houses, local citizens and planners established a historic zoning ordinance in 1931, even though it had no legal precedent and was established without enabling legislation. A board of architectural review, which had authority to review exterior changes to buildings within the district and to issue certificates of appropriateness if such changes were deemed acceptable, was also established. Without legal basis for this review authority, the regulatory district was viable largely because it had general community support.

Charleston became a prototype for many other early historic districts, including the Vieux Carré section of New Orleans, authorized through a Louisiana state constitutional amendment in 1936. San Antonio, Texas,

Historic Districts

Typical Charleston residence

followed suit in 1939; Alexandria, Virginia, in 1946; Williamsburg in 1947; Winston-Salem, North Carolina, in 1948; and the Georgetown section of Washington, D.C., in 1950.

Historic American Buildings Survey (HABS)

The recognition of historic areas received a boost in the 1930s, in the depths of the Depression, when President Roosevelt established many New Deal programs for the benefit of unemployed workers. The Civil Works Administration (CWA) provided for the employment of one thousand unemployed architects and photographers, who were made responsible for documenting historic structures throughout the United States. The Act established a policy "to preserve for public use historic sites, buildings and objects of national significance for the inspiration and benefit of the people of the United States." The American Institute of Architects (AIA) agreed to conduct the documentation program as a way to put unemployed architects to work.

In a tripartite agreement between the National Park Service, the Library of Congress, and the American Institute of Architects, the Historic

HABS drawing,
Emlen Physick House,
Cape May, NJ (1879)

American Buildings Survey (HABS) program was formally established in 1934. It can be seen as the first and only federal program to document historic structures and precursor of an increasing role for the federal government in historic preservation. As stated in the program's original mission statement, "The survey shall cover structures of all types from the smallest utilitarian structures to the largest and most monumental. Buildings of every description are to be included so that a complete picture of the culture of the times as reflected in the buildings of the period may be put on record."[4]

The Department of the Interior's National Park Service provided administration and funding and also established rigorous documentation standards. As a result, the data compiled in the 1930s remain among the best historical records of early structures, most of which have been demolished. It is an invaluable archive. The collection is now recorded on microfilm and microfiche and is available at more than a hundred libraries across the country.[5] A digital archive is now well underway.

As the country recovered from the Depression and entered World War II, the documentation programs languished. In the early 1950s, however, the HABS program was reactivated, this time using student architects and historians on summer teams overseen by architectural professors. Through their efforts, over 35,000 historic structures and sites have been recorded with over 360,000 measured drawings and large-format photographs. The original drawings are housed, serviced, and maintained at the Library of Congress. These archives are in the public domain, and may be used freely.

A companion program, the Historic American Engineering Record (HAER), was established in 1969 in an agreement with the American Society of Civil Engineers. While HABS focuses on endangered historic buildings of note, HAER emphasizes technology and engineering, such projects as canals, railroads, and bridges.

The HABS and HAER programs are now under the auspices of National Park Service's Cultural Resources Stewardships and Partnerships Program. Documentation continues through the preparation of measured drawings, written histories, and photography. The cost of the work is shared by municipalities, industries, historical societies, and preservation organizations.

The National Trust for Historic Preservation

As explained earlier, preservation efforts in the United States have historically taken two divergent roads. Private efforts primarily involved fundraising to save significant individual landmark buildings—the "George-Washington-Slept-Here" approach. On the other hand, government focused on the protection of natural landscapes, features, and parks. These two strands finally began to come together through the establishment of a new quasi-public organization, the National Trust for Historic Preservation.

The National Council for Historic Sites and Buildings, formed after World War II, evolved into the National Trust for Historic Preservation in 1949. The National Trust, inspired by its English namesake, was created with the purpose of linking the preservation efforts of the National Park Service and the federal government with activities of the private sector.

As laid out at a conference in Williamsburg in the late 1970s and adopted in 1983, the objectives of the National Trust were to:

1. Identify and act on important national preservation issues.
2. Support, broaden, and strengthen organized preservation efforts.
3. Target communications to those who affect the future of historic resources.
4. Expand private and public financial resources for preservation activities.[6]

The Trust encourages preservation in a number of ways, including publication of a magazine, *Preservation*. It also sponsors an annual conference that brings together prominent preservationists from around the country. The organization serves as an advocate agency to Congress; for example, it was instrumental in lobbying to retain the historic

preservation rehabilitation tax credit program when it was threatened in the 1980s.

One of the Trust's responsibilities is to assume ownership of historic properties that are problematic for the federal government to own. Acquisition of the first property the Trust accepted, Woodlawn Plantation in Virginia, led to an internal debate over whether such properties should be centrally administered and supported or independently administered and financially self-sufficient. As a result, over the years the Trust has accepted ownership of only twenty historic sites to be wholly administered—those of exceptional significance. Among these properties are the 1838 grand Gothic mansion Lyndhurst in Tarrytown, New York; Frank Lloyd Wright's home and studio in Oak Park, Illinois; the President Woodrow Wilson House in Washington, D.C.; and (under a different arrangement) the Lower East Side Tenement Museum in New York City. Donated properties typically come with endowments, but inflation has made most of these insufficient to cover costs. Because of administrative and funding difficulties, the Trust carefully evaluates the acceptance of additional properties. Because ownership can be burdensome, financially in some cases, the trust helps identify potential owners willing to preserve a property with protective covenants.

The National Trust is active in other ways. Each year the Trust presents its Endangered Properties List, which gives national attention to eleven historic places especially threatened with demolition or destruction. Also, it focuses public attention on the adverse impact of the federal government moving its facilities out of historic downtowns and encouraged the adoption of an executive order to locate federal functions in historic buildings.

The Trust developed other programs that complement its primary mission. These include the Main Street Program (see Chapter 9), which encourages the revitalization of older downtown areas (now administered through the National Main Street Center). The Trust also cooperated with the Justice Department in encouraging the adaptation of historic buildings to meet the requirements of the Americans with Disabilities Act (ADA).

Preservation since 1966: Federal, State, and Local Roles

THE FEDERAL ROLE

NATIONAL HISTORIC PRESERVATION ACT OF 1966

A general interest in preservation arose in the 1960s. This was closely aligned with and similar to the then-nascent environmental movement. The primary difference was that historic preservationists were concerned with protection of the built environment and environmentalists with the natural environment. The public was especially concerned about the destruction of both buildings and natural features caused by urban renewal, the interstate highway system, and other massive public works projects of the 1950s and 1960s.

In 1966, the National Trust for Historic Preservation published a report titled *With Heritage So Rich*.[7] This provocative and influential document illustrated what had been lost of American architectural heritage and proposed an expanded role for preservation supported by the federal government. The report included recommendations for accomplishing this:

1. A comprehensive survey of historically and architecturally significant buildings, sites, structures, districts, and objects, and their inclusion in a National Register.
2. A partnership of federal, state, and local governments to deal specifically with preservation, including the establishment of a national advisory council on historic preservation and the designation of preservation officers in every state.
3. A program of financial incentives for preservation to balance the incentives already available for new construction.

With Heritage So Rich was itself rich in ideas and did much to awaken a preservation consciousness at all levels.

These recommendations led to the National Historic Preservation Act of 1966, undoubtedly the most important historic preservation legislation ever passed by Congress. The new laws followed closely the recommendations of the previous year's report and included a strong national preservation policy statement. Among its many provisions, the Act established the National Register of Historic Places, encouraged the concept of locally regulated historic districts, authorized enabling legislation to fund preservation activities, encouraged the establishment of State Historic Preservation Offices (SHPOs), established an Advisory Council on Historic Preservation, and defined how federal preservation programs would rely on the voluntary cooperation of owners of historic properties and not interfere with ownership rights. These provisions are discussed in the following sections.

The significance of the National Historic Preservation Act of 1966 should not be underestimated. Until that time, preservation activities focused on established landmarks. Local historical organizations were interested in the restoration and maintenance only of structures with great significance. Those structures typically were used as a local museum; others received only a marker for recognition. Also at that time, only a handful of historic districts existed. Such districts were difficult to establish, as courts did not support local regulations imposing aesthetic restraints on property owners. Furthermore, local communities interested in preservation had almost no ties with preservation activities at the state and federal levels.

The 1966 Act changed this perspective. Historic preservation became an integral part of society, expanding interest and involvement at a level never previously imagined. There are now some 3,000 preservation organizations actively engaged in public education, advocacy, preservation and restoration projects of various kinds. In terms of geographic interest, distinctions among the regions are no longer drawn. Membership in the National Trust for Historic Preservation grew from 10,700 in 1966 to approximately 260,000 in 1999. More than thirty-five university graduate professional and technical curriculums directly related to historic preservation have been created.[8]

THE NATIONAL REGISTER OF HISTORIC PLACES

One important provision of the 1966 Act was the creation of the National Register of Historic Places. The National Register is the standard listing of the nation's inventory of recognized historic structures. It

*Old State Capitol Building,
St. Louis, Missouri*

should not be confused with the Historic American Buildings Survey, which was begun in 1933 as a method of documenting historic buildings through drawings and photographs. The National Register currently contains almost 70,000 listings representing nearly one million individual resources, and is maintained by the National Park Service. Information on these properties can be found on the National Register Information System (NRIS) data base on the Web or by contacting the State Historic Preservation office.

For inclusion in the National Register, properties must be nominated and approved. The necessary documentation for approval contains a detailed description of the property, including narrative statements of its history, context, and historic and architectural significance.

Copies of individual nominations are public records, and may be obtained through the National Park Service's Reference Desk in Washington, D.C. Some properties are listed under Multiple Property Submissions, and are listed collectively because they represent historical themes, property types, or geographic areas. A sample nomination form can be found on the National Park Service Web site.

Later amendments to the 1966 Act have modified some aspects of the National Register process, but the basic elements remain and make this an important archive.

Before nomination to the National Register, a property must be reviewed and approved by its state preservation board. As nominations do not necessarily come from owners, owner notification is part of this process, and owners may object to the designation. In such a case, the property can be determined to be "eligible for listing," which indicates its worthiness for inclusion. Nominations may also come from certified local governments (discussed below) and from other federal agencies. Chapter 3 describes the criteria and selection process used in the designation of properties for the National Register. This process is one of the most important aspects of preservation work.

Perhaps the best way to describe the National Register is to identify what it does and does not do, for there are common misconceptions about designation.

The National Register *does*:

- Identify historically significant buildings, structures, sites, objects, and districts according to the National Register Criteria for Evaluation.
- Encourage the preservation of historic properties by documenting their significance and by lending support to local preservation activities.
- Enable federal, state, and local agencies to consider historic properties in the early stages of planning projects.
- Provide a list identifying historic sites that might be affected by new development for review by the Advisory Council on Historic Preservation (discussed later in this chapter).
- Provide for review of federally funded, licensed, or sponsored projects that may affect historic properties.
- Make owners of historic properties eligible to apply for federal grants-in-aid for preservation activities.
- Encourage the rehabilitation of income-producing historic properties that meet preservation standards through tax incentives; discourage the demolition of income-producing properties through federal income tax disincentives.

Listing a property on the National Register *does not*:

- Restrict the rights of private property owners in the use, development, or sale of privately owned historic property.
- Lead automatically to local historic district or landmark designation.
- Stop federal, state, local, or private projects.
- Provide for review of state, local, or privately funded projects that may affect historic properties (although some states have tied such designation to environmental reviews).
- Guarantee that grant funds will be available for all significant historic properties.

• Provide tax benefits to owners of residential historic properties, unless those properties are rental and treated as income-producing by the Internal Revenue Service.

Some preservationists argue that the federal government should change this policy and legislate some form of protection for all properties listed on the National Register. Although it was politically necessary to leave such control out of the original act, historic preservation has since proved its worth, and many would argue that the ability of private developers to destroy national landmarks with impunity if they so choose is no longer justifiable.

THE CONCEPT OF HISTORIC DISTRICTS

The National Register redefined the concept of historic districts. Before 1966, only individual structures or objects were designated at the federal level. The new Act recognized that individual properties should be designated, but that in many instances it is necessary not only to preserve a building but also the historic context in which it and adjacent buildings are placed. Therefore, the idea of designating groups or assemblages of buildings as historic represented a significant conceptual shift.

ADVISORY COUNCIL ON HISTORIC PRESERVATION

The 1966 Act also established the Advisory Council on Historic Preservation. Its purposes were described in a later Annual Report to Congress:

> The Advisory Council on Historic Preservation is an independent Federal agency under the Executive Branch, which advises the President and the Congress on historic preservation policy. The Council also reviews and comments on Federal and federally assisted activities that affect properties listed in or eligible for listing in the National Register of Historic Places.[9]

In essence, the Council was established to provide a check against unwarranted demolition and destruction of historic resources as a result of federal activities and programs. It is an independent executive agency appointed by the President and is the only federal entity created solely to address historic preservation issues. It currently has twenty members, including the secretaries of the interior, transportation, housing and urban development, and agriculture.

SECTION 106 REVIEW

Most of the Advisory Council's budget and personnel resources are used each year to fulfill its primary mandate, a process known as *Section*

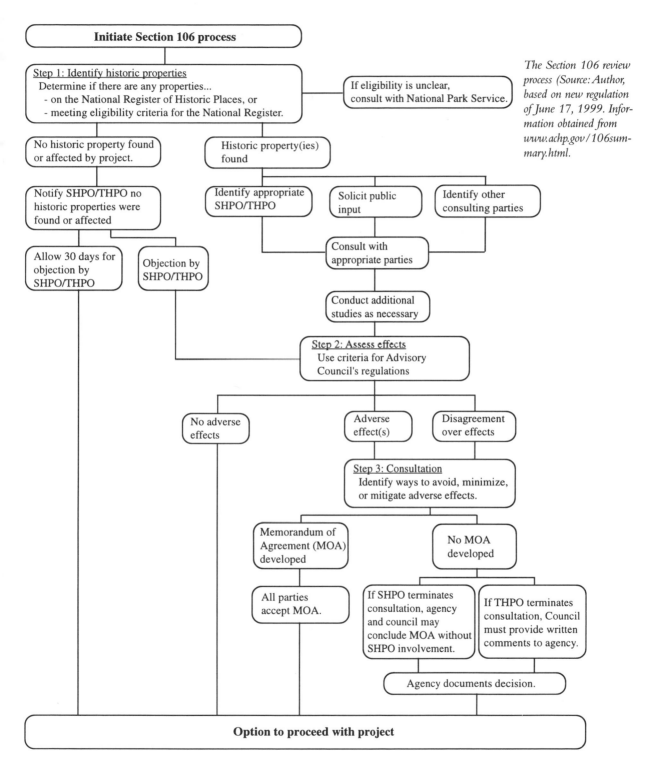

Initiate Section 106 process

Step 1: Identify historic properties
Determine if there are any properties...
- on the National Register of Historic Places, or
- meeting eligibility criteria for the National Register.

If eligibility is unclear, consult with National Park Service.

No historic property found or affected by project.

Historic property(ies) found

Notify SHPO/THPO no historic properties were found or affected

Identify appropriate SHPO/THPO

Solicit public input

Identify other consulting parties

Allow 30 days for objection by SHPO/THPO

Objection by SHPO/THPO

Consult with appropriate parties

Conduct additional studies as necessary

Step 2: Assess effects
Use criteria for Advisory Council's regulations

No adverse effects

Adverse effect(s)

Disagreement over effects

Step 3: Consultation
Identify ways to avoid, minimize, or mitigate adverse effects.

Memorandum of Agreement (MOA) developed

No MOA developed

All parties accept MOA.

If SHPO terminates consultation, agency and council may conclude MOA without SHPO involvement.

If THPO terminates consultation, Council must provide written comments to agency.

Agency documents decision.

Option to proceed with project

The Section 106 review process (Source: Author, based on new regulation of June 17, 1999. Information obtained from www.achp.gov/106summary.html.

The Preservation Movement in the United States • 49

106 review (referring to its source in the National Historic Preservation Act of 1966). This involves reviewing and commenting on federal projects and federally supported projects that affect historic properties—properties either on or eligible for the National Register. In any given year, thousands of projects are reviewed.

Section 106 review procedures are described in the Advisory Council's regulations, "Protection of Historic Properties." Simply stated, the process works thus:

1. The federal agency involved with the project identifies historic properties that may be affected and consults with the SHPO or the Tribal Historic Preservation Officer (THPO) to determine which properties are listed on or eligible for the National Register.
2. The agency determines for each historic property whether the proposed project will have (a) no effect, (b) no adverse effect, or (c) an adverse effect.
3. If an adverse outcome is anticipated, the agency consults with the SHPO and others to determine how to minimize the negative impact. This results in a Memorandum of Agreement (MOA), which outlines the mitigating measures to be taken.
4. If an MOA is executed, the agency can proceed with the project under its terms.

When no agreement can be reached among the parties interested in the project, the Advisory Council may try to develop an alternative agreement. As shown in the diagram, the Section 106 review process does not have the power to stop work even if it will have significant negative impact on a historic property. Likewise, it does not insist that certain procedures are followed in order to proceed with proposed work. The process mandates only the impact review itself and the opportunity of interested bodies to make comment. If the review shows that serious harm would be done to a designated property, federal funding may or may not be withdrawn, but a project cannot be prevented from proceeding minus such funding. The Act also requires special consideration and planning be undertaken for properties designated as National Historic landmarks.

The Federal Role Since 1966

Since the passage of the 1966 Act, the preservation movement has undergone significant changes. The Act not only instituted structural changes in preservation programs, as described above, but also changed the way preservation is thought of and who is involved.

First, the notion of historical significance underwent revision. Preservationists no longer focused on saving aged national landmarks as museum pieces. Instead, entire areas were delineated as historic districts. More recent buildings were recognized for their historic importance. A twentieth-century gas station or motel could be seen as an important representation of society's cultural heritage and therefore worthy of recognition. Buildings with local or statewide significance were seen as contributing to the larger historic context and worthy of National Register status alongside nationally recognized landmarks. But these buildings were not frozen in time as museum pieces. Through the new concept of adaptive use, alterations that enabled buildings to continue to contribute to the economic vitality of a community were allowed.

Thanks to the 1966 Act, many new preservation initiatives were undertaken. In 1968, the National Trust produced the first film on preservation for national distribution, which attracted more people to the cause. Also in 1968, American and Canadian preservationists linked together in an international organization focusing on conservation and restoration techniques, the Association for Preservation Technology (APT). In 1969, HAER was created to document engineering structures, complementing the existing HABS.

The tax incentive program for the rehabilitation of historic structures, created under the Tax Reform Act of 1976, represented an important change in the preservation movement. The bicentennial year brought a public celebration of United States heritage but also witnessed a significant shift from public-sector involvement to private-sector initiative. For the first time, investors who were not philosophical supporters of preservation became integral players because of new economic incentives. Rather than being perceived as obstructions to development, older structures were now viewed as financial opportunities, especially during the difficult economic times of the late 1970s and early 1980s. As Michael Tomlan, professor of historic preservation at Cornell University, has written, "It was in the 1980s that preservationists launched feverishly into the 'business' of preservation. The move was not without its irony: on one hand we preservationists continued to try to control development, while on the other we promoted business interests."[10]

Preservation also became an important tool of urban revitalization during this period. Through the Main Street Program, established by the National Trust in 1980 (see chapter 9), the preservation and adaptive use of older commercial buildings became an important tool of downtown renewal. This successful program changed perceptions of older and blighted downtowns and provided the framework for a complete revitalization program that transcended rehabilitation efforts to include recognition of the importance of organization, promotion, and economic restructuring.

As a result of these new perspectives, preservation advocates took a more activist role, sometimes with missionary zeal. Lobbying efforts by groups like the National Trust and Preservation Action pushed through other beneficial legislation. The ranks of preservation advocates swelled, tied closely with the environmental movement, which also grew after the passage of the National Environmental Policy Act of 1969. This act established a national policy on the protection and preservation of the nation's environment, including historic resources. It authorized a listing of environmental amenities and a process of review when such sites were impacted by federal actions or funding of development.

THE STATE ROLE

Many states had preservation programs prior to the National Historic Preservation Act of 1966, but they tended to be limited in scope. Typically, they included the operation of state-administered museums, historic sites, and highway or structure marker programs. As a result of the 1966 Act, states took on a larger and more uniform role.

STATE HISTORIC PRESERVATION OFFICES

The 1966 Act authorized grants to help establish state-level offices, which, in a federal/state partnership, eventually became the chief administrative agencies of most preservation programs. To be eligible for federal funding for preservation administration and projects, states were required to establish a State Historic Preservation Office (SPHO, pronounced variously as "shpoe" or "shippoe"). These offices were assigned a number of responsibilities, which they still have today:

1. Each SHPO is responsible for conducting systematic survey of historic properties and sites throughout its state. These surveys are intended to establish a list of individual structures or objects or districts that have historic significance. The surveys should indicate which properties need designation because they are threatened.

   Originally, the surveys were comprehensive in scope; they tried to recognize and document virtually every historic resource in a state. Lowered funding in recent years caused downscaling. The SHPOs now have two primary thrusts. The first is an effort to prioritize the survey work and to limit documentation to the most significant properties. Second, local areas are taught to do the survey work themselves in a manner consistent with the state's established procedures.

2. The SHPO processes nominations to the National Register of Historic Places. Although the National Park Service may override decisions made at the state level, this seldom occurs, and most of the processing and review work is carried out directly between the property nominator and the state office. The SHPO sends approved nominations, with comments, to the appropriate regional National Park Service office, where it is again reviewed and listing either granted or denied. The process may take as little as sixty days or as long as a year or more.

3. The SHPO administers grants to individual projects throughout the state, serving as the funding conduit from the national to the local level.

4. The SHPO advises and assists in the efforts of local agencies, but it cannot regulate. In the United States system of government, states authorize powers to local governments, but local government need not accept them. Thus, the power given by states to local governments to regulate historic properties does not necessarily mean that local governments take on this power. They may choose not to be involved in preservation regulation at all. Although the power to regulate resides with the state, typically the initiative for preservation lies at the local level.

5. The state office provides consultation on Section 106 review.

6. The SHPO's office reviews applications for federal investment tax credit and makes recommendation to the National Park Service. An increasing number of states are now also providing historic tax credits applicable to state income taxes.

In 1992, Congress adopted amendments to the 1966 Act allowing Native American tribes to assume any and all of the functions of SHPOs. Tribal Historic Preservation Officers (THPOs, discussed in the section on SHPOs) may maintain inventories and a register of places significant historically to the tribe. They may also nominate properties to the national register, conduct Section 106 reviews of federally supported projects on tribal land, and conduct education programs on the importance of preserving historic properties. Native Americans tend to preserve their heritage more through language, oral tradition, arts, crafts, and dance rather than through buildings, so the federal- and state-level programs may have a different emphasis, giving less importance to the preservation of historic structures.

Congress recognized the distinctive link between tribal cultures and tribal religions with the American Indian Religious Freedom Act of 1978. Indeed, the term *historic preservation* may not be inclusive enough to represent the appropriate meaning to Native Americans, for whom there is little difference between history and everyday life.

Historic preservation review boards are established in some states. Composed of professionals in the fields of American and architectural history, cultural geography, prehistoric and historic archaeology, historic preservation, and related disciplines, such boards can serve several functions. Most commonly, they review nominations submitted to the state for properties to be listed on the National Register and recommend that the SHPO accept or reject those nominations. In Michigan, the state board also serves an unusual role as the final board of appeal for property owners who do not agree with a determination made by a local historic district commission. This appeal procedure may be the most important responsibility of the board because it directly affects owners of historic properties. Although each case is unique, some issues are commonly raised by appellants. As part of the appeal process, the review board must determine whether:

· Retaining the historic resource will cause undue financial hardship to the owner and all feasible alternatives to eliminate the hardship have been exhausted.
· Retaining the resource is not in the interest of the majority of the community.
· The local commission failed to consider all relevant factors.
· The commission exceeded its authority or acted in an arbitrary and capricious manner.
· The commission followed an unlawful procedure resulting in material prejudice to the appellant.
· The resource constitutes a hazard to the public safety.
· The resource is a hazard to occupant safety.
· The resource is a deterrent to a major improvement project.[11]

Although each case must be decided on its own merits, it is inappropriate for the Michigan state review board to rethink the judgment of a local commission. The board determines only whether the local commission's action was within the rights provided by the local ordinance or whether rights of the property owner were not properly protected.

The Local Role

In many ways, historic preservation is most meaningful at the local level, where the process of designating historic structures is initiated. Preservation ordinances, regulations, and incentives are drafted at the local level, where authority is given to review and approve or disapprove changes to historic structures. Property owners deal directly with municipal officials. Thus, this is where the real protective power of historic preservation is found. This cannot be overemphasized. As historian Antoinette Lee, at the National Park Service, put it, "Architectural historians give you information; the neighborhoods give you passion."[12]

The roles of the various levels of government—federal, state, and local—are quite distinct. The federal role is to fund activities, set out an overall superstructure of preservation activities, and ensure consistency of approach from state to state. The federal government also monitors its own properties and activities and provides incentives to encourage appropriate work to historic buildings. But it has virtually no regulatory power and no ultimate power over owners of historic properties. At the state level, SHPOs encourage surveys of significant historic resources and facilitate federal activities, providing a link between the federal and local levels of government and state laws authorized for local programs.

But only at the local level can historic properties be regulated and protected through legal ordinance. These powers are reserved for local governments because of the underlying philosophy that each community should determine for itself what is historically significant, what is of value to the community, and what steps should be taken to provide protection. The process of administering local historic ordinances is in the hands of historic district commissions, which are made up of either appointed or elected local residents. The National Historic Preservation Act of 1966 encouraged local governments to establish such review agencies.

THE RANGE OF LOCAL GOVERNMENT PROGRAMS— THE CHARLESTON PRINCIPLES

The following document, referred to as the *Charleston Principles*, was written in 1990 and represents a national consensus on the activities of local governments and agencies in historic preservation.

A Call to Action for Community Conservation

Members of the national historic preservation community, assembled on October 20, 1990, in Charleston, South Carolina, for the 44th National Preservation Conference, sponsored by the National Trust for Historic Preservation, adopted unanimously the following principles for comprehensive local government programs to conserve community heritage and made a pledge to have these principles become part of the policy of their communities.

We call on local leaders to adopt and act on these principles in order to improve their citizens' quality of life, increase their economic well-being, and enhance their community's heritage and beauty.

Principle I: Identify historic places, both architectural and natural, that give the community its special character and that aid its future well-being.

Principle II: Adopt the preservation of historic places as a goal of planning for land use, economic development, housing for all income levels, and transportation.

Principle III: Create organizational, regulatory, and incentive mechanisms to facilitate preservation, and provide the leadership to make them work.

Principle IV: Develop revitalization strategies that capitalize on the existing value of historic residential and commercial neighborhoods and properties, and provide well designed affordable housing without displacing existing residents.

Principle V: Ensure that policies and decisions on community growth and development respect a community's heritage and enhance overall livability.

Principle VI: Demand excellence in design for new construction and in the stewardship of historic properties and places.

Principle VII: Use a community's heritage to educate citizens of all ages and to build civic pride.

Principle VIII: Recognize the cultural diversity of communities and empower a diverse constituency to acknowledge, identify, and preserve America's cultural and physical resources.

CERTIFIED LOCAL GOVERNMENTS

The National Historic Preservation Act was amended in 1980 to allow local communities to request their state government give them the status of Certified Local Government (CLG). This designation ties the local government more closely with the SHPO in administering preservation programs and makes it eligible for certain types of grants. To be eligible for CLG status, the local government must give evidence of the following:

1. It must have established a historic preservation commission with powers of review.
2. Its system of surveying historic properties must be tied to state office procedures.
3. It must be able and willing to enforce state and local preservation ordinances.

CLG status involves the local agency in the historic nomination review process, and the local commission must give preliminary approval for all historic nominations sent on to the state office. CLG status also conveys priority eligibility for federal and state preservation grants. Such grants may include the following:

- Survey and inventory of historic areas
- Survey of archeological sites
- Preparation of National Register nominations
- Staff support
- Developing published design guidelines
- Writing or amending preservation ordinances
- Preparation of preservation plans
- Preparing and publishing exhibits and brochures
- Special events

In addition, CLG grants may now be used for bricks-and-mortar work, such as the restoration or renovation of historic buildings.

The preservation movement has changed dramatically from its early years to today's organized and systematic activities. Local, state, and federal government agencies work to complement one another and support the nongovernmental action found across the country.

The history of historic preservation in the United States can be briefly recounted through dates important to the movement:

Important Dates in Historic Preservation

1816 Philadelphia State House (Independence Hall) saved from demolition.

1853 Mount Vernon Ladies' Association formed to save Washington's home.

1872 Yellowstone National Park made a federally protected area.

1889 First national funding for historic preservation: Congress appropriated $2,000 to preserve Casa Grande ruin in Arizona.

1906 Antiquities Act, the country's first national preservation legislation, passed, designating monuments on federal land and establishing penalties for destroying federally owned sites.

1910 Creation of the Society for the Preservation of New England Antiquities

1916 National Park Service established to administer areas too large to be preserved privately (e.g., Colonial National Historical Park in Virginia, including Jamestown; and Yorktown).

1926 John D. Rockefeller Jr. begins funding the restoration of Williamsburg, Virginia.

1929 Henry Ford establishes Greenfield Village.

1931 Charleston, South Carolina, establishes an "Old and Historic District," the country's first locally designated historic district.

1934 Historic American Buildings Survey (HABS) authorized by President Roosevelt.

1935 Historic Sites Act passed by Congress to establish historic preservation policy; it "established policy . . . to preserve for public use historic sites, buildings and objects of national significance for the inspiration and benefit of the people of the United States."

1949 National Trust for Historic Preservation established.

1966 National Historic Preservation Act passed; major provisions established preservation roles for federal, state, and local levels of government.

1976 Tax Reform Act removed incentive for demolition of older buildings and provided five-year rapid writeoff for certified rehabilitation of historic buildings.

1978 Revenue Act established investment tax credits for rehabilitation of historic buildings. U. S. Supreme Court upheld New York City's permit denial under local preservation law in *Penn Central Transportation Co. v. City of New York*

1980 Main Street Program established by the National Trust for Historic Preservation. Amendment of National Historic Preservation Act of 1966 and inclusion of provision for Certified Local Government status.

1981 Congress passed Economic Recovery Tax Act (ERTA), providing 25 percent tax incentive for rehabilitation of historic buildings.

1986 Tax Reform Act cut back some historic preservation tax incentives.

1988 Federal Abandoned Shipwrecks Act authorized state management of significant shipwrecks, and encourages maritime preservation.

1998 National Trust for Historic Preservation becomes independent of federal funding.

Chapter 3

Historic Districts and Ordinances

The first local historic district in the United States was established in Charleston, South Carolina, in 1931, although its establishment was encouraged decades earlier by Frederick Law Olmsted, the park and landscape planner. To establish the district, much work was put into documenting a large number of old structures in Charleston. Although the group of buildings surveyed was much larger, the final number, accepted in 1944, included 572 historic buildings. The second historic district was established in 1936 in the Vieux Carré section of New Orleans—the old French Quarter. These early efforts to establish historic districts helped keep both areas intact.

Background

Lower Pontalba Building, New Orleans, Louisiana, 1850–51. The Vieux Carré historic district preserves some of the first buildings to incorporate cast-iron galleries.

Nevertheless, the regulatory powers available to some agencies administering a historic district in that period were limited and maintaining the historic appearance of the district was desirable but not legally enforceable; controls could not be put on properties for aesthetic reasons alone and had to rely on the concept of *aesthetics plus*, the idea that there must be a reason beyond historic character (aesthetics) to justify regulatory control (e.g., building codes).

In 1954, the Supreme Court changed this with its *Berman* v. *Parker* decision, which established the right of local government to "tear down an old building to improve a neighborhood." The original purpose of this ruling, ironically, was to allow for the demolition of sound older housing for urban renewal. The initial application of the ruling was to beautify by clearing older structures, and led to excesses of urban renewal in the 1950s and 1960s, with city planners arguing that the demolition of older, rundown neighborhoods improved the appearance of the city. This ruling challenged the "aesthetics plus" concept, and established that aesthetics was enough of a reason by itself under the police power. Preservationists reinterpreted the ruling in their own favor, asserting that historic preservation ordinances could be established to protect older neighborhoods based solely on an area's visual importance to the historic fabric of the city. This became the more persuasive argument, and the aesthetic importance of historic structures was upheld by the courts.

Reasons to Establish a Historic District

Communities establish historic districts for a variety of reasons. Some create them simply as a way to protect significant historic properties. Some establish historic districts to protect against a specific threat of development, while others want to encourage development in an older area. Some communities use historic districts as a tool for maintaining property values and others because they contribute to an improved image of the community at large. Each of these motives is examined in the following case studies.

PROTECTION OF HISTORIC PROPERTIES—
ST. AUGUSTINE, FLORIDA

The St. Augustine Town Plan Historic District is the site of the oldest continuously occupied European settlement in the United States. Settled originally as a Spanish military base, the town grew around Castillo de San Marcos, the fort (1672–1756) and became the seat of Spanish power in Florida. The colonial buildings that remain date from the early 1700s and include the Oldest House (1706) and the Basilica Cathedral of St. Augustine (1797, restored 1887), one of the oldest Catholic establishments in the country.

*Pioneer Square, Seattle,
Washington*

CONTROL OF NEW DEVELOPMENT—SEATTLE, WASHINGTON

The Pioneer Square area of Seattle was the original Skid Row, named for the inclined street where logs were skidded down to the waterside for transport to other parts of the United States. In the 1950s and 1960s, the area was a run-down neighborhood, full of pawnshops and hotels housing transients. In response to concern over its problems, in 1963 the city supported a plan to revitalize this depressed area through the construction of new office buildings and parking structures and by demolishing most of the older buildings in the Square.

Some citizens, however, saw beyond the deterioration of the existing buildings and recognized the historic integrity inherent in the district. They made an effort to save the structures by establishing a designated historic district—an effort that succeeded. But the activists also were concerned about the needs of the city's transient population and wanted the neighborhood to continue serving them. In a most unusual coalition, the city responded by developing provisions in the city codes that encouraged the retention of the SROs and the establishment of social service agencies in the area.

Historic Districts and Ordinances • 61

Entrepreneurs purchased and began improving the deteriorating buildings. This spurred other redevelopment in the area, and the older buildings became desirable properties. As a result, the building valuations in the Pioneer Square area increased 600 percent in less than a decade. The district since has become a showcase example of urban mixed-use development.

REDEVELOPMENT INCENTIVE—
MANCHESTER NEIGHBORHOOD, PITTSBURGH, PENNSYLVANIA

In the 1960s, the Manchester neighborhood of Pittsburgh exhibited many of the signs of a dying residential area. Most of the housing had deteriorated, many buildings were abandoned, and the area was slated for demolition under the guise of urban renewal. Beneath the deterioration and neglect, however, was a stock of well-built structures, many with distinctive design features, in an area of prime residential potential because of its proximity to the downtown.

Arthur Ziegler, an English teacher, and James Van Trump, a local architectural historian, recognized Manchester's potential and decided to take action to save it. In 1964 they established the Pittsburgh History and Landmarks Foundation and encouraged others to participate in their efforts. Through the Foundation, an innovative preservation and rehabilitation program was established for the Manchester neighborhood. The Foundation persuaded the city's urban renewal agency to become a partner in the effort rather than an opponent.

A program to sell abandoned houses to qualified buyers was established with the help of the city. The houses were priced from $100 to $9,000. The conditions for their purchase were:

1. The city would restore the facade if the owner agreed to maintain the restored facade for twenty years. The owner could claim deduction for an easement valued at 10 percent of the appraised value of the restored house. (See chapter 8 for a description of easements.)
2. The city offered free plans and specifications for rehabilitation work as well as assistance with bidding and construction supervision.
3. The city made 3-percent loans available to owners. If the owner's income was low enough, the city offered an outright grant for the rehabilitation work.

Pittsburgh's commitment to the neighborhood through this program was unusually strong. Also surprising was the immediate success of the program. Fifty houses were sold in three days. In the next few years, the city invested just under $500,000 in the program, out of which more

Manchester neighborhood, Pittsburgh, Pennsylvania

than $3 million was generated in private rehabilitation funds. But perhaps most impressive of all was the change in the appearance and vitality of the neighborhood. While keeping its share of rehabilitated housing available for low-income families, the neighborhood attracted more affluent residents who appreciated the historic character of the buildings and the location, from which they could walk to work.

STATION SQUARE, PITTSBURGH, PENNSYLVANIA

Under Arthur Ziegler's continued leadership, in the mid-1970s the Pittsburgh History and Landmarks tackled a much bigger project. The Pittsburgh and Lake Erie Railroad owned an unused station building with an intact, lavishly ornamented Edwardian interior surrounded by forty acres of underutilized commercial buildings. The complex was across the river from downtown so, although it was a short walk away, most investors saw the area as having little potential. But Ziegler envisioned the adaptive use of the structures as an upscale shopping area, with shops and restaurants trading on the historic theme and the marvelous interior spaces. He noted that "Pittsburgh's nearest fashionable shopping district was in Manhattan, and Pittsburgh's last tourist came in 1946."[1]

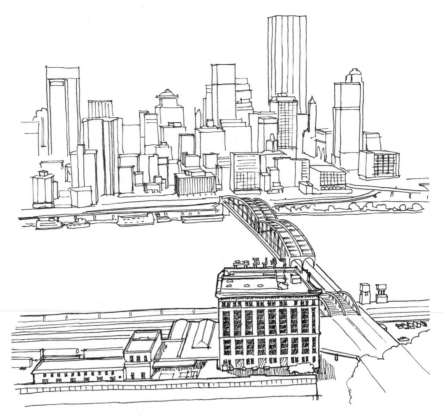

Station Square development,
Pittsburgh, Pennsylvania

Although leery investors scoffed, the development, known as Station Square, moved ahead with a $5 million grant from the local Allegheny Foundation and $2 million from Chuck Muer, a restaurateur who established a 500-seat restaurant in the station's grand concourse. The project's success was immediate. Although the experts had projected a maximum annual gross of $300,000, the project instead earned $3 million in the first year and became a successful draw for both tourists and Pittsburgh residents.

The journalist and urban critic Roberta Brandes Gratz described how this preservation/development project benefited the community:

> Station Square has turned into a genuinely reinvigorating project for Pittsburgh and an important catalyst for similar rejuvenation schemes. As sole developer, PHLF will convert the profits into an endowment for its revolving fund to underwrite local housing restoration for low- and moderate-income families, educational programs and other preservation projects. Station Square, furthermore, although developed by a not-for-profit organization, is paying full taxes.[2]

Stabilization of Property Values—Washington, D.C.

Does the establishment of a historic district inflate property values and taxes, based on the added prestige? Or do property values drop under the threat of increased regulation and loss of property rights? Most studies of the impact of historic districts on property values find that the primary effect is neither a rapid increase nor a decline; rather, such districts tend to stabilize property values.

Dennis Gale, a professor of urban and regional planning, looked more deeply at the question of whether historic district status tend to price moderate-income owners out of neighborhoods and found "little support for the argument that official recognition of the historic and architectural merits of residential neighborhoods leads to accelerating property values." Gale studied three historic districts in the District of Columbia, comparing tax assessments before and after designation. He found that growth rates in tax assessments were actually less after designation, perhaps because "fear of limits on property use, property changes and demolition permissions may have shifted investment activity to other neighborhoods."[3] There may be benefits, however, with historic designation, such as the right to oppose demolitions and protect an area against unwarranted and unnecessary clearance activities.

Public Relations and Promotion— Lowell, Massachusetts

In the nineteenth century, Lowell was at the center of New England's textile industry. When the textile industry moved to lower-cost, nonunion southern states in the 1920s, Lowell and other old industrial cities were largely abandoned. Large, well-built mill buildings remained, but most were vacant, and they lined the rivers as ghosts of former times. Lowell was one of the largest of the textile towns and was hit hard by the changed economy.

Preservation has been used as a tool for renewal, however, and Lowell now represents an important success story. In 1978, the city's center was designated a 137-acre preservation district under a National Historical Parks program. Since then, many of the textile buildings were restored as apartments for the elderly, a museum and tourist center were added in an old mill building, and Lowell has traded on the history of the textile industry as its primary historical and tourist attraction. The historic district is less an attempt to preserve a grouping of buildings than an effort to preserve the elements of an earlier local industry of national significance.

Lowell, Massachusetts

As a spinoff from this base, Lowell's downtown has been revitalized, with many new shops, continuing renovation, and reduced unemployment. The city now attracts new industry, boosting the local economy.

State Enabling Legislation for Historic Districts

CASE STUDY—STATE OF MICHIGAN LOCAL HISTORIC DISTRICTS ACT

Historic district commissions, with their powers of regulation, can be established at the local level only after the municipality has been given this right by state government through enabling legislation. Michigan's enabling act is typical in how it allows for the establishment of local historic districts and historic district commissions. The state legislation is Public Act 96 of 1992, the Local Historic Districts Act.

The purposes of the Act are defined as follows:

1. Safeguard the heritage of the local unit by preserving one or more historic districts in the local unit that reflect elements of the unit's history, architecture, archaeology, engineering, or culture.
2. Stabilize and improve property values in each district and the surrounding areas.
3. Foster civic beauty.
4. Strengthen the local economy.
5. Promote the use of historic districts for the education, pleasure, and welfare of the citizens of the local unit and of the state.

The Act provides for the following:

1. Establishment of historic districts.
2. Acquisition of certain resources for historic preservation purposes.
3. Preservation of historic and nonhistoric resources within historic districts.
4. Establishment of historic district commissions.
5. Maintenance of publicly owned resources by local units.
6. Certain types of assessments under certain circumstances.
7. Procedures.
8. Remedies and penalties.[4]

Some relevant sections of the Act illustrate how the state set up the parameters for local involvement.

Historic District Study Committee

Before establishing a historic district, the legislative body of the local unit shall appoint a historic district study committee. The committee shall contain a majority of persons who have a clearly demonstrated interest in or knowledge of historic preservation, and shall contain representation from one or more duly organized local historic preservation organizations. The committee shall do all of the following:

(a) Conduct a photographic inventory of resources within each proposed historic district following procedures established or approved by the [Michigan] Bureau [of History].

(b) Conduct basic research on each proposed historic district and the historic resources located within that district.

(c) Determine the total number of historic and nonhistoric resources within a proposed historic district and the percentage of historic resources of that total.

(d) Prepare a preliminary historic district study committee report.[5]

SETTING UP A HISTORIC DISTRICT COMMISSION

The act further provides:

The legislative body of a local unit may establish by ordinance a commission to be called the historic district commission. . . . Each member of the commission shall reside within the local unit. . . . The members shall be appointed by the . . . mayor [or township supervisor, village president, or chairperson of the board of commissioners]. The commission . . . shall include as a member, if available, a graduate of an accredited school of architecture.[6]

Historic properties may be designated either as individual structures or as part of a historic district. Here are factors to consider when deciding between designating individual properties versus a district.

A historic district should be established when a grouping of historic structures together has more importance and significance than the structures do individually. A district should have at least one unifying element or theme that ties together all or most of the structures within its boundaries and that justifies its creation. Establishing a historic district may be justified when a concentrated assemblage of historic structures represents an architectural period or style. For instance, many downtown districts are formed around groupings of nineteenth-century Italianate commercial buildings. The ground levels of these buildings often have undergone many changes, but the structures retain historic integrity on their upper levels as well as in the consistent height, scale, and exterior materials used. By creating such a downtown district, property owners institute controls and incentives that encourage retention or restoration of the district's historic integrity.

A district can also be based on an important era in the community's history. For instance, if mining played an important role in a town's development, a district may try to incorporate an assemblage of the remaining buildings that represent this industry.

In some situations, a district may comprise noncontiguous sites or structures if they have a common theme. Perhaps structures representing early settlement, for example, are scattered across a city. In this case, trying to collect the significant buildings within one physical district would mean substantial contortion of the boundary lines. A thematic district made up of noncontiguous elements would be the most appropriate approach, but this is relatively rare, since it does not capture the sense of place, an important factor.

Establishing the Boundaries of a District

By definition, boundaries differentiate between areas and, to some degree, separate them. Thus it is with historic districts. As soon as boundaries are established for a historic district, the city begins a pattern of differentiating areas on both sides of those boundaries. The creation of boundaries from the perspective of historical protection alone sometimes can be simplistic.[7]

Where should boundaries be established? The boundaries of a historic district are often defined by natural features and edges—logical boundaries that echo the images residents have of their community. A district may also be based on the early settlement patterns in a community. Although the logical edges of such a historic area may not be apparent, referring to early maps and descriptions may reveal important differentiations that become obvious solutions.

Boundaries may also be established to protect a historic area from adjacent growth and development that threatens to spill over. Such boundaries should recognize the economic forces that create the need for development and try to accommodate growth and change in some areas while protecting the historic fabric in others. The local planning department and other groups concerned with development issues should be consulted.

Establishing the boundaries of a district creates, by definition, one kind of area within and another without. In addition, the edges often acquire a distinctive pattern of change on their own. While the core of a district can grow and change within its defined environment, the fringe area always feels the boundary restrictions directly. These areas can become districts of their own, albeit with invisible and tacit boundaries.

Some study committees, concerned about omitting even a single historic property, attempt to cover every contingency with overly inclusive boundaries. This approach generally weakens the significant historic properties within, for the boundaries should have as much integrity as possible. It is usually better to be more selective and restrict boundaries to the smallest area that retains the strongest elements of the district's goals. In some states, proposed historic districts are considered for approval by SHPOs. In these cases, consideration is given to the ratio of historic properties to nonhistoric properties. The higher the proportion of historic structures, the more likely is the possibility the proposed district will be supported at higher levels of government. The integrity of the boundaries themselves should also be considered, and the SHPO's office looks negatively on proposed districts whose boundaries are gerrymandered to achieve the highest ratio of historic properties possible. The physical layout of a district (other than a thematic district comprising noncontiguous properties) should have an obvious logic.

The establishment of a historic district is a useful tool, but the consideration of each district and its boundaries must include a broad perspective of the city and the many forces and interactions that give it its vitality.

CASE STUDY—YPSILANTI, MICHIGAN

When creating a new historic district, either by proposing district boundaries or writing the ordinance, a question local preservationists must resolve philosophically is inclusiveness. Should a new district's boundaries embrace most of the community's historic buildings, even if this would include many nonhistoric buildings, or should the boundaries be more limited in scope? Should ordinance provisions make many changes subject to commission review to cover as many contingencies as possible? If so, how can the ordinance be written to accommodate the many building types with varying levels of historic significance typically found in a larger district?

Ypsilanti, population 22,000, took an inclusive approach. The person largely responsible for writing the ordinance, Jane (Bird) Schmiedeke, carefully reviewed the ordinances of sixteen other communities first. One of the best prototypes was New York City's ordinance; this indicated to Schmiedeke that the elements of a good ordinance can be used for cities of widely varying populations.

The intent of the Ypsilanti ordinance was to allow the city's historic district commission as much latitude for review as possible. Therefore, the district boundaries covered a large portion of the city. The district included many nonsignificant structures because they were seen as part of the context surrounding the historic structures. The ordinance also allowed for review by the commission of items not typically included by other communities, such as exterior paint colors and site landscaping. The following chart, prepared in 1984, lists items included in the Ypsilanti ordinance and compares these with ordinances for other Michigan communities.[8]

In the years since it was drafted, Ypsilanti's review process, like those in many other communities, has occasionally been criticized by property owners. One property owner, who began work without a building permit, was surprised when city officials said historic district commission review was also necessary. As a newspaper account described the situation:

> In 1990, George Davidson, owner of Campus Buick GMC Nissan at 34 E. Michigan Ave., ordered a $10,000 canvas awning to add a cozy touch to the establishment. As workers began installing it, city employees came along and stopped the work, saying it had to clear with the Historic District Commission. When presented with the drawing of the 100-foot-long awning, the commission said a section of it was too wide, so Davidson had to have it re-made at an extra $1,000.
>
> "I was new here and wasn't aware of the historic commission," says Davidson. "I have operated businesses in four other communities, but I have never had anything like this. I think it definitely discourages people from investing here. There are so many vacant stores downtown, which indicates something's wrong, and I believe the historic commission's restrictions have something to do with it."[9]

Ypsilanti Historic District Ordinance Provisions	Travers City	Grand Rapids	Adrian	Saline	Romeo	Detroit	Flint	Jackson	Kalamazoo	Muskegan	Northville	Commentary and Legends
PURPOSE: to safeguard heritage by preserving a district; stabilize and improve property values; foster civic beauty and pride; strengthen local economy; promote use of district for education, pleasure, and welfare of citizens	●	●	●	●	●	●	●	●	●	●	●	● = same as Ypsilanti's or similar O = no such provision in ordinance
AND encourage new construction and development harmonious with existing historic architecture and neighborhoods	O	O	O	O	O	O	O	O	O	O	O	The Ypsilanti HDO is the only ordinance in this comparison which specifically promotes or encourages new construction in the HD.
DEFINITIONS: eleven	8	3	0	1	0	13	23	2	1	4	0	
MEMBERS: must include an architect (or builder with known interest in preservation), two from list of preservation society members;	●	●	●	B	O	●	●	●	●	C	●	A. four from Historic District. B. Architect only. C. Architect and some from local Historical Societies D. Mayor and one from Planning Commission
AND one attorney, one elected official, two historians (two of above must reside in District)	O	O	A	O	O	O	O	O	O	O	D	
VARIANCES: duty to recommend to Zoning Board of Appeals any variances to standard requirements when they would serve to retain a neighborhood's historic appearance and/or character	O	O	●	O	●	O	●	O	O	●	●	The ability to provide such variances is vital to the protection of those features, other than buildings, whose retention is critical to the unique character of historic districts
ANNUAL REPORT: written and issued to the City Council obligatory	O	O	O	●	●	O	O	O	O	●	●	
REQUIRED TO REVIEW all applications for building permits in the Historic District	●	●	●	●	●	●	●	●	●	●	●	
AND to approve or disapprove such applications	●	●	●	●	O	●	●	●	●	●	●	
DESIGN CRITERIA: to guide Commission review and decisions	O	O	O	O	O	●	●	O	O	O	O	Some cities may employ criteria and standards not contained in their ordinances. It should be noted that the Ypsilanti ordinance actually incorporates designation criteria, design criteria, and minimum maintenance standards. In addition, the Ypsilanti HDC employs the Secretary of the Interior's Guidelines for Rehabilitation as a review guide.
PROCEDURES for designation of additional districts and landmarks	●	●	O	O	O	●	●	●	O	O	O	
AND designation criteria	O	O	O	O	O	●	O	O	O	O	O	
MAINTENANCE AND NEGLECT: Requirements	O	O	O	●	O	●	●	O	O	O	O	
Procedures	O	O	O	●	O	●	O	O	O	O	O	
Standards	O	O	O	●	O	●	O	O	O	O	O	
APPEAL: same as from decisions of Zoning Board of Appeals	●	O	E	●	O	●	F	●	●	●	G	The circuit court of appeals process is specified under PA 169 of 1970, the historic district enabling legislation. E. Planning Commission F. Building Code Board of Appeals G. City Council within 30 days
COMMERCIAL AREAS: included in separate District guidelines	Y	Y	N		Y		Y	N	Y	Y	Y	

This kind of surprise and chagrin is common among property owners unfamiliar with the review process, who see it as an intrusion on their rights of ownership. Although the Ypsilanti commission has control over virtually any exterior change within the district, its process has proved flexible and its authority to deny has needed to be exerted relatively rarely.

The long-term results were worth it. The city's continuing preservation activities have been effective in changing a general attitude of community neglect into one of concern and caring. The city's new-found sense of heritage restored pride in the community; a Heritage Festival has become a well-attended annual celebration of that pride.

Submitting Documentation for a Proposed District

If a community wishes to obtain National Register certification as a historic district, the following information must be submitted to its SHPO office:

1. A written explanation of reasons why the area should be considered a historic district, including a description of its historic significance.
2. A map describing the proposed boundaries for the district, along with justification for the location of those boundaries.
3. Calculation of the percentage of structures that contribute to the historic character of the proposed district versus the number of non-contributing buildings, and a map locating the buildings in each category.
4. Descriptions of the individual buildings or building groupings within the area, including descriptions of the architectural styles represented.
5. Photographs of the significant historic structures and typical streetscapes.

Scope of Powers of a Historic District and Landmarks Commission

A local historic district and landmarks commission can be involved in many activities relating to local history and preservation. The powers given to commissions are granted by local government and state law, although commissions often become involved in activities other than those specifically given through the ordinance. The following list, from *A Handbook on Historic Preservation Law,*[10] describes the powers that may be granted:

· To survey and identify historically and architecturally significant structures and areas.
· To designate and protect landmarks and their surroundings and landmark districts.

- To review applications for alteration, construction, or demolition of landmark buildings and all structures within a historic district.
- To require affirmative maintenance of historic structures.
- To make recommendations regarding zoning amendments and comments on the local comprehensive plan.
- To undertake educational programs and activities.
- To establish standards and procedures for designation and development review.
- To accept funds from federal, state, and private sources.
- To buy, sell, or accept donations of property.
- To exercise the power of eminent domain.
- To accept easements and other less-than-fee interests in property.

In some cases, the courts have invalidated designations because the criteria used were either too vague or absent entirely.[11] To determine whether designation is legally defensible, ask these questions: (1) Did the review body follow designation procedures as set forth by state and local laws? (2) Did owners receive legal notice of the proposed designation? (3) Were owners given an opportunity to challenge designation? (4) Did the local review body base its decision on the evidence before it?[12]

To be effective when reviewing proposals for additions or alterations to designated buildings, a commission must have the authority to deny. If it can only advise and recommend, then its powers and ability to protect are severely limited and depend more on the personal and moral suasion of its members than on sound review criteria. Chicago's commission has relied on advisory power; as a result, the city has lost many important landmarks and in previous decades its preservation program has sometimes been in disarray. Washington, D.C., and New Orleans have stronger ordinances giving commissions the right to deny but include an appeal procedure to the local elected council. New York City has some of the strongest ordinance provisions; until a hardship appeals panel for nonprofit owners was established in 1990, their commission had the final right of denial with no appeal except to the courts.

Writing an Effective Historic District and Landmarks Ordinance

A historic district and landmarks ordinance typically controls the exterior alteration and demolition of designated structures (and sometimes, as in New York City, Boston, Seattle, and Washington, that of the interior). Ordinances may also include control of new additions, maintenance, and repair. The extent of control is a decision made by the local community through its legislative body. Owners of designated properties must gain approval before making changes. The certificate of appropriateness (or other approval) they must obtain from the local historic district commission is based on the criteria established in the ordinance.

The historic district ordinance should not conflict with either the local zoning ordinance or building department regulations. Sometimes property owners have made changes based on the approval of one city agency only to find they are in conflict with another agency. Historic district ordinances may take precedence over other city ordinances, but this must be explicitly stated in the law. A historic district ordinance may also be established as an "overlay" ordinance, which builds on the existing zoning ordinance.

To be effective and legal, a historic district ordinance must satisfy three conditions: it should be well written, it should be needed, and it should be appropriate.

THE WELL-WRITTEN ORDINANCE

An ordinance must be able to withstand legal challenge, for owners who do not wish to abide by its restrictions may look for weaknesses in its construction. These considerations are important:

1. A good ordinance adheres to the provisions of its state enabling legislation but also includes sections providing for local concerns. For instance, the state may mandate that one member of a historic district commission be an architect. The local government may want to require an attorney as well, which it is free to do. However, each such additional provision tends to limit the flexibility of the city and the commission and should be carefully considered before inclusion.
2. An ordinance should be predictable in its application by the review agency. Clear and direct criteria and standards should be used so property owners can be fairly certain of how to gain approval when they apply to make changes. If approval by the commission is unpredictable, the ordinance is either weak in its formulation or in its application, either of which is unsatisfactory.
3. Before drafting an ordinance, it is worthwhile to review problems that other ordinances have typically encountered. Probably the most common problem is that an ordinance is too vague in its provisions and leaves too much to the discretion of the historic district commission or other review agency. In such a case, decisions are based as much on the personal dynamics of commission members or political considerations as on objective, rational standards.
4. To minimize misinterpretation or misapplication by local commissions, local ordinances may refer to the standards and guidelines established in the Standards of the Secretary of the Interior. This document

establishes nationally recognized criteria for determining the appropriate types of changes to make to historic buildings. (See chapter 7 for more about these guidelines.) Historic district commission members often have difficulty agreeing on aesthetic values. What appears visually compatible to one reviewer may be visually disruptive to another, and it is difficult to base such opinions on more than personal experience. To help overcome this problem, commissioners can refer to the Secretary of the Interior's standards, and by working together over time and reviewing previous cases, they can gradually develop a consensus viewpoint on what is appropriate design.

5. Problems often develop in ordinances when they attempt to define property maintenance provisions. It is one thing to review and approve changes to historic properties, for that process is undertaken by owners when they obtain a building permit. However, if an owner neglects the maintenance of a property and it falls into serious disrepair, then the commission must take the initiative and begin action against the owner. This concern was addressed in the 1975 case of *Maher v. City of New Orleans*: "Once it has been determined that the purpose of the Vieux Carré [historic district] legislation is a proper one, upkeep of buildings appears reasonably necessary to the accomplishment of the goals of the ordinance."[13] Because commissions rarely have power of enforcement, the city agency that does should be established at the outset (e.g., the building department).

6. If the commission is selective in its enforcement proceedings, an owner may claim that it singled him or her out unfairly, saying that similar problems at other properties are not being addressed. This argument may be awkward for the commission or the city to counter, but courts generally defer to commissions as expert bodies, and failure to enforce it in one case is not a legal defense in another.

A well-written ordinance describes how all the above concerns will be addressed by the commission. It is clear, consistent, and legally defensible.

LEGAL CRITERIA

A historic district ordinance is a legal document and must follow requirements of state and local government in its tenets. It should be evaluated according to three basic provisions.

First, its purpose should be to promote the public welfare. The purpose of government is to protect and promote the good of its citizens in general. Therefore, an evaluation of the provisions of an ordinance must show that its primary purpose is to benefit the community in general rather than a group of individual property owners.

Second, the means specified in the ordinance should be rational. The ordinance provisions should be similar in character to other city ordinances in how they are applied and not so convoluted that they lead to easy misinterpretation or misuse. For example, an ordinance requiring that all properties in the historic district have a green front door is irrational, for such a decree would not be based on historical precedent but rather created at the whim of the writers of the ordinance.

Third, the provisions of the ordinance should be fair, and should apply equally to everyone within a specified group. The local historic commission cannot use the ordinance to take action against one non-compliant property owner without taking similar action against others. The ordinance should not be unduly onerous or burdensome on those individuals. Indeed, if the ordinance is too restrictive on certain properties, their owners could argue that their property is subject to a legal taking (see below) and the city could be liable for compensation to those owners.

THE NECESSARY ORDINANCE

To be effective, an ordinance must fill a need. In some situations, historic buildings are protected and maintained through other agencies and no local ordinance is needed, for it would be either duplicative or ineffective in its application. In such an area, perhaps recognition by the municipality is enough. Historic buildings can be recognized by way of special resolutions, markers, and signage.

Elsewhere, an ordinance may not be necessary simply because properties are not threatened, and the political tradeoffs in pushing through an ordinance would be detrimental in other ways. Historically significant houses may be found in stable residential areas where no pressure for change is foreseen. Rather than draft an ordinance that attempts to anticipate future needs, it might be preferable to hold off on the legislative front. If the situation changes, the need for a protective ordinance can be more realistically assessed. This is not to say that local ordinances should be put off until the last possible moment, when the threat is all too real and the response must be reactive. Preservationists should always let the community know what areas and structures they consider historically significant and how they best can be protected.

THE APPROPRIATE ORDINANCE

An effective ordinance appropriately deals with the needs of the properties included in its jurisdiction. A boilerplate ordinance (one that simply copies another) should be avoided, for different communities have different needs and desires.

For example, the state of Alaska directs the establishment of historic districts with structures listed on the National Register of Historic Places, but supplements that by including districts "characteristic of the Russian-American period before 1867, the early territorial period before 1930, or early native heritage."[14] The Arkansas code directs that exterior changes to historic properties be approved by a local commission prior to the building of any structure, including "stone walls, fences, light fixtures, steps and paving, or any outdoor advertising."[15] The District of Columbia code says that anyone who is in violation through demolition or alteration of a protected structure shall be required to "restore the building or structure and its site to its appearance prior to the violation."[16] An ordinance dealing with a specific area in Indianapolis encourages preservation of Meridian Street "to preserve significant tourist attractions of historical and economic value by limiting or restricting any use in the area that would be inconsistent with its character."[17] Each of these examples illustrates how ordinances can reflect local concerns and needs.

Opposition to a Historic District

The proposed establishment of a historic district, covered by an ordinance, is met sometimes with opposition from groups with a variety of concerns. It is important to understand and address these concerns when putting forward the concept.

Surprisingly, opposition often comes from other agencies of local government. It may partially be based on the general fear of losing power to another city agency, in this case the local historic district commission. A historic district may be opposed because it can mean additional work for some city officials; perhaps the building department will need to coordinate its approvals for building permits with the historic commission, or the city planning department will need to wait for comments from the historic commission before making recommendations on projects before it. Other concerns may be financial. The cost of running the administration of a historic district commission (staff, office costs, project fees, and contracts) may come out of another agency's budget, either directly or indirectly. Also, the provisions of a historic district ordinance may limit capital improvements projects. For example, while the transportation department may want to widen a street to increase traffic flow, the historic district commission may not agree that it is in the city's best interests to do this in a historic district. All these concerns may arise when a new historic district is proposed.

Institutions also may not be in favor of historic districts, especially if they have a stake in the property. State institutions (colleges, hospitals, etc.) are typically not subject to local ordinances and need respond only to state regulations. Universities are frequently uncooperative with local historic district commissions. Generally speaking, the larger the institution, the more it can ignore local pressure for its structures to be included in a historic district. Yet, in most cases, these institutions represent important elements of a community's history and heritage; their lack of involvement in local historic designation efforts can cause serious discord in establishing a community's historic preservation goals.

Finally, historic districts may be opposed by private citizens, who assert their rights with the cry, "Don't tell me what I can and can't do with my own property." This attitude runs deep in the American psyche and represents a valid concern. However, legal precedents have already established the right of a city and its agencies to limit what people may and may not do with their property through zoning or building codes. When historic districts are proposed, these concerns come to the forefront because such regulations have been seen as intrinsic to a city's role and may not generally be recognized as appropriate by many citizens.

Otherwise, opposition is based largely on the amount of control being proposed. The best way to divert this criticism is to develop an ordinance that combines regulations with incentives—a carrot-and-stick approach.

Concerns and Comments

The following concerns, often heard when historic districts are proposed, represent the most common points of opposition. These concerns are heard especially when the designation of commercial buildings is proposed because owners fear the designation will limit their right to profit from their investment.

The suggested replies represent reasonable responses to these concerns.

CONCERN: Designation will add another level of bureaucracy to the city's approval process.

REPLY: When changes or additions are proposed to designated buildings, the review process of the historic district commission should be efficient, predictable, and integrated into the normal review of other city agencies. Approval or disapproval by the commission should be completed expeditiously (e.g., typically no more than sixty to ninety days from the time the application is submitted). The determination should be given in writing and the reasons for approval or disapproval should be given. As owners become accustomed to this procedure, it should take no longer than other approvals.

CONCERN: Designation will cause unnecessary hardship to property owners.

REPLY: The act of designation should not cause economic hardship. As a Virginia court found, the identification of an area as a historic district did not deprive the owners of any property rights.[18]

Designation should be based solely on historical or architectural significance and not on economic impact. However, historic preservation has been shown in many communities to help create economic revitalization. In residential areas, property values do not fall after such designation but rather stabilize, as designation implies more neighborhood stability and renewal. In commercial areas, designation has led to many new programs and revitalization proposals that have created a fresh image and new vitality for businesses.

If an economic hardship arises through inequitable property taxes or other regulations, it can be remedied by incentive programs described elsewhere (see Chapter 10). Owners who feel they are treated unfairly may typically appeal to the mayor, city council, or an appeals board.

CONCERN: Designation means I can't change or add on to my building.

REPLY: This is probably the most misunderstood and surprising concern, for most ordinances permit alterations and additions. Indeed, it would be foolish not to, because historic properties would be doomed to be museum pieces if they could not be updated.

Alterations and additions should be permitted if two conditions are met. First, the changes should not destroy the elements that give a property its historic integrity. For example, if the front facade is important as part of a district's streetscape, then an addition should be allowed at the rear. If the entire exterior is historically significant, then change can be made to the interior and an addition permitted if it complements the original structure. The guidelines for making such changes are described in the *Secretary of the Interior's Standards and Guidelines for Historic Rehabilitation* (see Chapter 7).

Second, alterations or additions should be subject to the review and approval of a historic district commission. This ensures that the standards are interpreted appropriately and consistently.

CONCERN: Designation is mandatory. Shouldn't it be voluntary?

REPLY: At first, this seems a valid approach. If ordinances allowed for voluntary designation, they would be acceptable to property owners. In fact, over 330 local governments are believed to have established owner consent requirements as part of their designation procedures.[19]

However, such ordinances are inherently weak from a preservation and a legal viewpoint, for they give owners the right to determine whether or not their buildings are historically significant—and owners may not be the best people to make this judgment. Some owners want to give high status to their property when its significance may be relatively insignificant, while others fear the restrictions that accompany designation and may insist that their important historic property not receive any form of designation.

Historic buildings should be recognized as such whether or not the owner agrees. The determination should be made by a qualified panel of experts; consistency in the designation process is important because historic buildings have no other protection from demolition or destructive alterations in any other way.

Owner consent also may be constitutionally invalid, for it fails to treat similar properties (historic properties) alike and regulates them in what could be considered an arbitrary manner.

CONCERN: It is unfair to give my building designation, for there are no firm criteria for selection. The list of proposed buildings seems arbitrary and based on subjective judgments only.

REPLY: The selection of properties to be designated and subject to the regulations of a local ordinance should be made by an impartial panel of individuals knowledgeable about local history and architectural history and styles. Serving on the selection committee is no easy task, for the merits of individual structures can be argued from many perspectives and consensus can be achieved at times only through much debate and reconsideration. The final list should present the reasons for each selection.

Although selection is to some degree subjective, as it must be, legal precedents have established that such a process has legal standing as long as (1) the selection decisions were made by qualified people, and (2) selection criteria were established beforehand. The selection criteria need not rely on cold, statistical logic but can be "soft," for complete objectivity is impossible when it comes to questions of historical importance. Courts have generally upheld the legality of such determinations and are not supposed to substitute their judgment for that of the expert selection committee.

Selection is ultimately based on two factors: historical or cultural significance and architectural significance. More specific criteria may be added, including such factors as age; number of buildings of a certain type extant in the community; listing on local, state, or federal registers; association with important local events; examples of fine craftsmanship, etc.

CONCERN: This ordinance has no sound legal basis and will be subject to lawsuits.

REPLY: Any ordinance designating and regulating historic buildings should be legally well founded. Many legal precedents uphold the right of local governments to enact preservation ordinances as a valid exercise of the police power, including the well-known *Penn Central* case of 1978 (see chapter 4). Such ordinances should also be compatible with state legislation, which is also necessary to establish local commissions and ordinances. An ordinance should be scrutinized by legal counsel, whether the city attorney or private counsel, for it is a document with many legal as well as economic ramifications and may be challenged by a disgruntled owner.

With such a basis in law, there is little reason to be concerned about the right to designate historic structures and individual landmarks through local ordinance. Over the past three decades, the right of local jurisdictions to designate historic districts has become as accepted a practice as the creation of zoning ordinances, which were earlier subjected to similar scrutiny and challenge.

Nevertheless, owners cannot be denied reasonable use of their property without due process of law. Therefore, if a preservation commission is considering a structure for designation, two steps should be included in the process: the owner should first be given adequate notice of the contemplated action (thirty- to sixty-day notice by registered mail is typical) and, second, notified and given a chance to speak at a public hearing.

A Limitation of Historic Districts

Often, a historic designation is given to a building largely on the basis of age. But age is relative and, by definition, constantly changing. Consider, for example, the situation of Oak Park, Illinois. In the early 1900s, Oak Park was one of the most desirable suburbs of Chicago. Its tree-lined streets were fronted by stately Victorian homes, many in the ebullient and showy Queen Anne style. The homes were tall, with steep roofs, turrets, and many gables. Into that setting Frank Lloyd Wright brought a new style for residential design, eventually known as the Prairie (or Wrightian) style, which was largely inspired by the broad midwestern plains (see chapter 5). Wright's houses were more horizontal than vertical, with low, sloped roofs and wide, overhanging eaves. There could not have been a sharper contrast to the Victorian houses in Oak Park than this new architectural style.

A question arises from this example. If Oak Park had had a historic ordinance and had set up a historic district commission to review new construction, would Frank Lloyd Wright's designs have been approved? Or would the commissioners have denied the requests because the

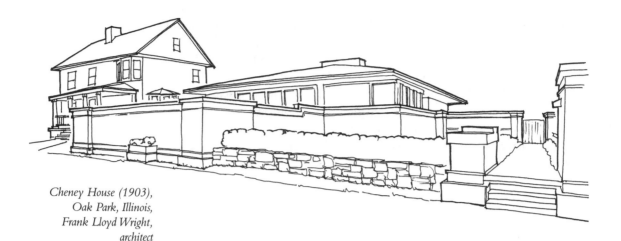

Cheney House (1903),
Oak Park, Illinois,
Frank Lloyd Wright,
architect

designs were incompatible with the residential character of the neighborhood? Today we recognize the brilliance of these early houses by Wright, which are among the nation's architectural treasures. Yet in 1910 or 1915 they were new, incompatible, and probably would have not been built if a strict review procedure had been required. What a tragedy in Oak Park that would have been.

In the same vein, we must ask ourselves today whether our historic requirements prevent the building of innovative and important architecture. In our attempt to protect against the worst designs, are we also not allowing the best to come out? Sometimes it is necessary to recognize significant architecture before it has had a chance to age; excellence must be nurtured and encouraged wherever it is found.

Chapter 4

The Legal Basis for Preservation

The legal basis for historic preservation ordinances and regulation was established with some difficulty. Land use law, which forms the framework for most historic preservation law, was based on the premise that property owners have the right to do as they wish with their properties and that this right could be infringed upon only if the use of the property was a nuisance to the community. The basic duty of government was to protect citizens from having bad things happen but not to insist on making good things happen. Thus, the government had no right or authority to regulate property for aesthetic purposes (or, in this case, historic character) and property owners had no legal obligation to contribute to the public welfare in the use of their property.

BERMAN V. PARKER

The zoning laws established in the early twentieth century had little impact on preservation, for historic structures were protected through ordinance only if regulations involved more than aesthetics and dealt with controlling a nuisance or protecting land uses. This "aesthetics plus" principle meant that regulation had to be justified by a reason beyond historic significance—for instance, economic benefit.

The important *Berman* v. *Parker* case, decided by the U.S. Supreme Court in 1954, changed this premise. The court determined that the District of Columbia could remove an unblighted building labeled "blighted" pursuant to a plan to address blight. This case established the principle that aesthetics alone is sufficient to justify government regulation. As Justice William Douglas wrote as part of the decision, "It is within the power of the legislature to determine that the community should be beautiful as well as healthy, spacious as well as clean."[1]

Preservationists realized this precedent could be used to justify protective historic ordinances and their protection of historic buildings. If a

The Legitimacy of Historic Review and Designation

city could regulate against "ugly" buildings based on aesthetics, it could also regulate for "beautiful" buildings. This case provided the backbone of historic preservation regulations.

FIGARSKY V. HISTORIC DISTRICT COMMISSION

In 1976 Connecticut's highest court dealt with a historic district's "vague aesthetic legislation." In *Figarsky v. Historic District Commission,*[2] an owner of an old structure facing the historic green in Norwich, Connecticut, was cited by the city's building inspector for having an unsafe structure. The building was part of the green's historic district, but because it had little individual significance, because it was in an altered condition, and because the owner had no good use for the vacant structure any longer, he requested a permit to demolish it. The commission denied the request, saying the structure was important because it blocked a view from the green to an encroaching commercial area and thus was important to preserving the character of the district. The "precedent" for this action had been established two years earlier in *Maher v. City of New Orleans,* where the court found a building in a historic district did not need to have individual significance to merit protection because "just as important is the preservation and protection of the setting and scene in which structures of architectural and historical significance are situated."[3]

In the Figarsky case, the owner felt the preservation of the general character of a district was not sufficient reason for the commission to deny a demolition permit, and appealed the commission's ruling, saying it had used "vague aesthetic legislation" and acted illegally, arbitrarily, and in abuse of its discretion. He wanted compensation to cover the cost of making sufficient repairs to satisfy the building inspector. However, the Connecticut court ruled that the city's not allowing the demolition of a structure needing substantial repairs was neither confiscatory nor an abuse of the commission's power and upheld the commission's denial of a demolition permit.

THE PENN CENTRAL DECISION

Historic preservation's most important legal precedent is the landmark 1978 U. S. Supreme Court decision *Penn Central Transportation Company. v. City of New York,*[4] commonly referred to as the *Penn Central* decision. The importance of this decision to historic preservation cannot be overstated, as it forms the legal justification for most historic preservation ordinances. The *Penn Central* case was significant because it dealt with the right of an owner to develop a property versus the right of a city to

Grand Central Station, New York City, 1913. Reed and Stem and Warren and Wetmore, architects

review and regulate the development of a designated historic property. The case became essentially the first Supreme Court decision dealing directly with historic preservation law.

Penn Central Transportation Company, the owner of Grand Central Terminal in New York City, had applied to the New York Landmarks Commission for permission to construct a fifty-five-story addition over the Grand Central Terminal building, which was designated as a landmark. The proposed addition was designed by Marcel Breuer and included a new structure cantilevering above the Terminal's existing facade. An alternative plan, submitted at the same time, included the removal of the building's features on the 42nd Street facade.

When the Landmarks Commission denied approval for the proposed tower based on the Terminal's historic designation, Penn Central claimed a taking (see below), sought to have the designation overturned, and asked the city for compensation for not being able to develop its property. Many saw the proposal as a desecration of this landmark building, which was important to the life of New York City. The case became a *cause célèbre*, with many notables, including Jacqueline Kennedy Onassis and architect Philip Johnson, marching in the streets to "save Grand Central."

A primary question this case presented was whether the city's new Landmark Law discriminated against a property owner who owned a historic structure designated as an individual landmark. Whereas zoning ordinances apply generally across all properties and the burden of such regulation is more or less evenly shared, landmark legislation applies to a minority of property owners, who must bear the burden of community good for all others. As made evident in this case, the imposition of the Landmarks Preservation Law "imposed a substantial cost on less than one one-tenth of one percent of the buildings in New York for the general benefit of all its people."[5]

The New York Court of Appeals earlier had ruled there was no taking because the preservation ordinance did not transfer control of the property to the city but only restricted appellants' exploitation of it. The Appeals Court held the owners had not been denied their rights because:

> (1) the same use of the Terminal was permitted as before; (2) the appellants had not shown that they could not earn a reasonable return on their investment in the Terminal itself; (3) even if the Terminal proper could never operate at a reasonable profit, some of the income from Penn Central's extensive real estate holdings in the area must realistically be imputed to the Terminal; and (4) the development rights above the Terminal, which were made transferable to numerous sites in the vicinity, provided significant compensation for loss of rights above the Terminal itself.[6]

The case went on to the U. S. Supreme Court, where in a six-to-three decision the validity of New York's preservation law was upheld as it applied to the *Penn Central* case. Justice William Brennan described the significance of the case at the beginning of his opinion:

> The question presented is whether a city may, as part of a comprehensive program to preserve historic landmarks and historic districts, place restrictions on the development of individual historic landmarks—in addition to those imposed by applicable zoning ordinances—without effecting a "taking" requiring the payment of "just compensation." Specifically, we must decide whether the application of New York City's Landmarks Preservation Law to the parcel of land occupied by Grand Central Terminal has "taken" its owners' property in violation of the Fifth and Fourteenth Amendments.[7]

In Justice Brennan's opinion, he cited the fact that government could not go on if it did not have the power to regulate the use of private property, or it had to pay for any diminution in land value or loss of potential value, based on changes in the general law. There are ample

ample examples of this, including zoning laws restricting the use of property and even the assessing of property taxes.[8]

This landmark (there is no other word to describe it) decision upheld the legitimacy of historic ordinances by recognizing that preserving historic resources is a permissible governmental goal and that the city's preservation ordinance was an appropriate means for accomplishing that goal. As such, the *Penn Central* decision formed the legal basis for legislatures to grant cities the right to establish controls to which the owners of historic properties would be subject.

It is interesting to note that during the 1990s Grand Central Terminal underwent a major restoration that has been recognized by residents of New York City and commuters as a return to its former glory.

With the *Penn Central* decision the Supreme Court upheld the legitimacy of historic preservation ordinances, but many questions were left unanswered. Primary among these was just how far a public agency could go in limiting the rights of private owners to develop their property. The commission's denial of Penn Central's proposal was upheld because, in the Court's opinion, the company had failed to show it was unable to get a "reasonable return" from its property. What the Court did not indicate was how much regulation would be considered too much.

If the owner was able to prove it was unable to make a "reasonable" return (left to other courts and other cases to decide), a taking could be claimed, in which case the public agency would need to compensate the owner for the loss of use of his or her property. A number of later court cases, not involving historic preservation regulations, have established the general limits of regulation before a taking could be claimed.

The Issue of Takings

The taking issue remains a primary concern to many historic district commissioners who are challenged by property owners. What should commissioners do to protect themselves from such legal challenges?

To avoid controversy about takings, a historic district commission should carefully describe the parts of the property included in the designation. Is just the principal structure designated? Are the ancillary buildings included? Is the entire site covered, or is the owner permitted to sell or develop sections of the property?

Sometimes a variance for new construction is given if an owner makes the case for economic hardship. However, the hardship must be more drastic than difficulty paying taxes or operating costs. The inability of an owner to maximize the property's economic return is also not

Takings and Local Historic District Commissions

sufficient justification. The owner must prove that the property's existing use is economically unfeasible and that sale, rental, or rehabilitation of the property is not possible.

In some jurisdictions, when historic buildings are owned by nonprofit organizations, the situation is considered differently. Religious organizations have long argued they should not be subject to the same requirements as other property owners. Obviously, their issue is not the economic question of reasonable return. Churches sometimes argue they serve a community and religious purpose and need to retain the right to change their property and buildings to best address that need.

In spite of the free exercise clause defined in the First Amendment, courts have generally upheld the right to designate religious buildings and have them subject to civic regulations. Just as they are subject to other land use and zoning regulations and fire and safety codes, they are subject to community interests with regard to historic designation.[9] If a proposed alteration or demolition is the only action that allows the property to continue in its religious role, then special treatment is generally supported.

St. Bartholomew's

The constitutional question of whether or not churches and religious buildings should be exempt from historic ordinances is an important one. This issue was dealt with most directly and publicly in the case of *St. Bartholomew's* v. *New York City Landmarks Preservation Commission* (1990).[10]

St. Bartholomew's is a prominent church located in the center of one of New York City's prime commercial districts. Built in 1919, the church was designed by Bertram Goodhue, one of the most important architects of the period, and is an excellent example of its kind. "St. Bartholomew's Church in New York City is many things to many people. To the passerby, it is a rare breathing space, an interval of gardens and terraces on Park Avenue between Fiftieth and Fifty-first Streets. To the aesthete, it is a beautiful edifice of soft brick and stone. To the religious, it is an oasis of faith in a spiritual wasteland, a monument to God in the land of mammon. And to the homeless, it is a haven where can be found a meal, clean clothes, a night's shelter."[11]

The New York City Landmarks Preservation Commission, recognizing the building's architectural significance and the importance of the architect and the history of the building, designated St. Bartholomew's a historic landmark in 1967. The rector and vestry had opposed the designation.

St. Bartholomew's Church,
New York City, 1919.
Sketch from photograph in
Preservation News
(February 1990)

By the early 1980s, the church had developed plans to replace its adjacent community house with a speculative high-rise office tower. The congregation felt the substantial income from the investment would both support maintenance costs for the aging structure and finance the church's community outreach and missionary programs. The estimated earnings of the proposed building were as high as $100 million. Following a series of public hearings, the Preservation Commission turned down the plans on the ground that the scale of the fifty-nine-story reflective glass tower was incompatible with the church. According to one commissioner, the project looked like "nothing so much as a noble work of man about to be crushed beneath a gargantuan ice cube tray."[12]

The church fought back. "People think we're vandals," said the church's senior warden. "But preservation of the church is very important to us. If we don't have more money we won't be able to preserve the very building that the preservationists are concerned about: the church sanctuary." To forbid construction would be to take the property out of the church's control and put it "in the hands of a secular agency."[13]

The parishioners were badly split on the issue. Some church members felt the commission had gone back on its promise to allow changes after designation. As one church member said, "We feel we were lied to at the time of the designation. We relied on a statement made then that would have allowed us to develop our property."[14] A commissioner responded that the 1967 agreement with the church permitted alterations to the property but did not permit the development of a skyscraper. "A one- or two-story addition is one thing, but a forty-seven-story office tower is different. We didn't say nothing could be done, we said this proposal was inappropriate."

Other parishioners were opposed to the development and formed the Committee to Oppose the Sale of St Bartholomew's Church. They charged that "this case is not about religion, but rather it is about a church's efforts, in partnership with a commercial real estate developer, to destroy its landmark property and to develop its site to the highest commercial value."[15]

The battle persisted for more than a decade. Three times the Landmarks Preservation Commission denied the church's plans—the original proposal for a 59-story glass tower, a second for a 49-story tower, and a third application based on economic hardship. The case went to the Federal District Court and then the U. S. Court of Appeals, where two questions were decided: (1) Did the church's historic designation violate the constitution's free exercise provision and (2) Did the denial represent a taking, and should the church therefore be compensated by the city for not being able to build the office tower?

The church's attorneys first argued the case on a series of general principles. They said the designation was against the First Amendment and interfered with the church's ability to develop money for its service programs, thus limiting free exercise of religious beliefs and activities. The court responded that as long as a rational basis for a law of general applicability exists (historic designation and review) and the church was not "impermissibly burden[ed]" in carrying out its religious activities, overruling the designation as illegal or unconstitutional was ungrounded.

Next, the church argued that previous cases had established that historic designation should not take away an owner's ability to make a "reasonable return" on its property. If designation took away the possibility of a reasonable return, then a taking could be claimed. The court, however, said that commercial and charitable entities were not alike. The church was a charitable organization and the reasonable return provision did not apply, as designation did not interfere with the carrying out of the church's religious purposes.

The church next argued that it had been denied due process in the initial decision on designation. The court responded that the requirements of due process had been met, as (1) prior notice was given of the designation, and (2) there had been a public hearing. The owner's approval was not necessary; the only requirement was that the owner be notified and given a chance to comment. The court thus rejected all three arguments of general principle and, therefore, the church's claims.

The church also argued specific points as applied in the case. The records showed that at the hardship hearing before the commission it argued it would be unable to fulfil its mission of community service and to maintain the main sanctuary without additional income. According to New York law, if it expected to satisfy the hardship provision, the church would have to prove

- That the landmarks designation interfered with its charitable purpose
- That the cost of renovating the building to suit that purpose would be too great for the church to bear
- That the church could not afford to maintain the buildings in its present financial condition.[16]

In a hearing with the Landmarks Commission, the church presented testimony that it did not have the resources to meet its needs. The court noted that the church had a stock portfolio more than sufficient to carry out the proposed renovations, and could increase its income by selling its air rights (see chapter 10). The St. Bartholomew's case is important for the legal precedent it clarified. It established that religious organizations are subject to historic preservation ordinances of local government, and that such regulations are not a violation of the First Amendment prohibition of interference with the free exercise of religion.

Voluntary Protective Covenants for Frank Lloyd Wright's Unity Temple

The owners of historic properties often are concerned about the restrictions placed on them through designation. The designation of religious properties is often more controversial than that of any other type of property. Though courts have upheld the right of municipalities to make such designations, churches are among the most vocal and active opponents of historic designation.

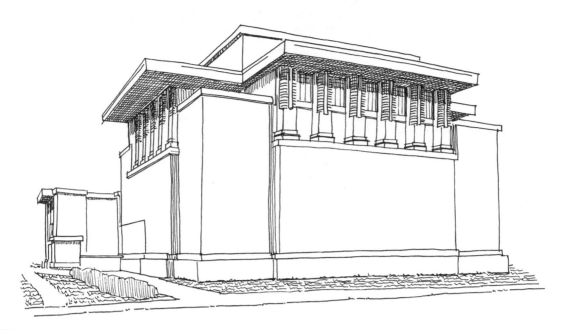

Unity Temple, Oak Park, Illinois, 1906, Frank Lloyd Wright, Architect

Unity Temple, an important early project of Frank Lloyd Wright, is another situation entirely. The Unity Temple congregation supported designation and made the landmark structure one of the first religious properties in the country to be voluntarily designated. An agreement guaranteed strict protection for both the exterior facade of the church and the public areas of its interior.

The designation is significant for a number of reasons. First, the owners voluntarily solicited the designation because they recognized the historic importance of the structure as one of Wright's most important projects and wanted to see it protected in perpetuity. Second, the designation included interior spaces, which are usually not designated because it is felt the infringement is too great. Third, protection was secured through an easement (see chapter 10). As part of this agreement, the Landmarks Preservation Council of Illinois annually inspects the structure to ensure that changes are not made without approval. The building must always be used as a church or similar entity to ensure that the interior spaces will remain as is. In return, the congregation's ability to solicit donations for the church's restoration work is increased, and the easement agreement assures donors that their money goes directly to the building fund rather than the church's general budget.

Chapter 5

The Documentation and Designation of Individual Historic Properties

Perhaps nothing comes closer to the heart of a preservationist than researching an individual historic property and preparing its nomination for designation as a historic structure listed on the National Register of Historic Places. The process of determining a structure's historical and architectural significance form the trunk of the tree from which all other limbs of preservation grow. Documentation is also one of the preservationist's most interesting activities, for the research is like a mystery hunt—bits and pieces of information are put together like clues, leading to the answers needed to document a structure's historic significance.

Like Sherlock Holmes's detective work, researching historic properties is both a craft and an art. The craft is in piecing together information on a property from disparate sources; the art is in its interpretation.

The term generally used to describe a property's relative importance is *historical significance.* This is established based on two primary factors: historical or cultural importance and architectural importance. Sometimes both contribute, in which case historical significance is enhanced.

Many factors may increase a historic property's significance; the more that apply, the greater the level of significance. As based on the *National Register's Criteria for Evaluation,*[1] the historical significance of a proposed property can be established based on any of four criteria:

1. The property is associated with events that have made a significant contribution to the road patterns of American history. For instance, if a city was established along an important rail line, the original railway station or complex of freight buildings from those early years could be considered significant to that city's local history.
2. The property is associated with the life of a significant person in the American past. This is the George-Washington-Slept-Here category. Generally, birthplaces and gravesites of important personages are not

Establishing a Property's Significance

designated because they are not uniquely representative of the person's significant years. More relevant and worthy of designation are buildings or sites that relate directly to significant events in that person's life. Fort Necessity Battlefield, where George Washington fought his first battle, and Ford Theater, where Abraham Lincoln was shot, are good examples.

3. The property embodies distinctive features of type, period, method of construction, or high artistic values, or represents a significant and distinguishable entity whose components may lack individual distinction. This category deals with architectural significance. Even if a property is not associated with an important event or person, it may be a good example of an architectural style or type of construction from a certain period. Selectivity is important in considering properties under this category, for every building represents a period and a style (even if a vernacular style). Therefore, selections should be based on how well the building represents its style. Does it retain most of its original features? Is the style relatively rare? Only the best should be chosen as representatives in this category.

4. The property and its site yield, or are likely to yield, important information in history or prehistory. Important evidence of older cultures is uncovered through archeological exploration. This evidence should be analyzed and documented as a historic resource before construction is permitted.

HISTORICAL SIGNIFICANCE

The importance of a historic property is evaluated according to its significance, which can be illustrated by a hypothetical significance thermometer. The following example shows how factors may affect historic significance.

A turn-of-the-century home is being considered for inclusion as a designated historic structure. The significance of each aspect of the property is assessed.

The home is quite old, which is a positive indicator. The house is also a good example of the Greek Revival architectural style, another positive indicator. As it has not been altered over time and is still largely in its original condition, its significance rises even more. Finally, the house was once owned by an important family in the town's history; this elevates it yet higher.

However, if a modern concrete porch had been built on the front of the house, this would lower its historic integrity and thus its level of significance. If the house had been moved to a new site, this would also

historical
unaltered
style
age

Significance thermometer

decrease its integrity, because a property's level of significance is negatively affected by relocation. The degree of significance lost depends on such factors as the appropriateness of the new site, the distance moved, and the number of changes necessary as a result of the move (e.g., building a new foundation).

Up and down goes the property's evaluation on the significance thermometer as each of these factors is considered. This process of evaluation continues until all relevant information is included.

Each community should determine for itself what minimum level of significance is appropriate for designation and regulation. Numbers should not be assigned for this evaluation because it is not a quantifiable evaluation; local historians determine whether the property is significant enough to qualify for designation based on their knowledge and experience. In communities where residents support preservation, the list of designated properties may be more inclusive than in communities where designation and regulation are opposed. For the former, the minimum threshold is low and many properties have enough significance to be protected. The latter community is more restrictive and only those properties high on the significance thermometer are likely to be included.

CRITERIA FOR EXCLUSION

Guidelines for identifying properties not considered appropriate for designation have been established by the National Park Service. Properties whose nomination to the National Register is not especially encouraged include:

1. Cemeteries and birthplaces, unless the property is the only remaining evidence from an important person's past. These properties are not considered appropriate because they have nothing to do with the person's historical importance. A cemetery or birthplace may qualify based on other criteria, however. For instance, Mount Auburn Cemetery in Cambridge, Massachusetts, is not currently listed but could be because it represents the first and best known of the nineteenth-century cemeteries laid out in the English landscape style.
2. Religious properties are generally excluded unless they have significant architectural merit. Every community has an abundance of prominent religious structures, which must have additional significance (religious status plus) to properly be considered. However, many churches are included on the basis of architectural merit.
3. Structures moved from their original sites are considered to have lost much of their integrity, and thus significance, and designations of such properties generally are discouraged.

The Documentation and Designation of Individual Historic Properties • 95

4. Similarly, reconstructed buildings generally are not included, except in cases where the work is based on authentic documents and is an integral part of a larger master plan.
5. The nomination of statues and commemorative structures is discouraged because they represent an event or person only indirectly.
6. Buildings less than fifty years old are rarely considered for listing.

RECONSIDERING THE AGE REQUIREMENT

The generally accepted criterion that a building must be a certain age to be considered historically significant is now being reconsidered, for many younger properties are obviously historically important. Some are even under threat of demolition.

One of Frank Lloyd Wright's most significant buildings, the Guggenheim Museum in New York City, was for many years threatened with a major alteration because it was considered a relatively small and inefficient building on a prime development parcel, on Fifth Avenue facing Central Park. Because it was less than thirty years old, the structure was not officially recognized as a landmark building and thus not protected, in spite of its architectural importance. Clearly, the building deserved the protection of historic designation despite its youth.

More recent examples represent how some structures have such great significance that they are immediately recognized as landmarks, and the inevitability of their historical importance is accepted. The AT&T

Guggenheim Museum,
Frank Lloyd Wright,
architect

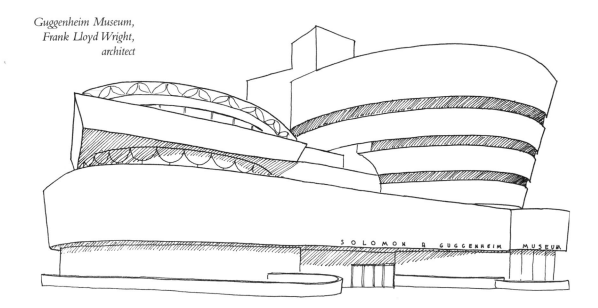

SOLOMON R GUGGENHEIM MUSEUM

An early McDonald's Restaurant, Downey, California

Building in New York City, designed by Philip Johnson and his partner, John Burgee, in 1984, is topped by a prominent Chippendale-style cap, a novel use of abstracted and amplified ornament. Although the building was criticized upon its completion, it immediately became an icon of the Postmodern style of architecture, and its place in architectural history was firmly established.

Other relatively new buildings that need recognition include the fast-disappearing examples of roadside commercial structures, such as diners, motels, and even an early McDonald's restaurant built in 1953 in Downey, California. These building types need to be identified and protected as important elements of our mid-twentieth-century lifestyle, with the best being designated.[2]

LITERATURE SEARCH

When designation is desired, the first step is to research and document the property. A literature search may yield important information. A good place to begin is with the owner of the property, or a former owner. Either may have old clippings about the building or even plans from the original construction or from a later construction project, including information about original conditions. The architectural firm that originally designed the building may still be in business and its files may include invaluable materials.

The land records in the building department may provide important information, including the title history and key dates for a property. Information may also be found in the local history section of a nearby

Documenting a
Historic Property

Photographs of Uniontown, Pennsylvania, from a local history book. Courtesy of Jack Gates

library. Collections of local archival information are often stored there and, although they may be difficult to search through, may yield material well worth the effort.

Sometimes a book is written about a historic structure to commemorate its construction and dedication; such a volume may have old photographs and stories of important personages from the period of its construction. The date of construction can also be used as a guide in searching old professional architecture and construction journals, which may have pertinent information (e.g., an article on the building describing the completion of its construction). State libraries and state archives may be useful, especially for deciphering the larger historical context of the building. For a very significant property, the Library of Congress may be a useful resource.

Dr. Leonard Eaton, professor emeritus of architectural history at the University of Michigan, has documented a number of buildings throughout the Midwest. In the process, he devised rules of thumb to use when researching historic buildings.

1. If possible, go and look at the building itself. Much can be gained by touching its walls and walking through its spaces.
2. Find all the documentation still available. Often, much of the work has been done already. Sometimes a complete set of plans is found in the attic or a file, or old photographs and histories provide evidence of original materials and furnishings. Look for primary sources; don't assume this information must be developed from second- or third-party sources.
3. Never overlook the obvious. The best source of information may not be the historians and experts but a custodian who still works in the building.
4. Consider the setting and its influence. A building is always better understood in its context, both of time and place. Try to visualize the environment at the time of the building's construction, as well as the social setting. This may lead to important clues for finding elements that are historically significant but could easily be overlooked in the structure's current context.[3]

ORAL TRADITIONS

Researchers often overlook the wealth of information found with people who lived for many years in or near a historic property. Much can be gained by asking property owners, tenants, and neighbors for information. Sometimes the best way is simply to ask them to tell the stories they know about the place—who lived there and what happened there.

Workmen and contractors, if they can be found, can also provide useful information on techniques of original construction or changes made over time. They may provide a historical context for construction methods appropriate to a period and help establish when work was completed. They may also describe the significance of craftsmanship techniques found at a property and give weight to arguments for the property's designation.

CITY LITHOGRAPHS (BIRD'S-EYE PERSPECTIVES)

In the nineteenth century, a group of traveling artists made their living by drawing detailed bird's-eye perspectives of the towns they stayed in. They sold lithographic copies to residents. The drawings were carefully prepared because their sales potential depended on accurate depictions from which residents could pick out views of their own homes and

businesses and those of their neighbors. A good-quality lithograph, suitable for framing, went for two to five dollars, so many were purchased; many are still readily found among household memorabilia.

The drawing and selling of city lithographs flourished from the 1850s until the end of the century. For historians they are rich documents that accurately portray a city during a particular time period. Excellent collections of city lithographs have been assembled by urban historian John Reps in his *Views and Viewmakers of Urban America* and *Bird's Eye Views: Historic Lithographs of North American Cities*.[4]

SANBORN INSURANCE MAPS

Sanborn maps are another readily available source of historical information. Published from the mid-1800s to the present day, they show in detail and with great accuracy buildings in approximately 12,000 U.S. cities. Buildings are shown by size, type of construction, condition, and use. Elements of building construction are shown by color: yellow indicates wood frame construction, pink indicates brick, blue indicates stone or concrete, and so on. Other symbols identify the roofing style, placement of windows, thickness of walls, height of buildings, and distance from sidewalks.

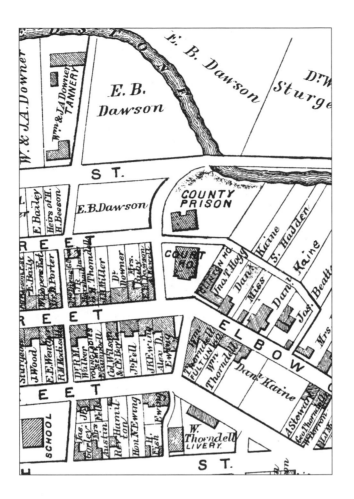

Sanborn insurance map, Uniontown, Pennsylvania. Copyright 1872 Sanborn Map Company, EDR Sanborn, Inc. (This Sanborn Map TM is reproduced with permission from EDR Sanborn, Inc. All further reproductions are prohibited without prior written permission from EDR Sanborn, Inc.)

Although developed primarily for insurance purposes, these maps have become important historical documents. Their publication dates vary from city to city; during certain periods they were released almost annually, while during other periods ten or twenty years passed between dates of publication.

Sanborn maps are indispensable for studying the changes of urbanized areas over decades. Use them with census information, archival photographs, old city directories and gazetteers, and other research materials to:

· Identify buildings and neighborhoods at various periods in history.
· Examine local businesses and view changes in a city's business and industrial base.
· Study the development of water, rail, and highway transportation in urban areas.
· Assess the environmental impact of new developments.[5]

The Documentation and Designation of Individual Historic Properties · 101

EDR Sanborn, Inc., the copyright holder to the Sanborn maps, owns in microfilm format the largest extant collection of them. The company and the Library of Congress in 1996 signed a cooperative agreement whereby EDR Sanborn would scan and provide to users of the National Digital Library and commercial users access to the maps in color digital format. Nearly one million maps will eventually be available on Web.

PHOTOGRAPHIC TECHNIQUES

Digital photography allows photos to be directly downloaded to computers. The digital images can be incorporated with computer drawings (computer-assisted drawing, or CAD) and replace drawn details. The digital photos can be used as part of the construction drawings; arrows, notes, and dimensions can be applied directly to them.

The use of digital cameras combined with notebook computers enables architects to work on CAD drawings directly at a project site, saving time and increasing the accuracy of their work. The resulting computer images can be sent as scanned images to other offices anywhere in the world instantaneously and returned in the same format.

Rectified photography is a relatively simple technique. Targets are placed on a structure at a set distance apart when photos are taken. The targets define the scale when used on a photograph of the structure and provide reference points for a superimposed grid. With such a grid drawn over a photograph, measurements of a structure can be derived for any elevation directly from the photo rather than from laborious

Digitized photo used on construction drawing

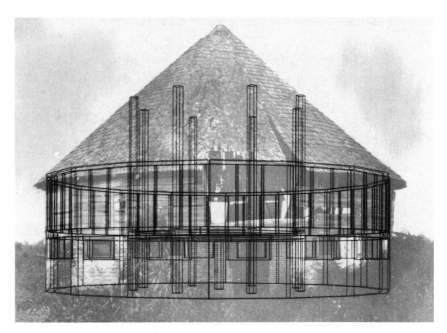

on-site measuring. Obviously, such derived measurements are not be as accurate as actual site measurements, but in many instances they are sufficiently precise. To measure some features, such as stone walls, the technique actually may be preferable because of the difficulty of recording details of the materials using drafting techniques.

A drawback of rectified photography is that it can be used on flat elevations only. Recesses or projections will change in scale and angled surfaces be distorted unless separately photographed with the camera lens parallel to the angled surface.

Photogrammetry is an expensive and highly accurate method for recording structures. Paired photos are viewed with a stereoscopic viewer, which allows for precise recording of all features, even very complex ones. The technique is recognized as the most sophisticated method for uniform and accurate documentation.[6]

Some architects and contractors use radar to locate building materials that cannot be seen by eye. For example, radar can show the location of metal anchors within masonry walls.

DOCUMENTING WITH MEASURED DRAWINGS

The documentation of structures can also be accomplished through the preparation of field-measured drawings. Such drawings allow the documenter to record notes and sketches based on direct observation. If

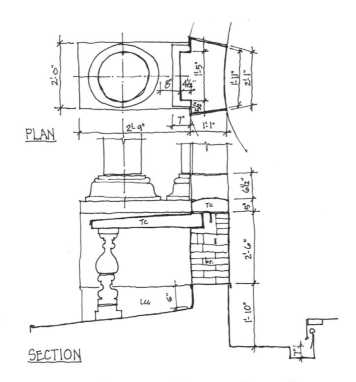

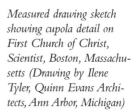

Measured drawing sketch showing cupola detail on First Church of Christ, Scientist, Boston, Massachusetts (Drawing by Ilene Tyler, Quinn Evans Architects, Ann Arbor, Michigan)

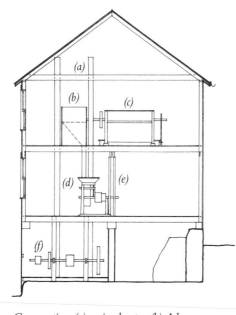

*Cross section: (a) grain elevator, (b) Advance
No. 1 Wheat Brush Scourer and Polisher,
(c) No. 4 Triple Scalper used as a bolter,
(d) Marmon and Nordyke grinders,
(e) chute, (f) equipment pulleys and shaft.*

*Documentation drawings
(cross-section view and
elevation) of Reese Grist
Mill, Greene County,
Pennsylvania*

done in an orderly manner, such sketches can be used to prepare final architectural drawings and provide important input for narrative text. Measured drawings are prepared in two steps. First, sketch plans must be made at the site, including drawings of the floor plans, elevations, and special details. It is usually easiest to draw on tracing paper placed over a grid of 1/4–inch squares, both of which are taped to a firm but lightweight drawing board. Each square of the grid can represent a given scaled area; for plans and elevations, a common scale is one square equals one square foot, or 1/4 inch = 1 foot.

Care must be taken to record information clearly, neatly, accurately, and unambiguously. To avoid misinterpretation of the information, the same person should sketch the drawings, record pertinent information, and prepare the finished drawings. Guidelines established by the Historic American Buildings Survey (HABS) should generally be followed. These define drafting techniques and allow for uniformity of documents as well as clear reproduction capability.

When collecting notes and dimensions for measured drawings, the most effective approach is for a team of two or three people to work together at the site. A draftsman prepares the sketch drawings and one or two assistants read dimensions from a tape measure. Measurements should be read off as running dimensions—that is, a long (100-foot) tape measure should be held at one corner of the structure and distances to doors, windows, and other elements on one wall read without moving the tape. This technique avoids the compilation of errors that would likely occur if the tape were shifted for each measurement.

Based on many factors associated with research on a property, a building may be nominated for designation as a historic structure. Information justifying this status is submitted to the State Historic Preservation Office (SHPO) for review. If approved, the building may be listed on the State Register of Historic Places. The application is then sent on to the office of the Secretary of the Interior in Washington, where, if once again approved, the building is given a National Register listing.

Nominations for National Register listing of a property include the following information:

- Historic and common name of building. Buildings often are referred to by the name of current or recent tenants, although their historical significance comes from an earlier period. Use the name most associated with the building's historical significance.
- Owner, address, and legal property description. Identify the owner and define exactly what parts of the property are included in the designation (e.g., accessory structures, such as garages, barns, and carriage houses; the entire site or the structure only; natural features).
- Date of construction. Include the dates of later additions. Indicate whether or not such additions are part of the designation.
- Architectural style and period. Describe the architectural style of a building whether or not this is the basis for designation. Also specify the architectural period represented by the building.
- Condition of building. Describe the structure's condition as excellent, good, fair, deteriorated, or ruins. Indicate whether or its original integrity is altered and if it has been moved from its original site.
- Narrative descriptions. Include brief descriptions that indicate both the building's historical importance and its architectural significance. Note unusual or important historical events with which the building is associated as well as unique architectural components that are representative of certain features or stylistic elements.
- Photographs. Include photographs of all the significant elevations as well as a photograph showing the building in its surrounding context.
- Preparer. Finally, indicate who prepared the submission and the date it was submitted.

Applying for Designation as a Historic Structure

Designation on the National Register of Historic Places gives national recognition to a historic property. The highest form of designation is a National Historic Landmark, which recognizes properties of national significance in American history and culture and includes their listing on the National Register. About 2,200 sites (approximately 3 percent of the properties on the National Register)[7] are National Historic Landmarks. Examples include Mt. Vernon, Pearl Harbor, Apollo Mission Control Center, Alcatraz, and the Martin Luther King Birthplace.

Because of concern that historic designation would give the federal government new powers over individual property owners, the designation provisions in the National Historic Preservation Act of 1966 did not allow for any direct regulatory power over private properties. In fact, since the 1980 amendment to the Act, such listing can only be done after notice to the owner and provided the owner does not object. If an owner objects, a historically significant property would be listed as "Register Eligible."

Once a property has been listed, it generally cannot lose this designation, even if the owner requests it, unless the basis of its significance were proved to have been lost. The same is true of buildings that have been designated as contributing historic structures in a listed historic district.

DEDESIGNATION

Sometimes it is necessary to remove a historic designation for a locally designated property. Dedesignation may be requested for a variety of reasons. Perhaps a formerly historic structure has been so changed—through conscious alterations, catastrophic damage (weather or fire), or neglect—that designation is no longer appropriate. The procedure for designation of historic structures is well understood, has been done many thousands of times, and has been upheld in courts as constitutionally valid. However, what is the procedure for dedesignation? The precedents for this are minimal and not well understood.

The procedure for removal is determined by the ordinance for designation. Under some ordinances, designation is so fixed that removing it can be accomplished only by abolishing the historic district commission or repealing the entire ordinance. This not only removes designation of the property in question but also all other properties subject to that ordinance or commission.

A properly drafted preservation law provides a recission procedure. Some communities have established procedures for dedesignation. For example, the Detroit city charter states that once a historic district is approved, properties can be removed with a majority vote of the property owners within the district.

What if an owner of a designated historic property consciously makes inappropriate changes or demolishes a structure without approval? What can be done? Often the penalty for such actions is so low (e.g., $500 fine) that such action is not discouraged. However, the owner may be sued in court to have the structure reconstructed, with a cloud on the property title until such work is completed. This is not satisfactory, however, as the damage has been done. Commonly, a commission and its community react with resignation, saying, "Well, we lost this one, but let's make sure it doesn't happen again."

In some cities, inappropriate alterations that were not approved are preservation commission violations or may be treated as building violations, and owners can be ticketed by the enforcing agency (e.g., the building department). The best way to avoid these problems is to institute an ongoing program of community surveillance and education. Neighborhood residents must be aware of ordinances and should be able to recognize when work does not follow its provisions. It is also helpful to have historic district commissioners serve as monitors for projects under construction.

The Secretary of the Interior may also find it necessary to dedesignate National Historic Landmark or National Register properties and districts if they lose too much of their historic integrity. Examples of properties being considered for dedesignation include Roosevelt Dam in Arizona, which has a massive concrete addition to its top and face; Central City, Colorado, the subject of a number of unsympathetic alterations and new construction related to newly established gambling facilities; and Orchestra Hall in Chicago, where remodeling has required extensive demolition of interior spaces.

Both the documentation and designation of individual historic properties are important aspects of historic preservation, for they represent the validation of a structure's historic significance and give it appropriate recognition. Individuals involved in such work find satisfaction in knowing their contribution continues the process of saving our architectural and cultural heritage.

Chapter 6

Architectural Styles

The Search for an American Style

Historic buildings are commonly described in terms of their architectural style. This enables us to place buildings in historic perspective, by describing styles that came before and came after. It also allows us to evaluate whether a building is a good or poor example of a particular period and style. A discussion of the architectural styles found in the United States is a discussion of a continuing search for an American style. For many generations, we have been searching for our cultural identity partially through our architecture. Americans have long wanted to define themselves as a culture separate from their primarily European roots. However, with no strong sense of our own history, the older heritage of a mother country inevitably was used as a starting point.

To trace the evolution of American architectural styles, then, is to follow a centuries-long process. It begins with European precedents and the ways in which early settlers imitated familiar styles based on examples from their homelands (primarily England). The search continues with experiments in the nineteenth century with both classical and romantic trends and culminates, at least for a while, in the twentieth century with a truly original American style.

This chapter presents a summary of major architectural styles that were prominent in American history, starting in the early colonial period; each succeeding style represents a shift in America's self-image. (For references on architectural styles, see the bibliography.)

English Styles

COLONIAL

Buildings constructed during the colonial period (generally considered to be up to 1776) were basic in plan and typically only one room deep. Common characteristics of early colonial houses in the north included steep roofs, which were needed to shed snow, and chimneys

Parson Capen House,
Topsfield, Massachusetts,
1683

placed centrally within the structure to keep the heat radiating within the building. Houses often had two stories for more centralized heating, with the upper floor projecting a foot or two over the lower wall at the front and giving some weather protection to the entry.

Structures were built with locally available natural materials. Pegged post-and-beam construction was common in the north because of the availability of hardwood. Early structures sometimes had thatch roofs, but these were soon replaced with more durable wood shingles. Rooms were added by extending the roof at the rear to form the familiar salt-box shape. Wattle and daub or brick infilled the walls, which were usually covered on the exterior with clapboard siding to provide protection from the elements. Small casement windows were common until the end of the seventeenth century, when sliding-sash double-hung windows became popular.

Other features were specific to certain locations or circumstances. For example, the Tyler-Wood Homestead was built during the colonial period but has a black band painted around the top of the chimney, reputed to signify a safe house on the Underground Railroad during the Civil War period. This suggestion is supported by a hideaway chute with false floor located behind an attic chimney.

In the southern coastal colonies, houses were unlike those in the north. They were typically constructed of brick, often had but one story, and the chimneys were located on the ends of the house to minimize heat buildup.

Cliveden Mansion,
Philadelphia, Pennsylvania,
1763–67

GEORGIAN

Colonial builders were not necessarily concerned with questions of architectural style; they dealt with construction details that related to basic existence. Late in the colonial period, however, settlers began the search for style and felt the need to present an identity through their

Georgian entrance with
Palladian window,
Princeton, New Jersey

buildings and to express a more civilized nature through architecture. British colonists initially established this identity by adapting the style with which they were most familiar—Georgian, named after King George III and the most prominent style of the eighteenth century in England.

Houses in the Georgian style were both formal and symmetrical. The style expressed a newly felt sense of civility through a formal arrangement of rooms and facade elements and in classical detailing. The style was largely influenced by the architecture of Palladio, a sixteenth-century Italian architect who derived and interpreted much of his detailing from classical Greek and Roman elements, including pediments, pilasters, and the familiar rounded Palladian window. Casement windows gave way to upward-sliding single-hung or double-hung windows, with each sash divided into as many as twenty individual panes.

FEDERAL

As indicated by the name, the federal style was popular during the period just after the Revolution, about 1780 to 1820. Although the elevations of federal-style buildings share classical detailing and symmetry with the Georgian style and are considered derivative of the earlier style, the detailing differed noticeably. Federal-style roofs had a shallower

Jones House, Libertytown, Maryland, ca. 1800

pitch; window and door detailing was lighter and simpler, and in some instances even delicate. While the Palladian window on Georgian buildings was typically a half-round arch over the center window, the federal-style adaptation usually placed an elliptical fanlight over an entrance that incorporated the sidelights under its arch.

THE CLASSICAL STYLES

GREEK REVIVAL (CLASSICAL REVIVAL)

Although Georgian and federal-style buildings featured some classical elements, the full replication of classical Greek and Roman buildings began only in the late eighteenth century, largely through the influence of Thomas Jefferson. While serving as minister to France, he became enamored of the Maison Carrée at Nîmes in southern France. This Greek-style temple structure was a prototype for Jefferson's design of the Virginia State Capitol in Richmond, completed in 1792. As the first public building in neoclassical temple form, the capitol building significantly influenced the design of other public structures. Soon the classical style, associated with the Greek city-states and republicanism, was accepted as the style most fitting to represent the new American republic. Jefferson's design for the University of Virginia in 1817, one of this country's best pieces of architecture, was a tour-de-force in this classical style.

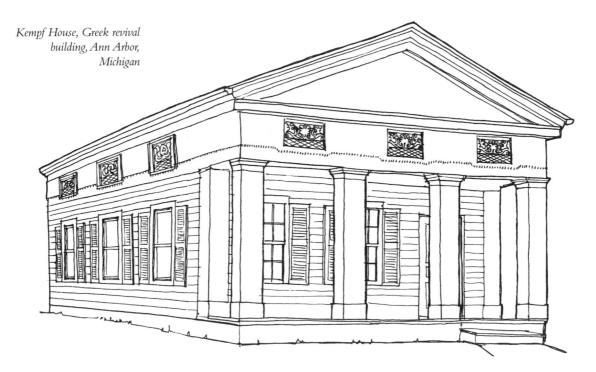

Kempf House, Greek revival building, Ann Arbor, Michigan

The classical revival style, more commonly referred to as Greek revival, is most readily distinguishable by two features: the pediment and freestanding Doric or Tuscan columns. Although the main structure can be white stucco, board siding, or red brick, the front elevation is typically enhanced with a white portico (porch) with full-width pediment and columns. The building is rectilinear and its interior spatial arrangement has height and width proportions and window arrangements that spring from the design needs of the temple form on which it is based.

Although long popular for certain building types, the Greek revival style owed its eventual decline to the inherent restrictiveness and inflexibility of its plan. As society grew increasingly urban, buildings closely placed along busy streets became more appropriate and workable than buildings situated temple-like on selected hilltops. This change in thinking was described by John Maass in his book *The Gingerbread Age*:

> The Victorians, of course, moralized on every possible occasion and they attacked the Greek style upon moral grounds. Actually, the Greek Revival had run its course in the [1840s] because it was no longer adequate. This beautiful, serene style is essentially an architecture of facades. Fenestration was always a problem in a porticoed building; even such a lover of the antique as Goethe had recognized that "columns and windows are a contradiction." The Greek temples had of course been windowless and the dwellings of the ancient Greeks and Romans were without columns. The ground plan of a Greek Revival building had to conform to the symmetrical elevation. This could be made to work in formal designs like royal palaces, state capitols and even town halls but it was a straitjacket for builders who were called upon to solve the everyday problems of an increasingly complex industrial civilization.[1]

ITALIANATE (RENAISSANCE REVIVAL)

The Italianate, another formal, symmetrical style, first came to prominence in the 1850s and remained popular through later revivals well into the twentieth century. Stylistic elements were derived from Italian Renaissance architecture and distinguished by an almost severe, blockish form similar to the Italian palazzo (hence the style's alternate name, Renaissance revival).

An important feature of the style is a wide, projecting cornice supported with elaborate bracketing. Windows with rounded or segmented arch tops typically have an eyebrow hood. Low-sloped or flat roofs make the roof form recede and give primary importance to the wall elevations.

The lack of projecting elements like the portico of the Greek revival makes Italianate buildings fit better on city streets, so this style became

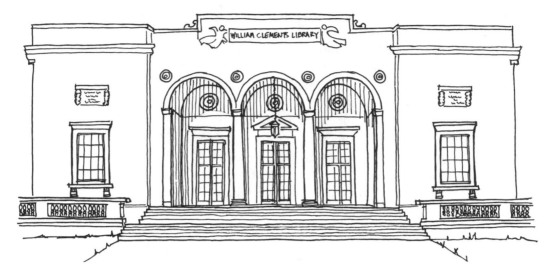

Italianate style, Clements Library, The University of Michigan

popular for downtown commercial buildings—in fact, the style of choice for common commercial buildings from the 1850s until the turn of the century. Because the timing of its ascendancy matched the period when most American cities beyond the east coast attained their most rapid growth, in many parts of the country downtowns large and small have a preponderance of storefronts in the Italianate style.

Italianate style house

Italianate storefront

BEAUX–ARTS (ACADEMIC) CLASSICISM

The French term *Beaux-Arts* means "fine arts" and refers to the architecture taught at the École des Beaux-Arts (School of Fine Arts) in Paris from the seventeenth century into the twentieth century. Perhaps the best-known example of the style is the Paris Opera House; prominent American buildings in this style include Union Station (1907) in Washington, D.C., the Boston Public Library (1895), and the Metropolitan Museum of Art (1895) in New York City.

Beaux-Arts (Academic) classicism as a style is characterized by grandiose, formal compositions with elaborate stone detailing. Multistory Greek columns or pediments typically are grouped in pairs to define projecting facades or pavilions. Symmetry is important on all of the facades and detailing much more exuberant than in other classical styles. Cornice lines have elaborate moldings and dentils, and both rooflines and windows included carefully detailed stone balustrades. Although Beaux-Arts structures commonly used rusticated stone bases, smooth stone exteriors, and grand masonry and marble interiors, steel framing was typically used in construction in the U.S.

World's Columbian Exposition,
Administration Building,
1893

Many American architects were trained at the École, including Richard Morris Hunt (in 1846, the first American to attend), Louis Sullivan, H. H. Richardson, and Bernard Maybeck. Their rigorous classical training greatly influenced the grand public architecture in the United States between the 1890s and 1920s.

The influence of the Beaux- Arts school was particularly strong at the World's Columbian Exposition, held in Chicago in 1893. The planners of the fair wanted to make it one of the most significant events of the age. Still recovering from the Great Fire of 1871, Chicago was to rise phoenixlike from the ashes. After the Civil War, many Americans toured Europe, and they returned aware that the United States had no city that could vie with the beauty of Paris or the prominent cities of Italy. Using Venice as a model, the Chicago Exposition and its waterfront location were designed to show, in a distillation of European culture and architecture, the best America could offer. The purpose of the enterprise was to demonstrate that America was a culture of destiny and its architecture could showcase that culture, even if only as a temporary facade that would last one summer.

Many of the country's most respected architects were commissioned to design structures for the fair. Led by architect and planner Daniel Burnham, a committee of architects was formed and given a free hand in the layout of the site plan and the buildings. Essentially, they searched for an architectural style to represent the new American culture. After much deliberation, the committee decided all major buildings along the Great White Way should be in the Beaux-Arts style, with its freely interpreted classical elements. The Beaux-Arts motif allowed buildings to be designed in a grand scale and provided an important uniformity to the Exposition's overall scheme.

The fair was a huge success. Great numbers of Midwesterners who had never visited a big city before came and saw what they considered the ideal world created by the architects. So great was the Exposition's architectural impact that the Beaux-Arts influence remained a force in architecture for another forty years.

THE ROMANTIC STYLES

GOTHIC REVIVAL

In the mid- to late nineteenth century, when many of the formal styles, with their controlled elegance and symmetry, were evolving toward grander structures and grandiose detailing, a newer movement

Delamater House, Rhinebeck, New York, 1844, in Carpenter Gothic style

arose that incorporated more romantic notions of architectural design. Influenced greatly by English landscape design, its free-flowing interpretation of nature and natural forms, and by contemporary landscape painting, the romantic period of architecture in the United States was ushered in by architect A. J. Downing. The son of a nurseryman, Downing was the author of an influential book, *Treatise on the Theory and Practice of Landscape Gardening* (1841). In his later books, *Cottage Residences* and *The Architecture of Country Houses*, he laid out design principles that provided a vivid counterpoint to the more prevalent formal styles.

The romantic style of choice was Gothic, considered the only "rational" style flexible enough to adapt to all of a building's functional requirements. As opposed to the symmetrical perfection sought in classical design, Gothic was a freely interpreted style subject to the whims of its designer.

Gothic revival style was expressed through pronounced features—most distinctively, the pointed arch form. This element is so integral to the style that any building with pointed arches can almost instantly be recognized as Gothic revival. Other elements common to the style include freely laid out, asymmetrical floor plans; tall, narrow windows; and steeply pitched roof forms. Window tracery and pinnacles may also be used.

Although at its roots a masonry style, wood frame buildings also were built in the Gothic mode and considered to be in a derivative Carpenter Gothic style. Typically they featured vertical board siding, elaborately cut decorative vergeboard trim under the eaves, and a veranda.

ITALIAN VILLA

The Italian Villa style became popular in the 1840s, when A. J. Downing included examples in his books and recommended it as both picturesque and practical. The distinguishing element of the Gothic revival style is the pointed arch, that of the Italian Villa style the prominently featured square tower, typically offset in a two-story *L-* or *T*-shaped floor plan. Additions can be incorporated freely without losing the essence of the style.

Balconies with balustrades are also common to the style, as are classically detailed verandas. Roofs with gentle slopes typically have wide projecting eaves supported by Italianate-style bracketing. Many of the windows are rounded at the top and set in groupings of two or three. Walls are either stone or stucco; only in less distinguished residences are they wood clapboard.

Italian Villa-style residence

RICHARDSONIAN ROMANESQUE (ROMANESQUE REVIVAL)

A style somewhat similar to Gothic in form, the Romanesque style, based on the ancient Roman basilica prototype, is differentiated by its use of rounded instead of pointed arch forms. Rounded arches are appropriated for windows and entrances but may also be used to enrich corbeling for belt or string courses.

The Romanesque style was popularized in the 1880s by Henry Hobson Richardson, an influential and dynamic architect of the period. Richardson was a large man with a commanding presence who exuded confidence, and represented the spirit of the age, a spirit that wanted to represent itself boldly to the world. Because of his personal influence, the new style became popularly known as Richardsonian Romanesque. During the relatively short span of twenty years, Richardsonian Romanesque style became an almost universal prototype for public buildings and was often used for churches, libraries, train stations, and other large institutional structures. Among Richardson's most representative

Richardsonian Romanesque residence, Chicago, Illinois

and important buildings are Trinity Church (1877) in Boston, the Allegheny County Courthouse and Jail (1888) in Pittsburgh, and the Marshall Field Wholesale Store (1887) in Chicago.

Most buildings in the Richardsonian Romanesque style have exteriors of heavy masonry punctuated with groupings of windows with transoms. A large arched opening forming a deeply recessed entrance is a signature. The proportions in Romanesque architecture are heavier than Gothic and do not stress verticality nearly as much. Monochromatic masonry emphasizes the prominent exterior forms of openings and

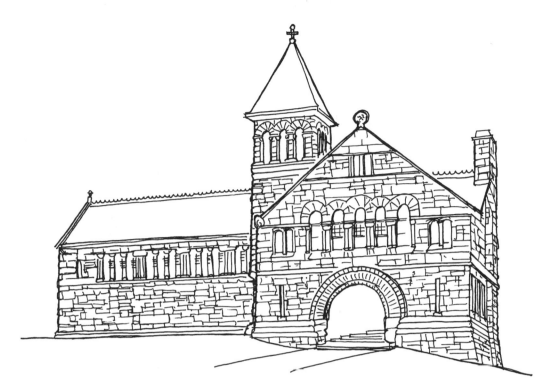

Oliver Ames Memorial Library (c. 1880), North Easton, Massachusetts. Richardsonian Romanesque style

recesses more than the details. Chimneys are low, in keeping with the horizontal massing, and eyebrow windows often provide openings through roofs.

SECOND EMPIRE

The Second Empire style is modeled on French architecture from the period of the Second Empire of Napoleon III. The Louvre Museum in Paris is the building that best represents its French roots.

In the United States, Second Empire style was elaborate and exotic enough to satisfy the need for pretension felt by many of those who had become rich during the Civil War. At the time, it was considered a modern style, one of the first based not on a historical style but on the contemporary environment of Paris of the 1870s. Prominent American examples of the style are the State, War, and Navy Building in Washington, D.C. (now the Executive Office Building), built between 1871 and 1875, and the Philadelphia City Hall (1874–81).

A distinguishing feature of Second Empire buildings is the distinctive upper-story mansard roof. However, lower stories were often classical in character and included Italianate detailing.

Ficke Mansion, Davenport,
Iowa, 1881–84

Second Empire style was commonly used for large residences, where a three-story structure with a mansard roof for the upper story could be kept more in scale with two-story structures. During the late nineteenth century it became a widespread, if not pervasive, style.

QUEEN ANNE

The Queen Anne style, most popular at the turn of the century as a residential style, represented the culmination of the picturesque, romantic styles of the nineteenth century, for it essentially proclaimed that anything goes. Closely associated with the Victorian era (Victorian is often discussed as an architectural style, but the term is correctly used only to represent the period of Queen Victoria's reign), Queen Anne designs thrived on decorative excess. Variety was encouraged, as was freedom of expression. The use of historical detailing is not predetermined in this style; instead, details casually intermingle. The overall effect is one of studied busyness—porches intermixed with turrets and roof gables. Wall

*Queen Anne-style
residence,
Port Townsend,
Washington*

surfaces are of masonry, wood shingles—either plane or fishscale—or clapboard and freely project and recess. Windows come in various sizes and shapes, often with small sections of leaded or colored glass. Brick chimneys are prominent and sculptural in form.

Although Queen Anne style was primarily used for residences, it found its way into some commercial structures. The style was more subdued in this building type, but it can be recognized in the freely expressed wall surfaces and roof combinations. A commercial structure with a gable roof form typically indicates Queen Anne elements.

A derivative of Queen Anne, often listed separately, is shingle style. Almost always used for residences, its overall forms and detailing follow the Queen Anne pattern, with its primary distinction the extensive use of wood shingles on the exterior walls. In some cases, shingles are found only on upper stories, but in the best examples shingles are used on virtually all the exterior surfaces, upper and lower, large and small.

Brophy College, Phoenix,
Arizona (1928).
Spanish colonial architecture

SPANISH COLONIAL (MISSION)

The Spanish colonial style remained a dominant architectural influence for centuries in the southwestern United States. Based on the heritage of the Spanish colonists, the style fit well with planning dictates put forward in King Philip of Spain's 1573 Law of the Indies. This required that buildings in the colonies be uniform in design for the sake of the beauty of the town. The style used building materials indigenous to the region, incorporating Indian adobe in thick, windowless walls for coolness in the desert climates and timber-supported flat roofs. Spanish colonial is known for the exuberant baroque detailing applied to plain stucco walls and surfaces. It remains a southwest style, extending from Texas to California and including Florida. Many excellent examples of the style are found in historic Santa Fe, New Mexico.

Because the Spanish colonial style was most often found in Spanish mission outposts, it is also called, in its more inclusive nomenclature, mission style. It lasted from 1600 to the mid-nineteenth century; a revival from the 1890s to World War II incorporated more architectural diversity and included residences, institutional buildings, and railroad stations. The style is still employed today, although typically constructed with more modern materials.

Tudor house

TUDOR

Primarily used for homes and residential club buildings, Tudor style comes from sixteenth-century England. Its proportions and detailing are medieval in character, with steeply sloped roofs, massive chimneys, exterior half-timbered construction with stucco infill, and tall, narrow windows with small panes and sometimes intricate muntin patterns. The steep gabled roof typical of the style usually has a cross-gable that accentuates the front facade and helps define the front entrance, often a heavy wooden door recessed in an arched opening.

This romantic style was especially popular from the turn of the century through the 1930s. It remains a common source for larger houses built as manors even today.

TWENTIETH-CENTURY STYLES

As America entered the twentieth century, the division remained between advocates of the romantic and the classical styles. Each felt their favored architecture represented the true spirit of the nation. In a way, American architects were frustrated because many styles had been embraced and were still in evidence.

This problem was pondered by traditionalist architect Bertram Goodhue in 1916 as he reconsidered architectural design for the new century. In an article he wrote for *The Craftsman*, Goodhue observed:

> I think you may expect me to say "Throw away traditions," but that I cannot do. I feel that we must hold tradition closely, it is our great background; as a matter of fact, good technique is born of tradition. We cannot start each generation at the beginning in our mastery of workmanship. The big universal progress in art moves on the wings of tradition. The nervousness about tradition in America springs from the fact that we have used it too much in place of imagination, in place of solid practical thought. Tradition has made us a little lazy about our own needs and our own inspirations. I feel that we should use tradition, and not be used by it.[2]

Even with this embrace of traditionalism, architects of the period realized the search was still on, for there was no one style America called its own. Every other great civilization had a style to represent it—why not this country?

THE CHICAGO SCHOOL OF ARCHITECTURE

But change was in the wind. More and more high-rises were being commissioned for larger cities, and they called for a new approach to architectural design. Even before the World's Columbian Exposition opened in 1893, the Reliance Building was built in downtown Chicago and pointed to an early solution to functional high-rise design.

By the early 1900s, the need for an architecture to satisfy the new functional needs of twentieth-century building types was more and more apparent. Traditional styles were still found acceptable for churches and residences, but businessmen, with their new skyscrapers, factories, and offices, sought a style to represent the entrepreneurial spirit of the times.

This led to a new style based not on historical precedents but on the utilitarian needs of tall, urban commercial buildings. The style was fully developed in the Loop area of downtown Chicago and became known as the Chicago School of architecture. Many of the best examples are still found there.

Chicago School buildings exploited new technologies and were possible because of two important developments: the advent of steel framing for tall structures and the invention of the first safe elevator by Elisha Otis. Other technologies also made high-rise construction possible, including improvements in foundation construction, wind bracing, and

Reliance Building,
Chicago, 1890–95

fireproofing.

Primary ornamentation of Chicago-style buildings was based on the repetition of windows across multistoried, rectangular facades. The most distinctive window unit, known as the Chicago window, filled the void between steel columns and was typically made up of double-hung windows for ventilation on either side and a large fixed glass picture window in the center.

GOTHIC REVIVAL AND THE CHICAGO TRIBUNE COMPETITION

After the 1893 Exposition closed, with its abundance of classical architecture, architects in this country became evenmore interested in finding an American idiom. The styles reinforced by the Exposition had served the nineteenth century but did not meet the needs of the twentieth century. High-rise, steel-framed structures had no historical precedent, and it was unclear what form or style they should adopt. Many architects of the period were uncomfortable with the new construction mode, which minimized the need for decorative exterior wall, and searched for a form appropriate for this design challenge.

Attempts to adapt earlier styles to the skyscraper led to incongruous

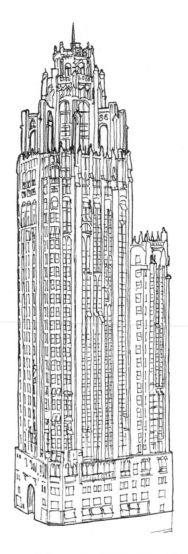

Tribune Tower, Chicago

Chicago Tribune Tower of the early 1920s. The Tribune Tower design competition was significant because it was a call to architects all over the world to present their best ideas for a prestigious high-rise building. With entries submitted by the world's most prominent architects, the competition brought to the fore all the current thinking on high-rise design. Some submissions were whimsical; others were precursors of the modern style. The winner was solidly in the historical revival style, a Gothic revival scheme that clearly represented the corporate tastes of the day. To many, the selection was a major disappointment and represented American unreadiness to take off the cloak of architectural historicism. The nation was unsure of the future and compensated by clinging too firmly to the past.

LOUIS SULLIVAN, FRANK LLOYD WRIGHT, AND THE PRAIRIE STYLE

Throughout his career, Chicago architect Louis Sullivan considered the question of functionalist design for a new age. He was an early architectural innovator, and his Transportation Building was the only non-classical building built on the Columbian Exposition's main concourse.

Sullivan's credo was "form follows function." This notion of having a building's design spring from its function rather than applying a decorative style was an entirely new way of looking at design. Architects of this school no longer perceived the function of a building and the style applied to it as separate decisions but acted on the assumption that the form of a building should be a direct expression of its function.

Sullivan gave first expression to the new skyscraper form by offering a new design approach for the high-rise building type. He defined high-rise buildings as having three parts: base, middle, and cap. Both the base

Wainwright Building (1890–91), St. Louis, Missouri, Louis Sullivan, architect

and the cap of a building were similar to those in traditional building styles, but the number of middle floors was seen as flexible; they could be arranged to express the typology's verticality, and any number of floors could be added without destroying the overall form. An early example of this approach is seen in Sullivan's Wainwright Building in St. Louis.

But Sullivan did not eschew decorative treatment. He simply redefined it in his own distinctive design vocabulary and created unique ornament to accent functional aspects. As a result, many architectural historians consider Sullivan the first modern architect. He was also the leading architect in a group that became known as the Prairie school, representing the architecture of the Midwest.

Sullivan's greatest pupil was Frank Lloyd Wright, who was to became America's most influential architect. Wright's genius was his ability to adopt the new principles of architectural design and make them distinctly his own. He developed a design vocabulary with horizontal, open floor plans representing the prairie, uniquely American in derivation and Midwestern in its influence. His style was not derived from any historical precedent but was formulated according to his own criteria, which represented perfectly the new freedom found in the American lifestyle.

The Robie House of 1906 in Chicago is one of the best examples of Wright's early work. Wide overhanging eaves and a strongly horizontal emphasis accentuated by low-sloped hip roofs are meant to represent

Robie House, Chicago, 1906, Frank Lloyd Wright, architect

protective yet expansive forms. The rooms are not constructed as traditional box forms; instead, walls are broken into planes, allowing rooms to become continuous spaces, flowing one into another naturally, with indoor spaces flowing as well into the outdoors.

Features of the Prairie style, as developed by Wright and others, typically include long bands of horizontal windows, recessed protected entrances, integral planters, and long, low chimneys at the intersection of the roof planes and usually defining the location of the family hearth. Stucco or red brick was used for exteriors; often Norman brick was chosen because its natural tones and longer, more horizontal form better represented the essence of the style.

BUNGALOW

The name *bungalow* derives from *bangla*, a style from India favored by the British for its broad overhangs and open porches, desirable in the warm climate. The style was adapted to the United States and was popular throughout the country from the turn of the century to the 1930s. Many older urban neighborhoods can easily be dated by the preponderance of this residential style.

The bungalow style is meant to give the appearance of a small, one-story cottage, even when used for larger houses. A definitive feature is a broad front porch, usually supported by substantial square or tapered columns resting on the porch rail. Typically, a front-sloping roof continues from the main house and sweeps over the porch in a continuous line. The bungalow-style house often has dormer windows in the center of the roof, facing front, with the result that a two-story house often looks like a low, one-story structure.

Bungalow-style house

CATALOG HOUSES

Although not a style, catalog or precut houses were an important and popular product from about 1900 to 1940. Houses were manufactured for buyers' lots and shipped in their entirety from the factory or mill. All lumber pieces were sized, numbered, and cut accurately to length at the factory, and doors, windows, hardware, decorative treatment, paint, and other building components were delivered as a package on one train-car or truck, ready to be quickly assembled on site.

Catalog houses included hundreds of designs in various popular architectural styles. They were indistinguishable from custom-built houses, except for the manufacturer's trademark (Sears, Aladdin, and numerous others) stamped on rafters and joists. Precut homes conferred the advantages of quick construction and low cost. Detailed instructions came with each kit, making it possible for owners to do much of the assembly themselves.

Until World War II, catalog houses were an important and large segment of the U.S. housing heritage. Enormous numbers of pre-cut houses still stand: according to Robert Schweitzer, who has studied catalog houses, the seven major national kit house companies operating from 1900 to 1940 shipped about half a million kit homes, and there are several hundred thousand still standing. (Chevy Chase, Maryland, boasts a large number and each year hosts a Kit House Historic Homes Tour.) Aside from an ever-increasing nostalgic interest and a growing respect for their historic value in the development of early 20th-century communities (a few Sears houses have even been listed in the National Register of Historic Places), they offer a level of quality in construction methods and materials that would be hard to duplicate. . . . They sometimes command prices that would stun the early owners.[3]

ART DECO/MODERNE

Art Deco is sometimes seen as the representative style of the 1930s. It was popular in such varied contexts as Hollywood fantasy sets and fair and exposition buildings. The name is taken from the exposition titled Arts Décoratifs et Industriels Moderne, held in Paris in 1925, to showcase innovative industrial design.

The chief characteristic of Art Deco is its stylized decoration, which represents a conscious rejection of the historical precedents found in most earlier styles and instead is based on geometric and naturalistic forms. In its attempt to be of the "modern" age, the forms and detailing of its decoration express a machine-age aesthetic.

Moderne (often considered a derivative of Art Deco) was an architectural expression of the streamlined design aesthetic that became

*The Berkeley Shore Hotel,
Miami, Florida*

popular in the 1930s and 1940s and remained so well into the 1950s. Based on the principle of airflow design used in aeronautic technology (during this period, tail fins were added to automobiles), the Moderne style was horizontal, as opposed to Art Deco's more vertical treatments, and used streamlining to look up-to-date. Instead of decorative treatment, it relied on horizontal banding of windows, canopies, and other

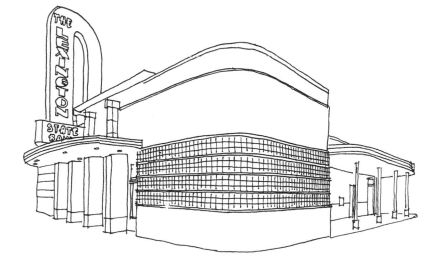

*Art Moderne-style bank,
converted from a Greyhound
bus station, Columbia,
South Carolina*

features to represent motion. The Moderne style incorporated high-technology materials, especially metal, marble, and other smooth, hard-surface finishes.

MODERN (INTERNATIONAL) STYLE

In the 1920s, a revolution was born in architecture. Louis Sullivan first expressed the principle that function should be the basis for design. What became known as modern or international style took this as a philosophical base and posited that superfluous decoration should be completely eliminated.

Whereas architects for two previous decades experimented with many new and eclectic approaches—including Art Deco and Prairie style—the modern movement established severe restraints that grew into an almost dogmatic approach to design. The style was based on three fundamental concepts:

1. Function, the prime motivation of design, was the only valid element to express.
2. New construction technologies should be utilized.
3. Completely free of historical references, modern architecture should express no period other than its own.

To modernists, the new style was both a product of its times and an immutable expression of truth. More a crusade than a preference, the modern style so completely dominated American architecture for thirty years that it seemed an important milestone had finally been reached—that the centuries-long search for a truly American style was over.

Ironically, the project that perhaps had more influence than any other in establishing the language of the modern style was the German Pavilion at the 1929 World's Fair in Barcelona, Spain (commonly known as the Barcelona Pavilion), designed by German architect Mies van der Rohe in 1927. With vertical marble slabs defining wall planes, light steel columns, and glass walls, it completely broke the mold of building as

German Pavilion, Barcelona, Spain, 1929, Ludwig Mies van der Rohe, architect

box. Using Frank Lloyd Wright's more organic schemes as a starting point, Mies's design used severe, crisp forms and new materials in a completely original way.

Mies later practiced in Chicago, where at the Armour (later Illinois) Institute of Technology he was for many years an influential professor of architecture. Among his most notable and influential projects were Lake Shore Drive Apartments, designed as a pair of towers and having a simplicity and straightforwardness that expressed the modern style in its purest form.

As these examples show, the modern style used materials in their purest form. Architects chose glass not only for windows but also for entire facades. The glass curtain wall became a common high-rise form. Steel, no longer covered over and ignored, was displayed freely and openly as a major design element. The goal was not only to express a universal style but to invent a universal building type that could be adapted for virtually all uses. This architectural tradition arose out of industrial design and structural engineering. Some in the architectural profession feared the trend, feeling it would eliminate the for architects as purveyors of design and styles.

Typical elements of the modern style are flat roofs with little or no overhang and flat, smooth cornices. Smooth wall surfaces appear engineered with one material and little relief, and windows are typically

Lake Shore Drive Apartments, Chicago, 1950–51

flush so they appear to be a continuation of the exterior walls rather than an opening in them. Large expanses of wall are broken only by projecting and penetrating planes, such as balconies and entrances. The absence of decoration is inherent in the style.

POSTMODERN STYLE

Postmodernism was initiated more as a movement than a style and its philosophy was more important than its design. With faint beginnings in the 1960s—expressed more often in architectural treatises than in actual buildings—its popularity peaked in the 1970s and early 1980s but continues to this day.

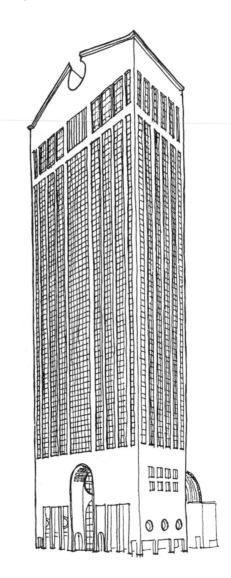

AT&T Building, New York City, Philip Johnson, architect

Postmodern design returned to the use of historical references. Many architects looked once again at historic design elements for inspiration. This postmodern period, as it has been termed, was a necessary catharsis to liberate designers from the severe restrictions of modernist dogma. Architects were relieved to again have the freedom to explore alternatives but were at the same time troubled by the loss of the design purity inherent in the modern. Robert Venturi expressed the postmodern manifesto in *Complexity and Contradiction in Architecture*:

> Architects can no longer afford to be intimidated by the puritanical moral language of orthodox Modern architecture. I like elements which are hybrid rather than "pure," compromising rather than "clean," distorted rather than "straightforward. . . .
>
> I am for richness of meaning rather than clarity of meaning; for the implicit function as well as the explicit function.[4]

Postmodern architects do not advocate wholesale duplication of earlier historical styles but select elements from earlier periods and reinterpret them in a decorative, sometimes whimsical, fashion. Elements such as column capitals and broken pediments have been enlarged to such a degree as to provide a completely different relationship of scale. Philip Johnson's famous—or notorious—AT&T Building in New York, for example, features a Chippendale broken pediment as the enormous cap on a high-rise building in the center of Manhattan.

Another branch of the postmodern movement addresses the issue of contextualism, whereby new designs fit within the vocabulary of their surrounding context (see chapter 7). Contextual design is especially important as a design principle for additions to historic buildings, taking features of the existing building or buildings and using them in a simpler, more contemporary way.

The rise of postmodern design is a concern for many old-line modernists because of its irreverence and unpredictability. Its anything-goes approach was a necessary antidote to the more purist approach of previous decades, however, and the style promises to settle into a period of less stridency and more accommodation as it continues.

Summary of Architectural Styles

The history of American architecture is the tale of a search for an architectural style to truly represent the new American culture. Beginning with the most basic colonial structures and extending through the Georgian and federal periods, builders first borrowed from familiar English styles. The search for a style then took architects and builders to other countries and other periods for their inspiration: Greek, Gothic,

Romanesque, Italianate, and French, and even back to England for the popular Queen Anne style.

Only in the twentieth century did architects develop forms unique to United States culture. Louis Sullivan and Frank Lloyd Wright originated a new aesthetic of the prairie. Contemporary art forms inspired the Art Deco and Moderne styles in the 1920s and 1930s.

But the search ended, at least temporarily, with the evolution of a style derived from the machine age—the modern (or international) style, whose roots lie in the Chicago School of architecture at the turn of the century. Although many important examples of modern architecture came from European architects in the 1920s and 1930s, it was the dominant style in the United States for most of this century. (The only major exception was residential architecture, which clung steadfastly to its traditional roots.) Only recently has modern architecture been joined by another style, still being defined, that combines elements of modern with inspiration from previous historic styles—the postmodern style.

Only some of the many architectural styles documented and categorized by American architectural historians are presented here. Many of the early revival styles had later revival periods as well, when the styles metamorphosed into newer forms. Likewise, the modern period is represented as a single style; this brief discussion does not reflect its many variations. The serious student may refer to more complete texts, such as those listed in the Bibliography, to better appreciate how the search for an American style followed many paths paralleling those represented here.

Chapter 7

Design Issues

From the 1930s through the 1960s, modernist-trained architects generally ignored older buildings and their styles and tried to design in a
modern mode. Respect for historical elements was not looked upon
favorably, which led to the covering or defacement of many elegant
nineteenth-century facades. Architectural critic Brent Brolin noted:

> The modernist architectural code of ethics maintained that history was
> irrelevant, that our age was unique and therefore our architecture must
> be cut off from the past. Just a few short decades ago modernists argued
> that everyone in the world, their tastes freed by the Movement, would
> soon want to live in the same kind of houses, in the same kind of mod-
> ern cities, all of which would reflect the spirit of our times. (While the
> "times" were always "ours," the decision as to which forms characterized
> them was always "theirs," the architectural elite.) Because of this over-
> whelming belief several generations of architects have felt little need to
> accommodate their work to the older, theoretically obsolete architecture
> around it.[1]

The stylistic straitjacket of Modernism has loosened. As architects
gained increased awareness of and appreciation for historic preservation,
they also saw the need to design new buildings that were compatible
with historic buildings. This design approach, called *contextualism*, yields
contemporary architecture that is sensitive to and compatible with the
context surrounding it.

Contextual design emphasizes compatibility and works to respect the
scale, height, setback, materials, and detailing of surrounding older buildings. This does not mean that new designs need to look old—in most
cases, this would be inappropriate. Rather, it means contemporary design
should blend with the old so that new and old are distinguishable but
compatible. This sense of continuity and basic sensitivity to the old has

been referred to as an "architectural genetic code,"[2] a code of craftsmanship worked out over generations of trial and error.

Matching, Compatible, or Contrasting?

When designing an addition to a historic building, or even a new building in a historic district, an architect or designer should look carefully at the question of contextualism. Generally, three design approaches can be taken—matching, contrasting, and compatible.

MATCHING

In the matching approach, new architecture imitates the old and is meant to fit in as a coherent piece of the historic fabric. Additions are designed in the same style as original buildings, using similar materials and detailing, at least on the public exterior.

Critics say this approach, because it does not clearly differentiate between old and new, may fool an observer into thinking a recent construction is much older and part of the original historic structure.

CONTRASTING

Contrasting design follows the logic that the new and old should be distinct because each is a product of its own era. Often, the contrasting approach uses simple, modernist surfaces and materials to serve as a counterfoil to the elaborate detailing of historic structures. The buildings may be designed either as background structures, with little identity of their own, or may frankly compete with their historic context; in the second case, the architect considers they will one day be historic structures themselves and seen as products of their own time.

Designers who use the contrasting approach perceive that most historic districts consist of a variety of architectural styles from many periods. They see no need to stay within this design context and instead feel they enrich the district through diversity.

COMPATIBLE

Compatible design, the most common of the three approaches, suggests that new design be sensitive to historic structures and compatible with them in terms of "size, scale, color, material, and character of the property, neighborhood or environment."[3] For example, the elaborately detailed windows of a historic building can be suggested in simpler form in a new addition, or a cornice similar in height and proportion designed with a simple horizontal line rather than the more elaborate dentils found on the original.

Achieving good new design in a historic district cannot be obtained by city ordinance It must come from architects and designers who understand the dynamics of contextualism and are sensitive to the relationship of new to old.

PROBLEMS AND SOLUTIONS IN CONTEXTUAL DESIGN

A TOWNHOUSE IN GREENWICH VILLAGE

A good way to understand contextual design is by example. The sketch shows two townhouses that are part of a block of similar townhouses located in the Greenwich Village neighborhood of New York City. The gap in the middle of the sketch represents a space created when, in 1971, a revolutionary group, the Weathermen, built bombs in the house on the site and accidentally detonated dynamite stored in the basement.

The empty site was purchased by new owners, who asked the architectural firm of Hardy, Holzman, Pfeiffer to design a new townhouse as infill. The architects faced the decision of how to approach the project: This was the only gap in a block-long progression of historic townhouses, all similar in design. Should they take a matching approach and restore the historic character of the block? Should they represent the contemporary new owners by designing a contrasting facade? Or should

Greenwich Village townhouses

Greenwich Village infill townhouse, Hardy, Holzman, Pfeiffer, architects

they try to blend the two and develop a contemporary facade compatible with the scale and detail of the original? There is no right or wrong approach; readers can better understand the issues by considering the problem and deciding what they would do.

The architects designed an infill structure that satisfied diverse criteria. The upper (third) floor was designed to match the adjacent townhouses, with a similar brick front and identical windows. However, the windows on the lower two floors were more contemporary, with the facade turned at an angle to the street. This angle, the architects explained, expressed the historic significance of the place by symbolizing the explosion of the previous structure. This attempt to use architectural design to represent a historical event was criticized by many as being both inappropriate and incompatible with adjacent buildings, but illustrates the latitude brought to the question of contextual design.

EAST CAMBRIDGE SAVINGS BANK

An example of a contextual design that illustrates the blending of older historic building elements with new construction is the 1978 addition to the East Cambridge Savings Bank in Cambridge, Massachusetts. The architect, Thomas M. Jones, chose to tie the old with the new in an innovative way. They removed the existing wall from the right side of the building and moved it intact to the street facade. The older facade served to shield the addition, which was inserted as a curved glass

wall connecting the original building with the reconstituted facade. The design differentiates clearly between old and new but also blends and integrates them in a satisfactory contextual design solution.

East Cambridge Savings Bank, Cambridge, Massachusetts, 1931, addition 1978

CHURCH COURT CONDOMINIUMS

Another interesting and complex architectural project using a contextual design approach is the Church Court condominiums in Boston. Architect Graham Gund purchased the shell of a burned-out church building, of which only the corner tower and two exterior walls

Church Court condominiums, Boston, exterior

Church Court condo-
miniums, Boston,
interior court

remained. Rather than demolish the structure, he incorporated it into the design of a new condominium complex. The stone walls of the old church serve as entrances to an interior court. The new building, where the condominium units are located, picks up design suggestions from the old church, but old and new elements are distinguishable. The project thus makes reference to the 1892 church and recognizes its former significance to the community but adapts the site and the remaining structure to a new use.

TYLER RESIDENCE

A small residential project illustrates contextual design at the scale of an individual house, a 1920s bungalow-style house. A master bedroom and bathroom were added to the rear, connecting the house to what had been a free-standing garage. The addition used the same siding and trim

Tyler residence: bungalow-style house, 1923, addition 1987

as the original house; new windows matched the old in appearance. The integrity of the original house was visually maintained, however, by stepping back the wall and roofline of the addition, making the addition subservient to and maintaining the visual prominence of the original structure.

DESIGN USING THE FACTORS OF TIME AND PLACE

The contextual reference so integral to the preservation movement is more than simple architectural detailing. Preservation's significant philosophical contribution to the design professions is a new awareness of both time and place.

Incorporating the element of time means recognizing that a new building does not represent its own time period only but also is part of a time continuum, as represented by Eisenman's arrow (see chapter 1). Contextual design accommodates buildings of both the past and the future. New design should recognize this continuum and be part of it.

How many contemporary architects, losing sight of this, design buildings that make no reference to what has come before? They pick the latest styles from a professional journal and make a design statement; unfortunately, that statement typically is "Forget the rest, my building is unique." A consciousness of good preservation design makes us realize that "the rest" does matter and shouldn't be forgotten. It encourages architects to see their statement as the most recent of many. They should recognize that their new building also will be old one day, and it should be able to age gracefully.

As the preservation movement has made architectural designers more conscious of the element of time, it has also made them more conscious of place. Sometimes architects work as if their new building had no neighbors. For them, place does not extend beyond the boundaries of their site. They ignore the context in which they work. The contextual approach reminds designers to look at what surrounds their new design and try to make it fit in. A good solution may result if the designer tries something as simple as showing surrounding buildings on a site plan. For instance, to get a better feel for context, architects can try placing a new building design not in the center of the site plan drawing but in a corner, giving more prominence to existing structures than to the one being designed.

The Need for Design Guidelines

Any discussion of contextual design must acknowledge the subjectivity of the issue. What one person deems appropriate may be condemned by another. This can lead to problems when proposals for new construction in historic districts are reviewed. It is unfair for property owners to be governed too subjectively, so procedures must be instituted to rationalize this process, both through the adoption of design guidelines and the establishment of design review committees. These are described in the following sections.

THE SECRETARY OF THE INTERIOR'S STANDARDS FOR REHABILITATING HISTORIC BUILDINGS

To address the public's need for design guidance, the National Park Service, acting on behalf of the Secretary of the Interior, publishes standards and guidelines for both the rehabilitation of historic buildings and new design in historic districts. The *Secretary of the Interior's Standards for Rehabilitation* present ten clear and brief standards that are commonly accepted. Supplemental to these standards, an extensive set of guidelines provides more specific guidance on exterior surfaces, roofs, windows, interiors—even sites and districts. These standards and guidelines, revised a number of times since their first publication in 1979, can be used and are sometimes adopted by historic district commissions to assist in determining whether or not to approve proposed changes. The standards and guidelines are nationally accepted and represent the best thinking on appropriate methods of intervention.

The ten standards for rehabilitation, as stated in the 1995 revisions, are:

1. "A property will be used as it was historically or be given a new use that requires minimal change to its distinctive materials, features, spaces, and spatial relationships."

   Commentary: As an example, take a historic church, no longer needed by its congregation, that has been sold. What is compatible with its historic use? Appropriate uses might include a community center or religious bookstore. Less appropriate uses include conversion to a boutique clothing store or a gym.

2. "The historic character of a property will be retained and preserved. The removal of distinctive materials or alteration of features, spaces, and spatial relationships that characterize a property will be avoided."

   Commentary: As part of a building's historic designation, the significant historic characteristics should be clearly defined. These historic features, whether arched windows, steeply sloped roof, or terra-cotta details, should be kept even if the structure is modified for a new use.

3. "Each property will be recognized as a physical record of its time, place, and use. Changes that create a false sense of historical development, such as adding conjectured features or elements from other historic properties, will not be undertaken."

   Commentary: Additions and alterations should not try to look original. To maintain the integrity of the original elements, the new should be clearly differentiated from the historic.

4. "Changes to a property that have acquired historic significance in their own right will be retained and preserved."

   Commentary: As an example, a black Carrara glass front was put on an 1880s Italianate commercial building when it was converted to a

Opera House with Carrara glass front, Howell, Michigan

jewelry store in the 1930s. This glass front may have developed historic significance of its own; hence, the building may be most appropriately restored as a 1930s artifact, leaving the glass in place.

5. "Distinctive materials, features, finishes, and construction techniques or examples of craftsmanship that characterize a property will be preserved."

Commentary: Perhaps a designated building has a magnificently crafted staircase in its foyer. Although the stair opening may not satisfy current fire safety codes for egress and other stairs will need to be built, plans should include the staircase as an elegant example of the building's original craftsmanship.

6. "Deteriorated historic features will be repaired rather than replaced. Where the severity of deterioration requires replacement of a distinctive feature, the new feature will match the old in design, color, texture, and, where possible, materials. Replacement of missing features will be substantiated by documentary and physical evidence."

Commentary: This typically applies to wood windows. It is commonly assumed old windows should be replaced with new, thermally efficient insulated units made of modern materials, such as vinyl. However, this standard urges owners to repair their original windows if possible and, if the windows are beyond repair, to replace them with similar painted wood sash to retain as much as possible the original appearance and proportion of muntins, whether using single or insulated panes.

7. "Chemical or physical treatments, if appropriate, will be undertaken using the gentlest means possible. Treatments that cause damage to historic materials will not be used."

Commentary: This guideline directly reflects on early attempts to restore painted brick buildings by sandblasting their exteriors. Often the integrity of the soft bricks was destroyed when the sandblasting removed the bricks' outer crust, resulting in the exposure of the soft inner area. Great care should be taken to use the gentlest means possible when restoring original materials.

8. "Archeological resources will be protected and preserved in place. If such resources must be disturbed, mitigation measures will be undertaken."

Commentary: Preservationists tend to limit their involvement to existing structures, but it is important to recognize the importance of preserving archeological artifacts as well.

9. "Additions, exterior alterations, or related new construction will not destroy historic materials, features, and spatial relationships that characterize the property. The new work will be differentiated from the

old and will be compatible with the historic materials, features, size, scale, proportion, and massing to protect the integrity of the property and its environment."

Commentary: Contemporary design in a historic district can be perfectly appropriate, as long as the new is designed with recognition for the old and is compatible with it. There is a danger in insisting on nostalgic design. As Garrison Keillor observed, "The past was copied, quoted, and constantly looked at until one day, the country looked more like it used to than it ever had before."[4]

10. "Additions and adjacent or related new construction will be undertaken in such a manner that, if removed in the future, the essential form and integrity of the historic property and its environment would be unimpaired."

Commentary: New construction, often designed for an economic lifespan of thirty to forty years, rarely lasts as long as original historic architecture. Therefore, new construction should be built adjacent to historic with the assumption that it will eventually be removed, at which time the old should still retain its original integrity.

The National Park Service also has developed standards and guidelines for preservation, restoration, and reconstruction.

DESIGN REVIEW BOARDS

One of the most controversial aspects of administering historic districts is the design review component. As described in chapter 3, a good ordinance includes sections describing the basis on which approval or disapproval for proposed changes is given. These may include provisions regarding the change of a roof slope, the location or type of window, or the enclosure of open front porches. When these are clearly and unambiguously described in the ordinance, few questions can arise.

In spite of how well an ordinance is written, however, questions do arise, and there will always be cases where changes proposed by the owner must be reviewed and interpreted. Procedures for design review should therefore be specified in anticipation. Is design review most capably performed by the historic district commissioners themselves? For most commissions, this is the established procedure. However, some cities assign the responsibility to a separate design review board, whose members have design backgrounds. These boards operate with mixed success.

In Portland, Oregon, residents generally feel the review board works well; virtually every downtown project is subject to its review. The review procedure serves as a public forum for discussion of a project's merits. Developers seem to favor this, for they get public reaction in a controlled, organized environment rather than in the unpredictable arenas of politics and the media.

Boulder, Colorado, is a city that accepts regulation as good for the community. It has a history of growth control ordinances and has passed laws that preserve solar access, control smoke from wood fires, and promote energy conservation.

In recent years, Boulder's downtown community has been increasingly concerned about growing competition from suburban shopping malls. To counter this problem, the city created an ordinance establishing design guidelines for the downtown in an attempt to ensure a pleasing environment. A citizens' board was set up to review all proposed downtown projects. Although project review is mandatory, compliance with the board's recommendations is voluntary.

A criticism of the ordinance is that the guidelines stifle creativity among architects. Other responses to the program were mixed. James Leese, AIA, then chairman of Boulder's planning board and president of Architecture Four Collaborative, says:

> Still, many local architects seem essentially sympathetic to the guidelines' major premise—that designs for an urban setting should respond to the urban context—even if the architects do not welcome the addition of yet another stage to a lengthy approval process. I can certainly understand that bringing downtown buildings up to some common level of acceptability is important. But I'm convinced that the guidelines must remain voluntary. It's OK to have a kind of 'dress code' for buildings, but a great designer must have the option of breaking the code for the sake of truly spectacular results. What we need is a board with the sensitivity and wisdom to allow excellence.[5]

The design review board of Scottsdale, Arizona, is made up of design professionals. Its agenda includes, but is not limited to, architectural review, site planning, and review of proposed developments as they relate to the surrounding environment and the community. As stated in the city's development guide, "Development Review is intended to enrich the lives of all the citizens of Scottsdale by promoting harmonious, safe, attractive and compatible developments."[6] The board has been instrumental in establishing a consistent design format, based on the traditional southwest adobe style, for all new development. Some residents have been critical of the stifling of creativity that comes with design review and the related pattern of homogeneous design, but most seem satisfied with the results.

In San Francisco, both city government and the public were concerned about the uncontrolled growth of the downtown and wanted to put a cap on new construction. A review board, appointed annually by the city planning director and made up of three respected individuals, now screens new projects, and approving only those adhering to strict design criteria. This procedure protects structures in the local historic districts by allowing developers to transfer their development rights to nonhistoric areas of the city (see chapter 10). It also encourages the redevelopment of blighted areas by giving incentives to build in those neighborhoods and disincentives in the downtown.

Such a review procedure tends to eliminate the worst projects; unfortunately, often it also discourages innovative solutions. Designers seek the common denominator that guarantees approval and submit designs that are generally mediocre. However, when the design review board is well respected and its determinations are shown to be in the public interest, this approach is a useful protection against inappropriate design.

FACADISM

Facadism involves preserving the historic facade of a building while demolishing or severely altering the remainder of the structure. This approach has been used in commercial historic districts subject to pressures for development and represents a compromise between retaining a historic streetscape and allowing more density with new construction. Facadism is viewed by some preservationists as a reasonable compromise because at least some of the original historic elements that face the street are retained. Others see it as an abomination that makes a mockery of history.

Much of the success of the technique depends on the design sensitivity of the architect or designer. Although sometimes done well as a form of preservation, facadism (also humorously referred to as *fasadism, facadectomy, or facadomy*) often results in preserving facades that bear little resemblance to their former historic context. As noted by preservation educator Michael Tomlan, "The overheated real estate market and preservationists' willingness to embrace the business community has led to a tendency to 'switch rather than fight.' The most obvious result is facadism—the deliberate demolition of all but one or more elevations of an old building."[7]

One project that illustrates the inherent illogic of protecting historic facades by disembodying them is located in downtown Salt Lake City, Utah. The construction of a giant mall, proposed for the downtown's

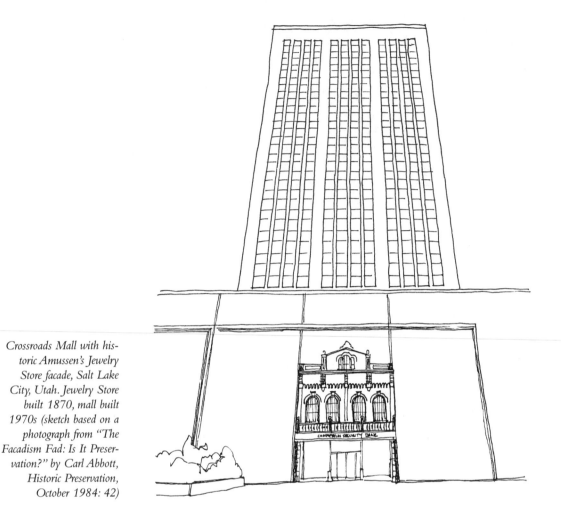

Crossroads Mall with historic Amussen's Jewelry Store facade, Salt Lake City, Utah. Jewelry Store built 1870, mall built 1970s (sketch based on a photograph from "The Facadism Fad: Is It Preservation?" by Carl Abbott, Historic Preservation, October 1984: 42)

main street, meant the destruction of a number of important historic commercial buildings. Preservationists rallied to save one of the most prominent, the landmark Amussen's Jewelry Store. Mall developers, however, saw the preservation of the entire building as intruding on the basic configuration of the mall's plan. To appease the preservationists, they agreed to preserve the building's facade and convert it to an entrance to a bank located within the mall. The result, as shown in the sketch, mocks the original building, forming what preservationist Stephan Churchill, then director of the Utah Heritage Foundation, called a "Disneyland paste-on that looks like a speck on a great big wall."[8]

In few cities has the facadism controversy been more heated than in Washington, D.C. A long-standing height limitation for buildings led to

Development on N Street, Washington, D.C.
Street facade for an eleven-story office block

intense development within those height parameters. To satisfy the historic ordinances, developers are willing to leave intact the three- or four-story facades of older buildings if they are permitted to build to the maximum height limit of ten stories directly behind the facade. They argue, often successfully, that the historic streetscape is not significantly altered with this increased density. Some preservationists feel that preserving the observer's impression of the historic streetscape is sufficient, even if new construction is inserted behind older facades.

Other preservationists view facadism as sacrilege and argue that entire buildings should be preserved to teach future generations about the epochs that produced them—even when the aesthetic value of the old buildings is not apparent to the man on the street.

Chapter 8

Preservation Technology

What Is Preservation Technology?

Preservation technology is the knowledge of techniques used to preserve historic building materials and systems. It deals principally with the conservation of building materials—identifying them, determining their condition, evaluating treatment options, and making recommendations for work to be done to them. Preservation technology involves a broad and deep knowledge of construction gained through experience in working with older buildings. Indeed, much of the historic integrity of a structure can be lost through inappropriate work, even when the goal is restoration.

Preservation technology is becoming increasingly important to architects and contractors alike, for they need people who are capable in working with historic building materials. Forecasters in the construction industry predict that soon more projects will involve the adaptive use of older buildings than new construction, so the demand for architectural conservators will continue to grow. Expertise in newer building materials, such as plastics, glass, high-strength steels, and concrete, will be in particular demand, for little attention has been paid to their long-term conservation.

Generally, preservationists focus on planning, economics, and administration. Preservation technology is a field of study that draws on architecture, construction, and conservation. Training in any of these areas contributes to good preparation for specialization in preservation technology. Architecture programs train students in design and methods of construction. A background in construction conveys beneficial practical experience. Programs offering a focus in conservation emphasize knowledge of the decay of materials and methods of mitigation. Also required, however, is a particular knowledge of historic building practices and interest in working directly on older buildings. With that interest, many avenues of appropriate education and training may be pursued.

Restoring a table at Frank Lloyd Wright's Fallingwater, Mill Run, Pennsylvania

Opportunities to gain expertise in preservation technology are numerous and varied. The Association for Preservation Technology (APT) is an interdisciplinary organization focusing on the practical application of technology to conservation of the built environment. Its journal and newsletter provide information on techniques for building conservation and include case studies of projects throughout the United States and Canada. (See Appendix 1, Preservation Resources, for contact information.)

Field schools provide opportunities for individuals to gain first-hand experience in preservation technology or special conservation methods. Examples of established schools include the Campbell Center for Historic Preservation Studies in Illinois, RESTORE in New York State, the National Park Service's Historic Preservation Training Center, and the Historic Windsor, Vermont's Preservation Institute. (See Appendix 1 for a full list of resources; see also the National Park Service's annual cultural resource training directory.)

The best and most common way of gaining expertise, however, is by learning directly with someone skilled in the field. Whether working under a restoration architect, a historic paint analysis consultant, or a master carpenter, the student will acquire practical experience not possible in a formal academic setting.

Conservation Ethics

Various approaches are appropriate to the conservation of historic structures. However, generally accepted guiding principles should be respected and followed with any approach. As described in the Guidelines of the Association for Preservation Technology, these ethical standards should be rigorously observed with any conservation work:

1. The condition of the building must be recorded before any intervention.
2. Historic evidence must not be destroyed, falsified, or removed.
3. Any intervention must be the minimum necessary.
4. Any intervention must be governed by unswerving respect for the aesthetic, historical, and physical integrity of cultural property.
5. All methods and materials used during treatment must be fully documented.[1]

Examples of Preservation Technology

ROOFS

Some examples can illustrate preservation techniques. Assume the roof of a historic building is leaking. Because the roof materials contribute to the historic significance of the structure, it is as important to identify the status of the original materials as it is necessary to determine the cause of the leaks. Care must be taken to inspect conditions properly before proceeding with work. Sometimes observations can be made from the ground, but this is usually inadequate. Looking at a roof up close may require extension ladders or a hydraulic lift if there is no hatch opening from an attic. Walking on the surface of the roof or leaning out of a dormer window allows you to probe for wetness, to observe torn or blistered membranes, molds or moss growing, broken tiles, and cracked flashing, and to determine how many layers of roofing have been placed over the original materials. It is also important to look at the underside of the roof structure for wet spots, staining, rotted materials, or efflorescence. This helps in understanding the construction methods, which may be contributing to the problems of deterioration.

All materials have an estimated useful life (usually expressed in a range of years from minimal to optimal). When exposed to weathering conditions, asphalt shingles and built-up bituminous roofing, for instance, have useful lives of fifteen to thirty years, whereas slate shingles can last eighty to a hundred years. If the underlying structure of the roof is protected properly by weathering materials, it could last indefinitely.

Roof materials are usually replaced rather than restored, unless the materials themselves are highly significant to the structure or they would be prohibitively expensive to replicate. If the roofing material is a special concrete tile, for instance, with a custom aggregate finish that cannot easily be replicated, the tiles should be removed so that a new waterproofing membrane can be installed underneath and the tiles reattached. A minimum number of tiles then could be fabricated to replace those completely broken or missing. The goal of both protecting the structure and retaining the original tiles is accomplished. However, if the tiles are terra-cotta and embedded in a solid concrete grout bonded to the roof structure, removal of the tiles would require such aggressive demolition methods that alternate methods must be considered. Covering the terra-cotta with sheet metal to match the shape of the tiles is one option. Another is to repair the individual tiles by patching and coating them with a water repellent and tuckpointing all the joints to minimize water penetration of the roofing system.

WINDOWS

Windows are another area of special concern in preservation technology. Openings in buildings are functionally important, of course, and are often significant to the historic style and details of a building. Unfortunately, they are also subject to heavy use and exposure to severe weathering. Owners often consider deteriorated windows or doors to be expendable and plan to replace them. In their concern about cost and energy conservation, owners feel the best solution is to replace existing windows with new insulated units. As discussed in chapter 7, however,

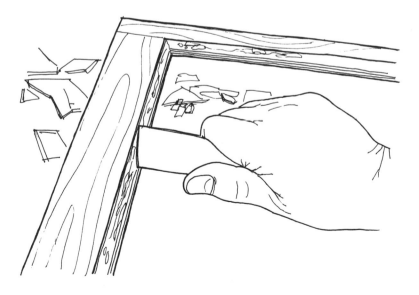

Deteriorated wood window

the Secretary of the Interior's *Standards for Rehabilitation* state that repair is preferable to replacement, and efforts should be made to repair the existing windows and doors if possible.

Several options are available to conserve and adapt wood window units. If the thickness of the sash is great enough (usually 1 3/4 inch), the wood is deep enough for routing; it can then accept insulated glass panels where originally there was only a single 1/8-inch-thick pane and still retain a beveled exterior glazing profile. For thinner sash, as found in most residential buildings, this option is not viable.

Also, the condition of the wood sash must be evaluated. Sometimes it may be fine with a new coat of paint, but typically the frames are loose and rotted at the lower rail. In that case, the wood sash must be taken apart, stripped of all old finishes, and the pieces reglued. Wood pieces that are severely rotted can be replaced; minor damage from rot can be consolidated with a special two-part epoxy treatment. Wood fillers and molding material can be used to rebuild a missing profile and to fill gouges or split wood. The same considerations can be given to the

Window detail, Wayne County Courthouse, Detroit, Michigan

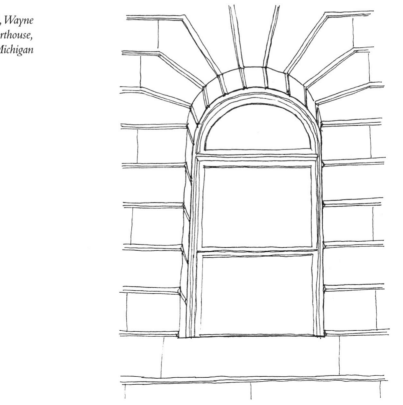

frames, exterior trim, and interior casing, all with the goal of conserving and retaining the original windows and doors in their original openings if possible.

CASE STUDY: WAYNE COUNTY COURTHOUSE, DETROIT

The 1897 Wayne County Courthouse in Detroit underwent a complete restoration in 1986. The existing windows were assumed to be no longer serviceable and in need of replacement. However, closer inspection showed that most were in excellent condition and only the paint coating had failed. Even better, when the paint was stripped from a sample unit the sash and frames were revealed as solid mahogany, an extremely hard and weather-resistant material. The sash was $1^3/4$ inch thick, so it easily could accommodate a new insulated glass panel. A wood shop was set up and relocated around the building as needed to remove, restore, and reinstall each window in its original frame. The exterior faces of the windows were painted and the interior restored with a clear finish to highlight the mahogany wood.

EXTERIOR MASONRY

Exterior masonry walls are subject to weathering, of course, and are also the victims of controversial experimentation with conservation treatments. Rough masonry surfaces attract dirt in a number of ways—from airborne pollutants, pigeons, human hands, and as the result of contact

Masonry repair

with metals. Masonry also suffers attack from acids in rain, the stress of moisture freezing and thawing in the walls, and impact damage caused by people and machines.

Conservation efforts address these problems separately. Repairs are usually executed before cleaning the walls to eliminate moisture penetration and further damage. Repair options include tuckpointing cracked and eroded mortar joints, replacing broken and damaged masonry, injecting epoxies at cracks, and patching with a cementitious compound tinted to match the adjacent masonry.

Once repaired, the walls should be cleaned using the "gentlest means possible."[2]

Before the work is carried out, materials and methods should be tested for their effectiveness and impact on the structure. A general cleaning using a low-pressure spray application of water to soften the dirt and rinse it away may be sufficient. If not, mild chemical cleaners can be tested and applied according to the manufacturer's instructions. An approved test panel is used to compare and approve results of the cleaning operation.

Special cleaning is usually needed for the most stubborn stains caused by bird repellent chemicals and runoff from copper flashing. Products that aggressively attack these stains are usually applied as a poultice to draw out the stain,, but they must be used with caution and then neutralized and rinsed off thoroughly. Additional treatments to consider include stone consolidants that penetrate and a water repellent to reduce water absorption by the masonry or to preserve a cleaner surface. These are extreme measures and should be used only with the utmost caution and knowledge of expected results based on tests. Abrasive cleaning is also used in rare instances, but it is generally not recommended unless all other methods are found ineffective.

CASE STUDY: THE FIRST CHURCH OF CHRIST, SCIENTIST, BOSTON

The First Church of Christ, Scientist, was founded on the teachings of Mary Baker Eddy in the latter part of the nineteenth century. When membership grew and meeting in members' homes was no longer feasible, a church was constructed in 1895 with seating for 1,500. Before the doors had even opened, membership had outgrown the Romanesque-style rustic granite building and plans were underway to construct an addition. The extension was completed less than ten years later in a classical style with elaborately carved granite and limestone walls topped with domes and a cupola of white glazed terracotta.

First Church of Christ, Scientist, Boston, Massachusetts

Maintenance on this structure has been diligent and sensitive over the years. In the 1950s, the steel framework of the central dome was repaired and the terra-cotta replaced. Even so, however, the building had never been cleaned properly. In the 1980s, many exterior materials had deteriorated and required intervention and comprehensive treatment to restore the church's appearance.

In 1987, conditions warranted an overview and analysis with recommendations for a comprehensive preservation plan to be implemented over a period of ten years. Blackened with carbon deposits, the building's carved limestone detailing of column capitals and large cornices was especially encrusted. The granite surfaces were eroding and flaking. The exterior conditions were evaluated and the various stone materials used in the facade tested, because the cause of erosion was unknown. Materials for cleaning and stabilizing the stone were also tested, both in the laboratory and on the site.

The first work undertaken included replacement of all the large flat roof areas, which required removing layers of asphalt roofing. Under-

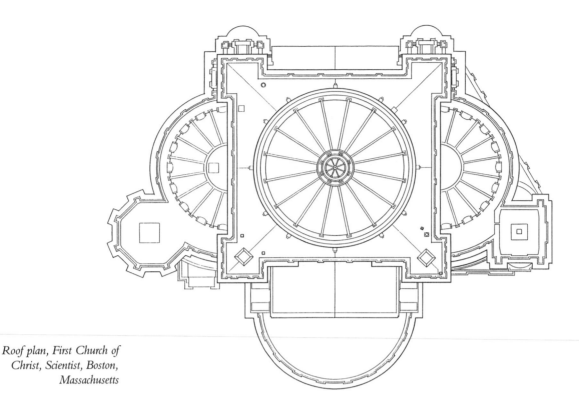

*Roof plan, First Church of
Christ, Scientist, Boston,
Massachusetts*

neath, the original materials were exposed to confirm their condition
and to provide clues as to the original treatment. In areas where flat-
seam copper roofing was found, the metal still provided a moderately
watertight membrane but, having been covered with asphalt, could not
be salvaged. In other areas, the original roofing made of slate pavers set
in asphalt directly on the concrete roof deck had leaked early and often,
and had been covered many times. To preserve the integrity of the structure and to provide a waterproof membrane, all of the old roofing materials were removed down to the concrete deck and a new lead-coated
copper roof installed.

The next phase was cleaning and repairing the exterior masonry at
the north wing and half dome. The information gained from the tests
carried out during the study was put to use. No harsh chemicals were
required to remove the carbon crusts; they were simply softened and
washed away with water. Specially formulated chemicals removed stubborn stains caused by pigeon repellents, copper and iron deposits, and
mildew. These were all tested before use by application to small, discreet
areas. Adjustments sometimes were made in the chemical itself, in the
concentration or dilution of the chemical, in the amount of dwell time

the chemical was left on the stone surfaces, and in the number of cycles or applications of the chemical that obtained the best results with the least impact on the stone.

Restorers decided not to utilize abrasive cleaning methods (i.e., sandblasting), as this would have removed fragile stone surface and detail. Acid rain was already visibly affecting some limestone areas. After the stone was carefully scraped with hand tools to remove larger flakes, abrasive materials were used to smooth the rough edges.

To protect cleaned surfaces, a water repellent was applied over entire walls. In addition to keeping the stone surfaces cleaner, the repellent prevents salts from leaching out of the limestone and washing over the granite surfaces below. Restorers determined that the granite is not of the most durable quality; it is susceptible to erosion and flaking due to a chemical reaction with the runoff from the limestone. Underneath the repellent, a coating was applied to the granite to strengthen and reinforce the cellular structure of the stone. Repairs at the exterior masonry also included patching deteriorated stone and repointing eroded and open mortar joints.

CONSTRUCTION CODES AND REGULATORY CONCERNS

Old historic buildings were constructed long before the establishment of modern building regulations. When they undergo rehabilitation, therefore, they are likely to be subject to more restrictive building code requirements than were in effect when they were built. Some of these regulations create hardship to owners of historic properties. It is important to understand these potential problems before proceeding with rehabilitation.

FIRE AND PANIC CODES

In the past, fires in one structure could result in entire blocks of downtown buildings being lost. As a result, over the decades stricter fire safety regulations have been enacted to give better protection. Although these regulations help in protecting property, their primary purpose is to allow for the safe exit of occupants.

Two means of egress: The primary goal of modern safety regulations is to provide for alternate means of egress (exit) for occupants of a building in case of fire. This means a building needs to include two ways out. Older buildings often had just one stairway connecting floors. When these buildings are updated, a second "fire-separated" stair must be added. The exception to this rule is small two-story buildings, which may require only one stairway.

Older commercial buildings (for instance, stores and hotels) often had a large open staircase leading to upper floors. Such a stair opening can draw fire rapidly upward like a chimney. Fire code regulations typically insist on the enclosure of such open stairs, often substantially changing the character of a historic interior.

Sprinkler systems: In older buildings, fire codes allow for some variance from their strictest provisions if developers install a sprinkler system—a thermally activated system of sprinkler heads that spray water when temperatures in a room reach a certain level. However, these systems can add considerable cost to even a small rehabilitation project and may also require the installation of a new main water supply line as well as new piping throughout the structure.

Other fire and panic code regulations may also apply, depending on how spaces are used and their occupancy level. All regulations should be interpreted by an architect or code official.

ACCESSIBILITY CODES

A movement to provide easier access to buildings for people with disabilities arose in the 1970s. People in wheelchairs and with other physical limitations often were not able to enter public buildings, restaurants, offices, and residential units. Accessibility (barrier-free) codes were adopted by many states, based on the principle that all persons should have full access to and use of buildings open to the public. With the passage of the Americans with Disabilities Act (ADA) of 1991, barrier-free laws were adopted nationally. Both new and rehabilitated buildings must now meet these requirements.

New buildings can readily allow for universal access in their initial designs, but barrier-free regulations often make the rehabilitation of older structures challenging. A common requirement is to provide a ramp for wheelchair access to an entry located a few steps above grade. Because older buildings often feature raised entrances with stairs, the construction of ramps has become common on historic buildings. The maximum permissible slope of such a ramp is 1 foot vertical for every 12 feet horizontal (if a handrail is used; without a handrail, the maximum slope is 1 foot for every 20 feet) . For example, an entrance three steps above grade level requires a ramp as long as 24 feet. Obviously, maintaining the historic character of the front entrance while adding such a prominent feature is a significant design challenge for architects and owners of historic properties.

To provide universal access to all floors inside, the installation of elevators often is necessary. This can be an expensive proposition, sometimes prohibitively so, especially if no section of the older building

Access ramp example

allows for the vertical openings required for an elevator shaft. One solution is to include elevators in an addition to the building that allows for such space. Sometimes, however, the rehabilitation of a historic building is prevented by the difficulty of satisfying access requirements.

Barrier-free codes also require spacious restroom facilities, with toilet stalls and open space large enough for the turning of a wheelchair. New buildings can be designed to accommodate these spatial needs, but the facilities of older buildings are usually much too tight, requiring tearing out walls and existing plumbing fixtures and installing new ones.

To the greatest extent possible, historic buildings must be made as accessible as nonhistoric or new buildings, but without threatening or destroying their significance. State Historic Preservation Offices can be helpful in determining whether full accessibility requirements would threaten or destroy a structure's significance and in finding acceptable alternatives. If full compliance is not possible, minimum requirements typically include all of the following:

- One accessible route from a site access point to an accessible entrance
- One accessible entrance
- If toilets are provided, one accessible rest room (may be unisex)
- Access to public spaces on the level of the accessible entrance; access to other public levels whenever practical
- Displays and written information located for viewing by a seated person

The National Park Service and its Preservation Assistance Division and Office on Accessibility has presented three levels of accessibility that can serve as guidelines for all projects. These should be seen in terms of an inverted pyramid, with the first approach being the most common and most desirable, and the second and third used less frequently and only when conditions leave no other choice. The first approach is to fully satisfy current accessibility standards, as required by law. This applies not only to new construction and new additions, which certainly should be able to meet current construction practices for accessibility, but also to rehabilitation of existing spaces if possible.

When not possible to fully comply with the accessibility standards for rehabilitation work, it is possible to utilize alternative standards following the process outlined in the ADA "Special Provisions" as well as local or state requirements. For instance, if a historic main door cannot be widened for wheelchairs without losing its historic character, perhaps an alternative entrance can be developed.

The third level of accessibility should be used only when either of the first two approaches is not feasible, and is a rare exception. This provides an alternative experience, which substitutes to some degree for lack of physical access. For example, if an upper floor of a historic museum is inaccessible to individuals in wheelchairs or with other disabilities, the experience of this space could be presented in a video and shown regularly in an area that is accessible, together with a display of some of the artifacts from the inaccessible space. It is not the ideal solution to the problem of providing access, but it may be the only reasonable one in certain circumstances.

ALTERNATIVE APPROACHES FOR PROVIDING ACCESSIBILITY
TO HISTORIC STRUCTURES

OPTION 1
Satisfy new construction standards

OPTION 2
Satisfy alternative standards

OPTION 3
Provide an alternative experience

Having a historic building should not be an excuse for not providing access to disabled persons, and every effort should be made to ensure a rich and satisfying experience for all individuals.

More information is available from the National Park Service; see Appendix I, Preservation Resources.

As the general level of sophistication increases in the preservation community, the need for better technical advice and construction skills becomes increasingly important. Through apprenticeships, training centers, and organizations such as the Association for Preservation Technology, more opportunities are available for individuals to develop skills in preservation technology, and these skills are desired and requested by others, including architects, building contractors, and preservations administrators.

Chapter 9

Downtown Revitalization

The Role of Preservation in Downtown Planning

The goals of city planners and preservationists sometimes are at odds. Planners look for ways to encourage growth in their community, while preservationists are out in front of bulldozers trying to stop new development. Or so it seems. . . .

Not surprisingly, it can be difficult for city officials to resolve this dilemma. Growth is good. It leads to a larger tax base, which is always a priority. Although preservation of existing historic structures may be considered important, it is typically seen as a secondary goal.

But what is growth, and how is it most beneficial? Of course there are several views. As E. F Schumacher wrote in *Small Is Beautiful: Economics As If People Mattered*, "In a sense, everyone believes in growth, and rightly so, because growth is an essential feature of life. The whole point, however, is to give to the idea of growth a qualitative determination . . ."[1]

If cities are to rely on growth as a yardstick of health, growth must be seen in terms of the quality of life rather than simply physical and economic growth. And isn't quality-of-life growth directly tied to a community's image of itself? And isn't that image, to a large degree, a recognition of and respect for its heritage? Growth *is* good, and historic preservation should be seen as an important component of it.

WHY REVITALIZE DOWNTOWNS?

Preservationists must consider what to do with older downtowns. Should they be saved? Maybe they have served their purpose and are no longer needed. Why try to prolong the life of these urban dinosaurs? These are valid questions.

Where should growth in our cities be encouraged—in the center city or on the urban fringe? In the past decades, as a society we have directed our attention to the suburbs and away from traditional urban cores.

Many older downtowns have been largely forgotten as activity destination points.

What caused the deterioration of downtown vitality? Much of it slowly bled out by misdirected planning policies. New office complexes with high-rise structures were overemphasized, and not enough attention was paid to existing smaller businesses and downtown residential uses. The goal was to increase the tax base and generate revenues. But recent studies show the emphasis on the big project versus the small may be wrong.

There is growing disenchantment with the proposition that downtown office buildings provide a municipal government with more taxes and jobs than the selective retention of smaller buildings and promotion of urban housing. We know for sure that downtown high-rise concentrations bring with them increased air pollution, clogged freeways and bridges, loss of light and air, destruction of smaller historic buildings, and soaring housing costs. Now experts such as MIT economist David Burch question whether high-rises actually account for as much job development as we previously had thought, in contrast to the known growth of jobs in the small-business sector. Often, this sector cannot afford the rents charged by the new high-rise office buildings, and the result is net job losses downtown—not gains.[2]

"Other economic studies have shown that residential housing in downtown areas actually may benefit a city more than new office construction. This was the conclusion of the Washington, D.C., zoning commission when it rezoned the city's downtown to include residential development. We, for example, that downtown residents contribute twice as much in retail purchases and sales taxes as daytime office workers. For cities such as Washington that collect personal income taxes, new downtown permanent residences should account for many more overall tax dollars than an equivalent amount of commercial office space. Moreover, additional residents should help create a lively twenty-four-hour downtown area, with more shoppers, theatergoers, and "eyes on the street"—and that means a lot less crime."[3]

The health of downtowns cannot be ignored. The revitalization of city centers can serve many purposes, giving them a prominent and important role in their communities. The main considerations are the following:

Existing infrastructure: Downtowns have streets, sewer and water lines and other utilities, and a central location. It is wasteful for American cities to discard this built-up infrastructure and pay to duplicate it at the city's perimeter. From both an economic and an environmental stand-

*Quincy Market, downtown
Boston, Massachusetts*

point, throwing away downtowns rather than recycling them is a poor decision for our society.

Community focus: Downtowns traditionally provided a focus for local communities, giving a sense of identity to their residents. Downtown, they could associate a place with the concept of community, and this did much to create a common sense of purpose. Without this focus on local culture, residents do not feel they belong to a community, and it becomes difficult to raise support for local projects and activities. The need for a place with which to identify is increasingly important in a mobile society. With the loss of downtown comes the loss of the community's center. To borrow Gertrude Stein's words describing Oakland, California, "There is no there there."

Greater diversity: Downtowns have greater functional diversity than many of the newer centers built on the city fringe. They still serve as centers for retail stores, financial institutions, public agencies and local government offices, public transportation, historic areas, and cultural and educational institutions. This diversity comes in varying degrees but always gives downtowns an inherent, long-lasting strength. By contrast, many newer developments are unifunctional, devoted only to specialty retailing, quick-stop shopping, or single-size residential developments. They are therefore more vulnerable to changing times, and indeed may become obsolete much sooner than downtowns. Many suburban developments from the 1950s and 1960s have already been abandoned, to be replaced with more recently built fringe developments.

Employment: Statistically, downtowns are still the greatest employment sectors within cities, with many people coming to the downtown district daily to work. This provides the potential for a regular and continuing user base for functions located in the area.

Downtowns also serve as incubators for new businesses, allowing a supportive environment for small entrepreneurs. Studies show that the highest proportion of new jobs comes from small, start-up businesses, the kind that flourish in the supportive environment of a downtown. A study conducted at the Massachusetts Institute of Technology revealed that 50 percent of all new jobs are generated from expansion of existing small businesses. The retention and prosperity of such businesses is vital to the economic stability and growth of any community.[4]

Centers of trade: Downtowns continue to be the center of distribution of goods and services. Although for many decades there has been a pattern of dispersion of businesses to other sections of cities, downtowns retain a substantial share of these functions and therefore the potential for many other activities to consolidate around them. Most downtowns have a high proportion of locally owned businesses. Revitalization of these cores helps support them and keeps consumer spending within the local economy.

Sprawl reduction: Keeping retail functions in a centralized location lessens the tendency toward suburban sprawl. Centralization allows better utilization of public transportation systems and reduces the need for resources devoted to automobiles.

Historic character: When the inherent historic character of older downtowns is preserved, they become tourist attractions, enhancing both the local economy and the sense of community pride. Over time it has become obvious that historic preservation is good for business.

Evaluating the Health of Downtowns

Preservationists traditionally have worked to save historic buildings. Yet a program intent only on saving downtown buildings is not enough, for the issue is not just the deterioration of the physical environment of the downtown but also the decline of its economic and social environment.

After many years researching the issues of downtown revitalization, looking at downtown health in sixteen smaller cities, a study by the author to determine what factors have had the greatest impact on the health of the downtowns found the preservation of the physical elements, including the preservation of older buildings, historic facades, and a traditional streetscape, was important, but only in combination with the preservation and encouragement of critical functional aspects of the downtown environment.[5] In other words, the preservation of an old downtown drugstore building should be combined with an attempt to preserve the drugstore business itself, or a similar customer-oriented business. The functions (the "verbs" described in chapter 1) are what define downtown as a focus of community life, not simply the physical groupings of buildings (the "nouns"). Downtown preservation, therefore, has goals beyond the physical preservation of buildings. For example, revitalization efforts should encourage existing businesses to remain in the downtown, for many residents associate specific businesses with downtown's viability as a commercial district. Yet many are family-owned businesses that haven't changed in years; ways must be found to update their operations, to make them vital and competitive in a changing market, without losing their historic integrity.

An article about this study of downtown health outlined how revitalization strategies should include a careful analysis of the downtown business mix:

> [The study indicated] a primary strategy should include encouraging the right mix of businesses. Local policy makers should promote browsing, shopping, retail stores, and other functions which encourage the leisurely use of the downtown, reestablishing it as a focus of community life.
>
> [L]eisurely shopping could be enhanced through streetscape improvements. Improvements such as benches, mini-parks and walkways, if properly located, could coerce shoppers to walk by a greater number of storefronts. Downtown should be seen as a pleasant place to spend time, rather than simply a place to quickly pick up convenience goods.
>
> The study also showed that the existence of identifiable downtown landmarks, such as a courthouse or a grouping of historic buildings, helped establish the image of downtown as a district rather than simply individual structures without strong relationships to each other. This sense

of downtown as a district gives a cohesive image, and helps identify the downtown not as a place to come for a single purpose, but rather a place to come for a variety of reasons.[6]

Promoters of downtown development should recognize the need to bring new businesses to older downtowns. These core areas should not be seen as museums where time stands still but as organisms that continually evolve into new forms. The continuity of such districts relies on their ability to change over time, and because they are made up of commercial establishments, they need to change much more than other districts.

A common conflict is encountered when preservationists encourage the restoration of downtown facades and storefronts. They may fail to recognize that a retail establishment needs to periodically update its image and present a fresh face. It is generally accepted that retail stores should have a new image—and a new storefront—at least every five to ten years. The restoration of the storefront can provide a new and positive image; a historic image is marketable and well accepted by the public. Thus, restoration or rehabilitation of a storefront can by itself draw customers. The problem arises when, five or ten years later, the business is ready for another new image. What does the preservationist suggest then?

The preservation of downtowns is a relatively recent movement; the problem of updating the postpreservation look has not been confronted in most communities. This issue is unique to downtown preservation efforts, and flexibility must be the key. Whereas the goal in residential and institutional restorations is to retain and restore as much of the original as possible, the goal of many commercial projects is to retain the basic historical integrity of the structure while allowing the freedom to change, to provide for the image needs of the current business.

The National Trust for Historic Preservation established the Main Street Program in 1980. Mary Means, the initiator and first director of the program, felt that preservationists were focusing too much on saving individual landmark buildings and not enough on the more complex problems of downtown districts. Downtown revitalization was seen by preservationists as a problem for others because it involves issues of marketing, economic development, and urban infrastructure.

The original concept for the Main Street Program was based on three pilot projects—in Galesburg, Illinois; Hot Springs, South Dakota; and

The Main Street Program

Madison, Indiana, where involvement began in 1977. Administered through the National Main Street Center in Washington, D.C., the program is intended to show that rehabilitation of older commercial buildings can be an important part of a downtown revitalization effort. Indeed, preservation can lead to economic development and downtown promotion, and these efforts should be seen as inextricably linked to the same goals.

From the three pilot cities, the program expanded to include thirty cities over three years. Each received an experienced community development project manager, whose salary for three years was paid through the program. The Main Street program was so successful that it became a nationwide effort; the number of cities across the United States requesting designation as Main Street communities was so great the National Trust was no longer able to directly support each one.

Since its inception, total public and private reinvestment in Main Street Program communities is over $11 billion. The Main Street Center recently tabulated that the program led to the rehabilitation of almost 60,000 buildings, over 174,000 new jobs, and to $35 reinvested for every $1 spent.[7] The positive results of this program are obvious.

The National Main Street Center in Washington, D.C., also serves as a national clearinghouse for information and resources for communities following the Main Street approach. It provides resources to local officials and downtown development managers and coordinates regular National Town Meeting conferences, which communicate a wealth of how-to techniques.

THE FOUR-POINT APPROACH

Encouraged by the results of the pilot projects, the Main Street Center's approach to downtown revitalization is based on four key ingredients:

1. *Organization*: Perhaps the most difficult aspect of any revitalization effort is to create the organizational framework that brings together interest groups and individuals. Each comes to the table with its own agenda and sphere of interest. The merchants' association may be interested in the promotion of retail sales, the Chamber of Commerce in job creation, and city government in providing municipal services. Without coordination, these efforts may not be mutually supportive and in some cases may be at odds. The Main Street Program's project manager usually attempted to bring the groups together under an umbrella organization that deals directly and exclusively with the concerns of downtown.

2. *Promotion*: In many communities, the downtown is largely overlooked by citizens who shift their consumer shopping patterns. To counter this, the Main Street Program showed that downtowns need to compete by promoting themselves and presenting an attractive new image. Promotions were considered critical to attracting people downtown. By targeting groups that the downtown should try to attract (e.g., families with children, young professionals, tourists, etc.), the creation of sales and special events establishes downtown as a place of activity where something new and interesting is occurring.

3. *Design*: Although physical improvements alone are not enough to revitalize an area, storefront rehabilitation and streetscape improvements provide visual proof that something is happening in a downtown. Thus, the design aspect of the Main Street Program was important because it provides evidence of revitalization activity in the course of creating a more desirable environment.

4. *Economic restructuring*: Financial support for a revitalization program was the last critical component in the Main Street Program's approach. This effort attempts to find financial resources for revitalization work. A typical strategy may enlist local banks in a revolving loan program that funds rehabilitation work. In the past, downtowns were largely ignored by local lending institutions, who saw little business potential there. When banks are convinced to give their support jointly, none feels greatly exposed to risk. The Main Street Program demonstrated that property values can be substantially increased with a coordinated revitalization program.

The four-point approach works most effectively when combined with eight principles to be applied when developing revitalization strategies:

1. *Comprehensiveness*: A single project cannot revitalize a downtown or commercial neighborhood. An ongoing series of initiatives is vital to build community support and create lasting progress.

2. *Incrementation*: Small projects make a big difference. They demonstrate that a Main Street is alive and hone the skills and confidence the program needs to tackle more complex problems.

3. *Self-help*: Although the National Main Street Center can provide valuable direction and hands-on technical assistance, only local leadership can initiate long-term success by fostering and demonstrating community involvement and commitment to the revitalization effort.

4. *Public-private partnership*: Every local Main Street program needs the support and expertise of both the public and private sectors. For an effective partnership, each must recognize the strengths and weaknesses of the other.

5. *Identification of and capitalization on existing assets*: A key goal of the National Main Street Center is to help communities recognize and make the best use of their unique offerings. Local assets provide the solid foundation for a successful Main Street initiative.
6. *Quality*: From storefront design to promotional campaigns to special events, high quality must be the main goal in all activities.
7. *Change*: Changing community attitudes and habits is essential to bringing about a commercial district renaissance. A carefully planned Main Street program helps to shift public perceptions and practices to support and sustain the revitalization process.
8. *Action orientation*: Frequent, visible changes in the look and activities of the commercial district reinforce the perception of positive change. Small but dramatic improvements early in the process remind the community that the revitalization effort is underway.[8]

EVALUATION OF THE MAIN STREET PROGRAM

The Main Street Program, successful in its efforts since 1980, is one of the best approaches yet developed for revitalizing aging downtowns. To date, hundreds of communities have aligned themselves in some way with the Main Street Program, although many have adopted its strategies without receiving direct support from the National Main Street Center.

When the Main Street program fails in a community, it is usually for one of these reasons:

· The project manager was not working full time, and could not follow through properly on initiatives.
· Some downtown groups were unhappy with the new show in town and sabotaged efforts of the Main Street project office.
· The board of directors tried to accommodate too many groups and became large and unwieldy.

An important criticism of the Main Street program is that it doesn't stress the historical aspect of historic preservation enough. The program encourages reuse of older buildings and stresses economic and retailing revitalization, but says little about dealing with local history. Historian Dan Morrill made the following observation after attending a Main Street conference in Washington, D.C.:

Increasingly, preservationists are forgetting, ignoring, or overlooking the essential purpose which should underlie their activities—the preservation of history.

Huntington, West Virginia,
a Main Street Program
downtown

I appreciate and applaud the aspirations and accomplishments of the National Main Street Center.... Not once during my three-day sojourn in Washington, however, did I hear a speaker mention the necessity or even the desirability of performing historical research. I spent a lot of time touring the bars with two fellows from Mississippi (we Southerners stick together) and they told me that they thought history was boring. They didn't come to the Main Street Center to learn about the past. Jefferson Davis who? They owned a couple of bedraggled buildings on some bayou or other and were looking for those wonderful . . . investment tax credits.

My Mississippi cohorts asked me what I did for a living. I told them I was an historian. "A what?" they drawled. A look of dismay and disbelief crept across their faces. I could almost hear the query which began to percolate in the marrow of their bones: "What's an historian doing at the Main Street Center of the National Trust for Historic Preservation?"[9]

OTHER ENDEAVORS OF THE MAIN STREET PROGRAM

In recent years the Main Street Center has expanded its activities beyond small cities and begun to support programs in large cities through its Urban Main Street Program. It also conducts training courses for downtown revitalization efforts; use of its comprehensive how-to manual is now widespread. In addition, the program has sponsored a number of national video conferences on Main Street revitalization. The annual Great American Main Street Awards, which give national recognition to communities that successfully follow the Main Street approach, are among the program's other achievements.

Zoning and Downtown Revitalization

Can older downtowns be revitalized through the use of conventional land use regulations and zoning? Some planners feel an innovative approach to zoning may be sufficient to encourage renewal activities. An editorial from Small Town magazine laid out an interesting perspective:

> This country desperately needs an enlightened public policy concerning downtowns and their relationship to overall land use. Zoning must reflect the downtown's role as the community social center. Therefore, zoning codes need to begin the process of pulling multiple uses back downtown. For example, the code should say that government must stay downtown and that shipping must stay downtown. Also, downtown is where the movie theater and other entertainment businesses must locate. It is also the place for offices and for service businesses. Zoning should exclude these uses from other areas and it should do away with such designations as commercial highway strip, planned shopping center, etc.
>
> In our rush to modernize, we've forgotten the fundamental truth that people need a central meeting place. The old downtown served that function once. Nothing has ever replaced that crucial foundation for community in those places that destroyed their downtowns. The most important agenda item for all concerned citizens and public officials is not the sewer or water system, or the roads or the police. It is how to forge and maintain a special sense of community. The solution starts downtown.[10]

Zoning is a powerful tool wielded by cities—perhaps its most powerful tool. Preservationists should understand this power and use it for their own purposes. The power to comment officially on proposed changes to a zoning ordinance or master plan should be within the scope of a historic district commission. Commissions, seeing only design review as their responsibility, thus limit their involvement to this level. However, the development of the surrounding area can play a key role in preserving the integrity of a historic structure. Commissions should see it as part of their responsibility to make comment whenever proposed changes affect designated properties.

Such coordination has other benefits as well. It encourages a municipality to consider historic significance as a regular part of all their deliberations and supports the development of plans and ordinances that are compatible with historic district goals.

Preservationists have a special interest in their community that is expressed in protection of its historic heritage. However, other residents have many interests, and preservation may or may not be one of them. Preservationists should recognize that many people with varying perspectives affect a city's changing physical environment. They can then better understand how to protect their community's historic structures, integrating that process with the natural and inevitable course of change and development.

People representing many points of view can affect the course of change in a community. Sometimes their goals seem counter to preservation goals, but with understanding and an innovative approach this need not be. Understanding of the goals, or the agenda, of the other players helps preservationists better deal with concerns as they arise.

CITY OR MUNICIPAL COUNCIL

The city council is made up of elected representatives who are responsible to their constituents in the community. Because of this, the council's actions may be based on political expedience. Whereas other city agencies follow policy, the city council makes policy.

Most actions of a local historic commission are subject in some form or other to review by the council, as commission members are typically appointed either by the mayor or council. Historic ordinances also are subject to review and approval by the council, as is the designation of new districts or individual historic structures. Therefore, the council support for the work of a historic district commission is necessary, but it should not be taken for granted. Some council members are aware of the vital role of the commission but others are not, and may view the commission's work as extraneous and unnecessary, or even as an impediment to the community's ability to grow and prosper. Because council giveth, council also taketh away, or at least is empowered to do so. It is therefore incumbent on preservation activists and commission members to regularly educate and inform council members on preservation issues. This is important not only when a big vote is coming up; a regular awareness program that includes an annual preservation awards program, the provision of printed updates on preservation issues, and the release of news features on historically significant structures should be established.

PLANNING COMMISSION AND PLANNING DEPARTMENT

Although lumped together for purposes of discussion here, a city's planning department and its planning commission are usually entirely different bodies. Each fulfills a function of planning for community growth, but from differing perspectives. The planning commission is made up of appointees from the community, serving the city as volunteers. The commission represents the interests of the community at large and includes time on its agenda for residents to voice their opinions on proposals. The planning department, on the other hand, is made up of professional planners, not necessarily from the community, who are responsible for providing the technical and professional backup essential for planning commissioners and city council members to make determinations.

The underlying purpose of both the planning commission and planning department staff is to review development proposals to see if the plans are in the best interests of the community, to approve or reject the plans, and then advise the city council of their determinations. As such, they provide an important overview function and can recognize how each proposed project fits in with the longer-range goals of the community. If preservation and downtown revitalization are defined as important goals, then planners can do much to encourage compatible development and discourage inappropriate proposals.

DOWNTOWN DEVELOPMENT AUTHORITIES

Downtown development authorities (DDAs) were instituted in the 1970s as a way to deal with the special needs of older downtowns. State enabling legislation allowed for their establishments, with the twin goals of preventing downtown deterioration and promoting economic growth and revitalization.

TAX INCREMENT FINANCING

DDAs are essentially revenue allocation authorities that encourage public and private development activities in downtowns. A common financial basis for DDAs is tax increment financing (TIF). TIF districts work like this: The city determines the initial assessed value of property within a defined downtown district; this base amount goes into general fund revenues. However, in each year thereafter the municipal treasurer transmits to the DDA all monies that exceed this base amount. This so-called captured assessed value makes up the tax increment revenue. With TIF, any increase in the base amount created by new development within the downtown district is allocated exclusively to the DDA for use on designated projects within its boundaries. Such financing capitalizes on and makes use of the increased tax base created by economic development. DDAs may also create a second source of revenue from the sale of municipal bonds based on the new increment financing.

In many communities DDAs are closely tied to downtown preservation efforts. In some, the DDA office serves also as the Main Street program office, with overlapping activities and personnel and little to distinguish among them. Main Street program costs thus are largely funded through tax increment funds captured within the DDA boundaries.

DDAs are limited in the ways they can use their revenues. Projects are financed as public improvements and are intended to encourage private investment, but must not directly benefit private individuals. For instance, street and sidewalk improvements within the downtown are an appropriate use of DDA funds, but improvements to individual structures generally are not unless they are part of a general program available to all. Often DDAs work in conjunction with local banks, the DDA paying for public improvements and banks establishing a loan fund pool for individual property owners.

One of the problems faced by new DDAs is that, in a slow-growth downtown, initial new development is required to prime the pump. Without initial new development, no revenues can accrue for the authority to use to attract more development, which would in turn bring in more revenues and other development. The creation of a new DDA should therefore be timed to tie in with new development already planned within the district.

On the reverse side of the coin, some DDAs are so successful in creating new development that the revenues generated greatly exceed their needs. Once established, it is difficult for a DDA to give up its economic power base; within its domain it can rival the city itself. This creates concern and jealousy from other city agencies, as revenues that formerly would have gone into the city's general fund are now diverted into this special downtown agency. Public schools generally suffer the most from this diversion of resources, hence school boards are often been the biggest critics of the DDA concept. For this reason, an increasingly important provision in DDA ordinances is the termination clause. Typically such causes stipulate that the authority will be dissolved by city council upon completion of its purposes. If these purposes are clearly stated and the scope well defined, council can act appropriately. However, if the authority's purposes are loosely defined and open to interpretation, the city may find it difficult to regain control.

DEVELOPERS

Developers are in the business of looking for good economic opportunities. Whether representing themselves or the interests of others, developers' primary goal is to maximize return on investment dollars. Often this pits developers against the advocates of preservation. The best investment opportunities are typically found in "hot" locations, and these locations today are often the same locations that were hot in previous generations. Such locations include the main four corners of a downtown (known by economists as the 100-percent corner) and areas adjacent to established institutions or businesses. Older buildings in these prime locations may be underutilized and not considered the highest and best use for the property by ambitious developers. According to this perspective, historic structures stand in the way of progress.

Preservationists can best work with developers by defining the rules of the game. It is important to establish a public list of structures and historic districts determined to be in need of protection, along with a well-thought-out ordinance that clearly defines what will and will not be permitted in the way of development. Developers tend to steer away from areas of conflict and look for opportunities in which cooperation from the city and its agencies is assured and where opposition from special-interest groups and residents is minimal. Generally, only after developers invest a considerable amount of money in a project and then see opposition from preservationists developing as a belated response do they dig in for battle to protect their initial investment.

Preservationists may need to take a cynical, hard stance in order to influence developers. As stated by Arthur Frommer, noted travel writer, who spoke to preservationists in Chicago:

> Adopt a more confrontational approach to the real estate developers; subordinate your normal tendency to gentility: it will not work. The developers are motivated by that most powerful of urges—short-term financial gain—a drive far stronger in most instances than the principled motives of the public advocating preservation. They will always find reasons for demolition where the dollar is at stake. They will run roughshod over your most urgent pleas.
>
> In other cities, I have heard preservationists speak about enlisting the developers to participate in joint committees and cooperative planning. We are told they should be met at the doors to council chambers with coffee and cake, an outstretched arm of friendship.
>
> In my opinion, they should be met with injunctions and orders to show cause, with summonses and motion papers, the only language they understand. Then they will negotiate.[11]

ARCHITECTS

Architects generally take a broader view of development than do developers. When working on a proposal for a new project in a historic area, an architect considers the larger community interest as well as the existing physical context in which a new structure is being placed. For two reasons architects are usually more sympathetic to historic interests. First, their training is professional, and the consideration of larger community interests is part of their professional obligation. Second, architects study historic buildings and styles in their schooling and have a greater appreciation for historic architecture.

Nevertheless, architects are paid by their clients and are agents for their clients' interests. They have both a financial and an emotional investment in their project proposals, and if changes are necessary because of local opposition from preservationists, they must absorb redesign costs and suffer some loss of professional prestige. It is important, therefore, for preservationists to review project proposals early in the design process. If a historic district commission review is one of the last steps in the development process, it may be too late to insist on substantive design changes. Instead, reviewing and commenting at an early stage is an excellent way to minimize conflict. Printed guidelines describing appropriate design in a historic context are also helpful. These should include examples of how new designs can be compatible to old through the use of proper scale, proportion, setback, materials, and so on.

Downtown revitalization is one of the most complex and one of the most important of preservation activities, for it not only brings to life a historic district but in many cases serves to restore the economic and cultural heart of a community. Preservationists bring many perspectives to the revitalization of downtowns and make many arguments about the relative importance of their various approaches. But, as the Main Street Program and the many activities of the National Trust's National Main Street Center show, historic preservation can provide a core for such efforts and can achieve success well beyond the simple preservation of old buildings.

Chapter 10

Preservation Economics

The Economic
Burdens and
Benefits of
Preservation

The economics of historic preservation is an important issue. The cost/benefit financial analysis for rehabilitation of a historic property is typically more complicated than for new construction, and a number of factors must be considered. Someone once described historic preservation as a very expensive art form. The preservation of a painting or an antique dresser cannot be compared with the cost of preserving a Greek revival house. But the preservation of a structure might be seen as more important than saving a painting or piece of furniture, for there history has taken place. Historic buildings "are vehicles of culture . . . and in their evolved states, whole works of art, in whose intangible elements the true value lies, because it is there that we find the signs of life."[1]

Although there are many economic benefits in rehabilitation, there may be no inexpensive way to preserve an important older building. In some cases, the costs of simple maintenance alone can be a financial burden for a family or community organization that is responsible for a historic structure. Costs of full restoration can run even higher, and often require special materials and workmanship.

What can be done to alleviate this financial burden? Who should be responsible for paying for preservation? Can financial incentives be created to offset such costs? These questions must be confronted in order to make preservation acceptable to society in general and especially to owners of historic structures who bear the responsibility for their upkeep.

COSTS OF REHABILITATION VERSUS NEW CONSTRUCTION

Rehabilitation can seem an expensive option for a commercial developer, for there are drawbacks to rehabbing older structures: spaces not easily adapted to current needs, problems of deterioration not apparent at the beginning of work, difficulty in finding appropriate construction materials.

Yet rehab can also pay. Studies show that rehab can save money compared to new construction. According to one study:

> *Rehabilitation costs per square foot are often significantly less than the costs of new construction.* Case studies presented at the National Trust for Historic Preservation conference on the "Economic Benefits of Preserving Old Buildings" demonstrated that the cost of rehabilitating old structures generally runs 25–33 percent less than comparable new construction. In those cases where the costs are equivalent, the preservation project provided greater amenities—time saved in construction, more space in either height or volume, or the right location. These amenities frequently produced other economic benefits to a developer through higher occupancy rates and rents. In addition, rehabilitation oftentimes bypasses lengthy development review processes, local neighborhood opposition, and zoning delays.[2]

The costs of rehabilitation can be seen in other ways as well. A government study found that rehabilitation construction uses 23 percent less energy than new construction, the primary reason being that the work is more labor intensive than material intensive, depleting fewer natural resources.[3]

"Conservation of the Urban Environment," a report prepared by the Office of Archaeology and Historic Preservation in the Department of the Interior, explained this in more detail. The reliance on labor-intensive work

> . . . is important not only in terms of the employment potential of historic preservation, but also in terms of an individual project's multiplier impact on a local economy. Dependent on the size and sophistication of a locality, a higher proportion of construction materials will come from outside the area than will construction labor. For funds that are spent in a local economy, a higher percentage of funds remains as a stimulant in that locality from projects that are labor intensive. Thus, funds utilized in historic preservation projects have greater impact on employment than funds used in the construction of new buildings such as hospitals, schools, and office buildings because of (1) the greater labor intensity of preservation projects, and (2) through this labor intensity the higher multiplier.[4]

Testimony by the General Services Administration indicated that rehabilitation creates two to five times as many jobs as new construction for a given expenditure of money, and that this was especially important because older buildings are often found in areas of the city that have the highest rates of unemployment and underemployment.[5]

Many other economic advantages accrue to historic preservation—too many to list here. They are thoroughly documented, however, in *The Economics of Historic Preservation* by the recognized expert on this topic, Donovan Rypkema. He lists and describes a hundred arguments supporting the commonsense economics of historic preservation, among them that historic preservation creates more jobs than the same amount of new construction by having a higher proportion of a project's costs related to labor and less to materials; historic preservation is an important part of the quality-of-life equation; historic preservation programs effectively target areas appropriate for public attention; historic preservation is a fiscally responsible reaction to the high cost of landfill; and the most effective method of preventing suburban sprawl is through more intensive use of buildings and sites already in place within the community.[6]

TAX ASSESSMENTS FOR HISTORIC PROPERTIES

Owners of designated historic properties often complain they are taxed unfairly. Local tax assessors may evaluate a historic property in a downtown area based on the property's potential for development. Thus an owner who restores a two-story residence in a prime area may have to pay a property tax rate comparable to that of a newer and larger commercial building. It is patently unfair to penalize the owner of a historic property for maintaining it rather than replacing it with a building that would allow more intensive use.

Because downtown preservation (where this type of inequity is most commonly found) is a relatively recent phenomenon, few legal precedents address such cases, and it remains unclear whether or not special provisions can be made in assessments for certified historic properties. The decision in *1827 M Street* v. *District of Columbia* was that the assessment could not be raised based on the property's "highest and best use" as long as it was either designated or under official review for designation. This emphasizes the importance of designation as a way to protect owners of historic properties.[7]

Steps can be taken by local governments to mitigate the disincentive of higher assessments. Some cities are empowered to defer tax increases for a number of years; this power can be invoked when the restoration of a historic property is completed. Some preservation ordinances allow for a reduction in property taxes for designated historic properties.[8] These tax rebates compensate owners by recognizing the potential inequity of owning a historic property; they typically are tied to ordinances that regulate the owner's right to demolish or alter the exterior of a property. In some communities, local lending institutions agree to jointly offer a program of below-market-rate or guaranteed loans to owners of historic commercial properties who wish to restore or rehabilitate their buildings. Through such programs, historic districts are able to withstand the pressures for demolition.

EASEMENTS

Ownership of a historic building can be a financial burden due to the expense of proper restoration or rehabilitation. A method of easing this burden, available to owners of both commercial and noncommercial properties, is the use of easements. An easement gives an interest in a portion of a real property to a qualifying organization. The owner retains use of the entire property but agrees to relinquish part of the bundle of rights inherent to property ownership in return for favorable tax treatment.

Easements, then, are a potentially valuable means to both protect historic buildings and provide value to their owners. For example, using an easement the owner of a property with a historic facade can agree to give up the right to change the facade in perpetuity. This right is given to a qualifying organization, which must be tax-exempt under Section 501(c)(3) of the Internal Revenue Code; such an organization, typically a local historical foundation, is responsible for checking on the condition of the property regularly to ensure it satisfies the provisions of the easement. The current owner and all future owners are bound to the easement provisions.

In return, the current owner can claim as a charitable donation for income tax purposes the value of the easement. This may be beneficial to the owner if the historic use value is lower than the fair market value without the easement.

An example is an actual property in Alexandria, Virginia, a community near Washington, D.C., with high property values. The property includes a significant historic house and carriage house (shown in solid black in the sketch). The two structures and land had a total market value of $200,000. However, a developer offered $1 million for the property, subject to approval to build eighteen townhouses as shown. The owner, recognizing this much greater value, wanted to sell, but the local historic district commission would not approve such intensive development of the property.

The owner felt he was being treated unfairly and said he should be compensated by the city for the $800,000 loss of potential profit resulting solely from the historic district commission's designation. The

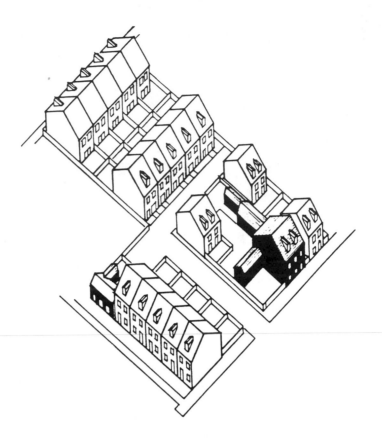

*Sketch of Alexandria
project by M. Hamilton
Morton Jr., AIA*

courts, however, have consistently upheld a community's right to deny inappropriate development of historic properties, as long as owners continue to get a reasonable return on their property, even if it isn't the highest and best return. (Refer to the precedent-setting *Penn Central* decision discussed in chapter 4.)

In this case, however, the owner was able to recoup some of the loss in potential income by donating a real property easement. An agreement in perpetuity attached to the property title said the property would remain undeveloped, with the right to develop donated to the local historic commission. In return, the owner could claim a personal income tax deduction for the $800,000 difference. Depending on the owner's tax bracket, this could be a large proportion of the total amount and serve as considerable compensation for not being able to develop.[9]

Although this seems an equitable solution, questions immediately arise:

Question: Who determines the value of the easement?

A well-qualified appraiser who has had experience with similar appraisals should determine the fair market value of the easement.[10]

Question: Who checks over the years to ensure that the easement component remains unaltered?

A not-for-profit organization must inspect the condition of the property covered by the easement at least once a year to see that it is not altered and is properly maintained. The organization may be chosen from a local or statewide preservation group, a local historical society or the State Historic Preservation Office (SHPO).

You can appreciate why easements are not often used for historic structures and why they occasionally lead to complications. The program is good in theory but less so in practice. A Government Accounting Office (GAO) study found that easements were typically overvalued by appraisers, often at 200 percent or more of their actual value.[11] A high appraisal is in the owner's interest. Few appraisers are experienced in evaluating easements and therefore do not have comparable information from which to extrapolate values. Owners also find it difficult to identify not-for-profit associations willing to hold an easement, typically without compensation. This responsibility has great potential for problems to the accepting body but little in the way of reward. Many receiving organizations are now requiring an endowment with the easement to defray the cost of administering it. Finally, owners are discouraged by the perpetual nature of easements, which decreases the overall value of their property for future sale, but of course that is the basis of the dedication of the easement.

When properly set up and administered, however, easements are a good way to maintain a property's historic integrity. They permit a community to hold onto important elements of its architectural heritage and benefit owners, who earn tax breaks while ensuring that the integrity of a historic property is protected for posterity.

TRANSFER OF DEVELOPMENT RIGHTS

In densely developed urban areas, smaller historic buildings can be threatened by economic forces. The demolition of a historic structure allows a property to be redeveloped to its highest and best use. Owners of these properties may feel limited by historic designation, which can prohibit them from realizing potential higher profits from their property. A transfer of development rights (TDR) provision, if established by a city, may help alleviate this financial inequity.

A TDR program allows owners of buildings in zoning districts where more intense development is permitted to sell that development potential to owners of other sites. As shown in the diagram, development rights are literally purchased by another owner for use on a second site.

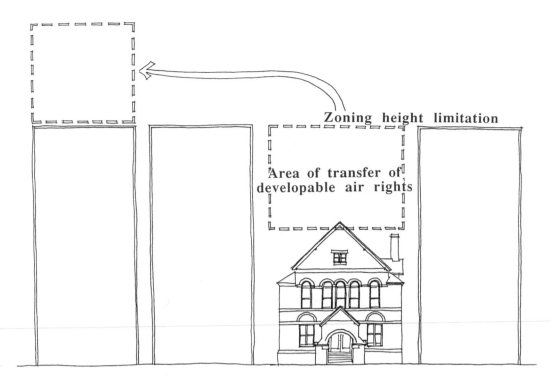

Zoning height limitation

Area of transfer of developable air rights

Schematic drawing of a development rights transfer program

The city of Philadelphia has a TDR program that came about when an ordinance was passed to prevent the demolition of a landmark downtown building. At the same time, an old gentleman's agreement was broken not to build a downtown building higher that the hat on the sculpture of William Penn on the City Hall. It was recognized by city officials that development should be encouraged while the historic character of the downtown district preserved. The Philadelphia TDR program allowed for this and had three goals when it was established in 1991:

1. To provide an economic incentive for rehabilitation to locally designated landmarks.
2. To protect the 1984 local historic preservation ordinance from court challenge by offering relief to city-certified property owners on land zoned for more profitable use.
3. To establish a new and innovative incentive for nonprofit owners of historic properties to maintain and rehabilitate their buildings.[12]

More than two hundred owners of historic structures were eligible to sell development rights through the TDR option. This incentive was combined with two other development programs: an enhanced real estate tax abatement program that included historic properties, and a large revolving loan fund.

San Francisco considered and subsequently adopted a TDR program as a way to encourage preservation, described in *A Preservation Strategy for Downtown San Francisco,* which proposed the following recommendations for the use of TDRs:[13]

- Permit transfer of development rights only from significant buildings.
- Permit transfers within the same zoning district at a 1:1 and in special development districts at a 1.5–2:1 ratio.
- Allow an automatic right to use TDRs on eligible receiving sites up to the maximum permissible floor area ratio (FAR) or maximum achievable FAR under height and bulk limits.
- Require valid occupancy or current use as a condition for transfers.
- Permit a bonus transfer for restoration.
- Record a permanent reduction in development potential and maintenance agreement in the city's favor upon transfer.
- Encourage city support in organizing a trust to create an initial bank that would ensure an active market in TDRs.
- Prohibit the demolition or significant alteration of the highest-rated buildings except in restricted, special circumstances. The study highlighted this protection as a critical component of the proposed TDR program.

TAX BENEFITS

Although the federal government lay much of the groundwork for preservation efforts through the National Historic Preservation Act of 1966, little was done up to that time to give financial incentives for preservation. Without financial incentives, preservation remained an idealistic issue removed from the mainstream of development. Indeed, developers were given an income tax deduction incentive for expenses incurred in the demolition of older buildings. This was without prior determination whether the buildings had historic significance and should be protected from demolition.

These types of tax deductions encouraged the wholesale demolition of many older urban neighborhoods, which were destroyed one after another under the guise of urban renewal programs. Many sites were torn down to make way for new development that did not materialize, leaving behind the eyesore of vacant lots. Those areas that were "developed" often fared no better. Urban renewal generated the construction of limited-access highways in the city's core, allowing suburbanites speedy access to downtown offices. Superblocks replaced the traditional urban neighborhoods of small blocks of two- and three-story rowhouses and walkups with a new order of high-rise apartments.

When the horrors of the urban renewal projects of the 1960s and '70s became apparent, the federal government responded in a limited way. In 1976, the Tax Reform Act was a first step in recognizing the inadequacies of legislation protecting existing neighborhoods and historic structures.[14] The Act stated that developers could no longer consider the cost of demolition of historic structures as a deductible business expense; previously, developers essentially were reimbursed for demolition. The Act also permitted accelerated depreciation for substantial rehabilitation of historic structures used in a trade or business or held for income producing purposes, which allowed owners to take greater tax deductions in the early years.

The 1978 Tax Act went further by establishing a tax credit program for rehabilitating older buildings.[15] The Rehabilitation Investment Tax Credit (RITC) program allowed developers a 10 percent tax credit for the costs of rehabilitating a historic structure used in a trade or business or held for income producing purposes. The credit is a reasonable incentive, for unlike a tax deduction, which is a reduction from gross income claimed on the tax form, a tax credit is subtracted directly from the amount of tax owed and represents a much higher savings.

Because the new RITC could be taken only for rehabilitation work on historic structures, a procedure was needed for determining what structures qualified as historic. To accommodate this, the National Park Service had as a primary responsibility the review and approval of eligibility for certified historic structure (CHS) status. This status became a rehabilitated structure's mark of eligibility for the new tax credits, provided its rehabilitation was certified by the National Park Service as complying with the Secretary of the Interior's Standards.

The RITC program was an immediate success. A 1979 study showed that $1.3 million in tax credits had generated $27 million in rehabilitation work. Between 1976 and 1986, nearly 17,000 projects, valued at $11 billion, took advantage of the program.[16] The focus of urban projects shifted dramatically from demolition to rehabilitation. One prominent preservation consultant, speaking at a preservation forum, concluded, "The tax credits have been enormously successful in cities and towns around the country in encouraging the preservation of historic buildings."[17] Congressman Richard Gephardt, speaking at the 1994 National Trust conference, referred to the tax credits as "the most important feature for urban redevelopment and urban renewal" in the 1980s.[18]

Another preservation stalwart, Nellie Longsworth, concurred, explaining the significance of the credits in revitalizing downtowns: "All kinds of things have been tried to stop the deterioration of downtowns. The first program that ever really worked was the investment tax credit."[19]

Because of the success and increasing public support for it, the federal government expanded the RITC program in 1981 as part of the Economic Recovery Tax Act (ERTA).[20] The new Act increased the tax credit to 25 percent for certified historic structures, a substantial return on investment. The Act also added two new categories, allowing a 20 percent credit for any income-producing building over forty years old and a 15 percent credit for any over thirty years old. The Act led to the creation of many new historic districts, for through this device structures that had not been recognized as historically significant on their own qualified for the 25 percent credit as "contributing" structures.

The tax credit program's purpose was not to restore significant older buildings as museum pieces but to return them to use to meet current housing, retail, industrial, and commercial needs. Even developers with no previous interest in historic preservation wanted to become involved because of the financial opportunities. This stimulation of private investment in housing through a public program was unparalleled by any other government housing program.

Between the years 1981, when the Economic Recovery Tax Act was passed by Congress creating the 25 percent rehabilitation tax credit, and 1985, the tax credit program alone led to the investment of an estimated $8.2 billion dollars in over 11,000 structures.[21] Certainly the tax credits provided the engine to make the historic rehab program run during this critical period.

The program made some strange bedfellows. Whereas old-line preservationists had for many years opposed most of the proposals presented by developers, now preservationists and developers both supported the program, the former because it saved historic buildings and the latter largely because it was profitable. The biggest financial beneficiaries were high-tax-bracket investors looking for ways to decrease their tax burdens. They considered investment possibilities primarily on the basis of whether they qualified for tax credits, and as passive investors they were little concerned with whether businesses contained within the structure succeeded or failed, as long as they as building owners received the program's tax breaks.

In 1984, the GAO looked into the impact the program was having on the federal treasury and became alarmed at its success. The GAO calculated that the taxes lost through these credits had increased from $2.5

million annually in 1978 to $210 million in 1984, and an increase was projected to $700 million annually by 1988. In a time of fiscal cutbacks, this kind of largesse could not pass unnoticed.

The GAO also discovered some serious abuses in the program. Some 17 percent of the owners claiming tax credits did not qualify and their buildings had not been approved. If a building were sold within five years of its rehabilitation, the owner forfeited the tax credit on a prorated basis and was liable for a recapture tax; however, the study found that fully 40 percent of the owners who sold within five years had not paid the recapture tax. Finally, a serious abuse was found in the use of easements. For properties where an easement had been donated and the owner was able to take a tax deduction based on its value, it was found that the average easement had been overvalued by more than 200 percent.

Congress decided to clamp down on this and many other tax shelter programs, and the historic rehabilitation tax credit program was put in serious jeopardy of termination. It was saved only because of a strong lobbying effort by groups impressed by the incredible success of the program in retaining and refurbishing older buildings and historic districts in cities throughout the country. The 1986 changes in the tax law trimmed the program but also included some necessary changes.

The 1986 Tax Act established limits on the program. Credits could be taken only by individuals who were actively involved in the property as owners or long-term lessees; passive investors could no longer piggyback on the investment activity of others only to take advantage of tax credits. Also, tax credits were scaled back to 20 percent for Certified Historic Structures (CHSs) and to 10 percent for nonhistoric structures built before 1936. These new values, although lower, were an improvement in some ways. With the previous values of 25 percent for a CHS and 20 percent for a building over forty years old not certified as a historic structure, many owners and developers had preferred working on the latter type of property, for the rehabilitation standards were less strict and rehab work was not delayed while certification was obtained. As a result, more secondary buildings were rehabbed than significant historic structures. This distorted the program's goals. The new values rectified the situation by giving primary encouragement to the historic structures.

However, with the changes made in 1986, investment in historic structures began to decline significantly. There were various reasons for the downturn—more restrictions, a lower tax break, the prior completion of many of the easiest and most lucrative rehab projects. Money shifted from investment in historic structures to other types of development, and the golden days of the RITC program were over.

Since 1994, a primary effort has been directed at establishing a rehabilitation tax credit for homeowners. Because they do not have income producing property, they have been left out as beneficiaries of the tax credit program, although many would argue their contribution to preservation is just as important as that of other owners.

Using the Rehabilitation Investment Tax Credits

The RITC program has done much to stimulate interest in rehabilitating older structures but has changed considerably since its inception. The current program operates according to the following provisions.[22]

what buildings qualify?

Buildings may qualify for RITCs either as historic or nonhistoric. To be considered historic, a building must be a Certified Historic Structure (listed on the National Register) or be certified as a contributing structure in a historic district recognized by the Secretary of the Interior. Owners can claim a 20 percent tax credit on the costs of rehab for historic buildings. A nonhistoric building, built before 1936, is eligible for a 10 percent credit.

Historic buildings may earn the 20 percent credit only if they are income-producing or used in a trade or business. Residential rental units also qualify. For the 10 percent credit, a nonhistoric building must be nonresidential.

Individuals or limited partnerships can take the credit only if they are building owners or leaseholders whose base lease equals thirty-nine years for commercial properties, twenty-seven and a half years for residential.

qualified expenditures

Expenditures that qualify for RITCs are essentially those connected with the rehabilitation or restoration of the structure. The Secretary of the Interior must certify that the work is consistent with the historic character of the building; this approval is conveyed by the National Park Service. If the work is incompatible or inappropriate, the project may be denied certification for a tax credit.

examples of qualified expenditures:
· Rehabilitation costs
· Construction interest and taxes
· Architectural and engineering fees
· Legal and professional fees
· Developers' fees
· General and administrative costs

The cost of other work, such as additions to the structure or construction related to rehabilitation or restoration, does not qualify as a certified expenditure.

EXAMPLES OF NONQUALIFIED EXPENDITURES:
- Acquisition costs
- Enlargement costs
- Acquisition interest and taxes
- Realtors' fees
- Paving and landscaping costs
- Sales and marketing costs.[23]

SUBSTANTIAL REHABILITATION REQUIREMENT

Other provisions must be met for rehab expenses to qualify for a RITC. First, the work done must be considered "substantial rehabilitation." To satisfy this requirement, the work must exceed the value of the adjusted basis cost of the building or $5,000, whichever is greater. The adjusted basis of the building is the owner's cost of the property (less the value of the land) plus the cost of any capital improvements less depreciation taken.

Consider a commercial building for which the owner paid $100,000 five years ago. If the value of the land alone is $45,000 of that figure, the owner has made $10,000 in improvements, and has depreciated the property at $6,000 per year, the adjusted basis would equal:

Cost of property	100,000
Less value of land	–45,000
	55,000
Plus improvements	+10,000
	65,000
Depreciation (5 years @ 6,000)	–30,000
Adjusted basis	$35,000

The rehab expenditures must exceed $35,000 to qualify, as it is the greater of $5,000 or the value of the adjusted basis.

PRIOR USE REQUIREMENT

To be eligible, a structure must have been used as a building prior to its rehabilitation and cannot, for example, be a caboose or grain silo converted to use as a habitable building.

WALL RETENTION REQUIREMENT

If the rehabbed building is a qualified nonhistoric structure (qualified because it was built prior to 1936 and is not located in a historic district), it must also meet the wall retention requirement. To satisfy this requirement, a certain proportion of the exterior walls and framework must be retained as follows:

- At least 75 percent of the external walls must be retained either as external or internal walls.
- At least 50 percent of the external walls must be retained as external walls.
- At least 75 percent of the internal structural framework must be retained.

FINANCIAL METHODS

An important incentive of the RITC program is the use of tax credits rather than tax deductions. Tax credits provide a dollar-for-dollar direct reduction in income tax owed, while deductions reduce taxes based on an individual's percentage tax bracket. As an example, assume the rehab cost for a project is $100,000, with an incentive of 20 percent or $20,000. As a credit, the owner could reduce his or her federal income tax owed by $20,000; this is a savings of the full $20,000. However, as a deduction, the actual savings would be $20,000 times the individual's tax bracket (e.g., $20,000 x 28% tax bracket = $5,600). This illustrates the significant advantage to the tax credit.

CONDITIONS OF USE FOR REHAB TAX CREDITS

To be eligible for the tax credit, the work on a rehab project must be certified by the National Park Service. This can be arranged by completing a series of applications filed with the appropriate State Historic Preservation Office (SHPO). These applications are reviewed by the SHPO and then forwarded with recommendations to the National Park Service for approval or denial. The decision of the National Park Service is the final one. The applications include:

Part I—Evaluation of Significance: This part usually contains a narrative describing the history of the building so the National Park Service can determine if the building contributes to the historic district within which it is located. (Buildings listed in the National Register individually are automatically certified historic structures, and no Part I is required.)

Part II—Description of Rehabilitation: This part is intended to provide both the SHPO and the National Park Service with a narrative, pictures that outline the architectural and historical features of the building as they currently exist, and a description of the proposed work to be undertaken. It is usually recommended that both Parts I and II be filed before work is started on the project.

Part III—Request for Certification of Completed Work: This final part of the application process is intended to notify the state and the National Park Service that the project is completed and that the owners are requesting that the project be reviewed for certification. It includes pictures of the completed rehabilitation. In some cases, the building is subject to an on-site visit by the SHPO or the National Park Service.[24]

The RITCs may be used to offset up to $25,000 of personal income tax liability; beyond that amount, they may offset 75 percent of such liability. Credits not used in one tax year may be carried forward or back a number of years, defined by the Internal Revenue Service. Credits may be used only by individual taxpayers or closely held corporate taxpayers (five or fewer shareholders owning more than 50 percent of the stock). They do not apply to work done to buildings owned by other types of corporations or nontaxpaying institutions.

If the building is sold, exchanged, or converted to personal use within five years of the credit being taken, the tax credit must be repaid at a recapture rate of 20 percent for every year under the five-year minimum. For example, if the building is sold after three years, the owner must repay 40 percent of the credit taken. The new owner is ineligible for any portion of the credit.

An example illustrates the important tax advantages of the RITC program to a property investor. Assume $1 million is invested in the construction of a new building. With straight-line depreciation over thirty-one and a half years (the standard rate), the accrued tax benefits would be $80,638. For comparison, assume an investor purchases a historic property for $250,000 and spends $750,000 to rehabilitate it. The same total amount of money is spent on this property as on the new construction. However, with the resulting 20 percent credit for rehab and a similar depreciation rate, the tax benefits would total $204,906, yielding more than two and one-half times the benefits. (Both examples give present value of the tax benefits, assuming a 10 percent discount and 28 percent tax rate.)

It is important to realize that the tax credit program is complicated and subject to change. The description here is only is a general overview of the major provisions. Before work is actually begun on any such project, owners should review current tax law and obtain the advice of a reliable financial advisor.

FINANCIAL ANALYSIS TECHNIQUES

PRO FORMA ANALYSIS

Many variables pertain to the financial feasibility of rehabbing an older commercial building. How can these be systematically accommodated so as to calculate a project's potential?

Pro forma analysis is a technique commonly used for projecting the financial future of a project for a given number of years. It figures dollars in versus dollars out. This bottom-line comparison must be favorable for an investor to consider a rehab project. Pro forma analysis begins with a baseline year, usually the current year, and considers how the financial status of a project will change over three, five, or even ten years based on certain assumptions made by the analyst. Five years is the most common time span, long enough for the project to "settle in," to cover most start-up costs, and to develop a normal occupancy rate, yet not so long that projections are too hypothetical.

CASE STUDY—REHAB OF AN OLDER COMMERCIAL STRUCTURE

To illustrate the elements of a pro forma analysis, here is a case study of a typical two-story, turn-of-the-century commercial building. The property is for sale at an asking price of $195,000. Located one block from Main Street in the downtown, it is in an area with good potential for growth in offices, stores, or residences. The property has not been improved in more than forty years.

The following analysis assesses the feasibility of investing in the rehab of this property and presents, item by item, the factors to consider. A financial datasheet that gives a complete overview of the analysis is included. After each item is explained, some assumptions are changed to illustrate their impact. In this way a complete financial picture of the project is developed.

FINAL PRICE

The first piece of information needed about the project is how much it will cost to purchase. Assuming the asking price for the property is $195,000, a seller may accept less. For this analysis, we will assume an offer of 5 to 10 percent below the asking price will be acceptable. Therefore, a final price of $175,000 is assumed.

Building for Pro Forma
Case Study

COSTS OF REHABILITATION

The costs of rehabilitation can be calculated in a number of ways. Initially, a project architect gives preliminary estimates based on prices from similar projects, also incorporating figures from cost-estimating books. (Contractors' bids provide more accurate estimates but are difficult to obtain until the project is actually designed and plans and specifications available, a process that follows rather than precedes the feasibility analysis). Typically, a preliminary cost estimate is based on an overall dollar-per-square-foot value. This quick and easy approach generalizes many of the project details—one factor may be estimated low, another high—but the result for any but the smallest projects should be reasonable. The square-foot cost amount can also be obtained by talking with builders or realtors in the area, who can estimate it based on their experience with similar projects.

For the case study project, a preliminary cost estimate was established at $40 per square foot for 7,200 square feet (SF). This is added to the cost of demolition, which together form the project's "hard" costs of $298,000.

The "soft" costs for the project include nonconstruction costs—professional fees for the architect, appraiser, and attorney, costs of the mortgage during construction (assumed to be six months), closing costs, permits, and start-up costs. For this project, these total $52,756.

PRO FORMA for Building Rehab
Projected Typical Year

	Assumed final price	175,000
A	Cost of rehab	361,655
	Total Project Cost	536,655
	Loan to Value Ratio LTV	80%
	Mortgage Amount	429,324
	Cash Investment	107,331
	INCOME	
B	Total Gross Rent	86,400
	Less assumed 10% vacancy	8,640
	Gross Effective Income	77,760
C	Less Operating Expenses	27,640
D	Less Debt Service (Annual)	44,709
	Before Tax Cash Flow	5,411
	ROI #1	5.0%
E	Return on Taxes	5,067
	ROI #2	4.7%
F	Appreciation	16,100
	ROI #3	15.0%
	TOTAL ANNUAL ROI	25%
	TOTAL ROI with Credit	38%

Debt coverage ratio   1.12
(Net income/Debt service)

A   Cost of Rehab

a	Soft costs	52,835
b	Hard Costs	298,000
c	Rent-up Costs	10,820
	Sub-total	361,655

B   Gross Rent

Leaseable SF(1stFl)	3,600
Rent/SF (#1)	14
Rental Income, 1st	50,400
Leaseable SF(2ndFl)	3,600
Rent/SF (#2)	10
Rental Income, 2nd	36,000
Leaseable SF(other)	0
Rent/SF (other)	0
Rental Income, other	0
Total Gross Rent	86,400

C   Operating Expenses

Taxes	12,880
Insurance	1,800
Mgt. (5% G.Rent)	4,320
Legal/ Acc't. (2%)	1,728
Leaseup Fee (3%)	2,592
Repair/Maint. (5%)	4,320
Sub-total	27,640

D   Debt Service

Mortgage	429,324
Interest Rate (%)	8.5%
No. of years	20
Mo. Payment	3,726

a   Soft Costs

Architect (6% of constr.)	17,280
Appraisal	2,000
Attorney's fees	3,000
Debt service (6 mo.)	22,355
Closing costs	3,000
Permits	1,200
Constr. startup costs	4,000
Sub-total	52,835

b   Hard Costs

Demolition	10,000
Construction	288,000
Sub-total	298,000

c   Rent-up Costs

Advertising	4,000
Office Costs	2,000
Cleaning	500
RealtorLeasingFee(5%)	4,320
Sub-total	10,820

Construction

Total SqFt Rehabbed	7,200
Cost per SqFt	40

E   Return on Taxes

Without Rehab Tax Credit		With Rehab Tax Credit	
Total Prop. Value	536,655	*Rehab Tax Credit (%)*	*20%*
Less Value of Land	30,000	*Total Value*	*72,331*
Depreciable base	506,655	*Depreciable base*	*434,324*
No. of years	39.0	*No. of years*	*39.0*
Annual depreciation	12,991	*Annual depreciation*	*11,137*
Tax bracket	39%	*Tax bracket*	*39%*
Return on taxes	**5,067**	*Normal Return on Taxes*	*4,343*
		Tax Credit (over 5 yrs)	*14,466*
		Total return on taxes	*18,809*
		ROI #2	*17.5%*

F   Appreciation

Property Value	536,655
Annual Apprec.	3%
Sub-total	16,100

Pro Forma Analysis Sheet

A final rehab cost was "rent-up" costs—the costs of advertising, marketing, and office expenses in finding initial tenants, in this case $10,820.

TOTAL PROJECT COSTS

The price paid for the property plus the costs of rehabilitation are added to obtain the total project cost. This is the amount that must eventually be recouped if the investment is to be profitable. In this example, the total is $536,576.

LOAN-TO-VALUE (LTV) RATIO

To raise the total of $536,576, two sources were used—investors and lending agencies. Investors are individuals willing to put up their own money in the hope of a significant return or for tax advantages. Lenders are institutions, such as banks, who lend money as a business.

Banks and other lenders are unwilling to put up all the money for a real estate project; they insist some funds be developed through other resources. (They assume if the project fails, they will recoup enough in value to cover their portion of the investment.) The percentage of total costs a lender is willing to risk is established as the loan-to-value ratio. Typically, this is 75 to 80 percent of the project's value if the project is determined to have a sound financial basis; this, in large part, is decided on the basis of a thorough feasibility analysis, such as this one. Based on an LTV ratio of 80 percent, the case study project could expect a mortgage from the bank of $429,261, requiring $107,315 in cash from investors.

The initial total cost of the project is now determined. The project cost is $536,576, but the amount that must be raised is $107,315; the remainder is a mortgage, with its cost covered as part of the project's expense.

To the analysis must now be added calculations of ongoing income and expenditures. Their impact must be determined on an annual basis (referred to as *annualizing*)—that is, converting all information into an income or expenditure over a one-year span.

TOTAL GROSS RENT

The annual rental income derived from the project is projected based on market data figures for the local area. The typical rate for ground-floor commercial space in the downtown area is currently $10 to $18 per square foot per year. Because the property borders a main shopping street, a rate of $14/SF is assumed for ground-floor rental. The second floor could be leased for offices at $10/SF (the basement is assumed to have no rental value). Based on the square footages for each floor as shown, a total gross rent (annualized) of $86,400 is anticipated.

PROJECTED VACANCY RATE

Not all of a project's space can be leased all the time, even in a very good market. Initially it takes months or years to come up to full occupancy at full market rates. An average vacancy rate of 10 percent is assumed.

GROSS EFFECTIVE INCOME

By reducing the gross rent figures by the projected vacancy rate, the expected annual income, called the *gross effective income*, can be calculated. This is shown to be $77,760.

OPERATING EXPENSES

Balanced against the gross effective income are ongoing project expenses. These include taxes, insurance, project management costs, legal and accounting fees, and normal repair and maintenance. The cost of utilities may either be included as a project expense or passed along to tenants if the lease so specifies. The case study assumes the tenant pays for utilities. These expenses are projected at $27,638 for a typical year.

DEBT SERVICE

The annual debt service is based on the total mortgage amount (in this case, $429,261), the mortgage interest rate, and the number of years of payments. The case study uses an interest percentage rate of 8.5 percent paid over twenty years or 240 months. A monthly payment is derived using an amortization calculation and then converted to an annual payment. Such calculations can be done quickly by a bank loan officer or by one of many simple computer programs now available.

RETURN ON INVESTMENT (ROI)

The whole purpose of a pro forma analysis is to determine how much an investor can expect to get as return of an initial investment. This is referred to as *return on investment* (ROI). Will it be as much as could be expected from other types of investments, such as the stock market or a money market bank account? Is the return high enough to be worth the extra risk involved and that the money may be tied up for an extended period? What are the local market conditions? How are they likely to change over the course of two, five, or ten years? Changes in some of these factors can dramatically alter the financial outlook of a project, while others will have surprisingly little impact on the total return.

A rewarding aspect of investing in real estate is that there are three ways to make a return on the initial investment. Together these three types of ROI can add up to a significant total return—one that justifies the greater risk and involvement. The three types of ROI found in real estate are cash flow, return on taxes, and appreciation.

BEFORE-TAX CASH FLOW (ROI #1)

Cash flow is the amount returned annually to an investor as cash. This represents the most direct type of return, although it is typically the lowest in the early years of a project and may initially even be negative, meaning additional cash must be put into the project over the short term.

Cash flow is determined by deducting the annual amounts for operating expenses and debt service from the annual gross effective income. For the case study, the annual cash flow is $5,571.

To determine this as a percentage ROI, the cash flow amount is divided by the amount of the original cash investment, which is $107,315. This represents a return of 5.2 percent; 10 percent is considered a fair cash return on this kind of investment. (Note that the mortgage amount is not included as part of the cash investment, as this was not part of the investor's capital and was previously accommodated in the calculations under debt service.) One rule of thumb is that the cash return should be at least double the percentage that could be earned in a bank savings account.

RETURN ON TAXES (ROI #2)

Many investors, especially those in high tax brackets, are less concerned with cash return than they are with the tax advantages of real estate investment. For them, historic building rehabs provide some of the best tax opportunities available.

The calculation of the return on taxes is shown on the datasheet in Box E. Annual tax return is based on the depreciable value of a property. The depreciable value is the total value of the property less the value of the land (a basic assumption of tax law is that a building depreciates (decreases) in value over time, but the land it is on does not). With a land market value of $30,000 (established through local appraisal), the case study example has a depreciable base value of $506,576. A building's value, under current tax law, can be depreciated over 39 years. This allows an annual depreciation of $12,989 in this example.

To calculate the investor's actual return on taxes, this annual depreciable amount ($12,989) is multiplied by the individual's tax bracket.

Assuming the investor is in a high tax bracket, the total state and federal tax may be around 39 percent, giving an annual tax return of $5,066. As with ROI #1, this amount is compared to the initial cash investment of $107,315, for an ROI #2 of 4.7 percent annually.

In addition, the rehabilitation costs of a CHS can be partially recovered through the RITC provisions. As noted above, the rehabilitation of such a building could make investors eligible for a tax credit totaling 20 percent of the rehab costs. Assuming the case study building is a CHS, an additional total credit of $72,315 (20 percent of the rehabilitation cost of $361,576) can be applied (shown in the box "With Rehab Tax Credit"). The calculation assumes the investor does not apply the entire $72,315 amount to one tax year but spreads this credit over five years, giving an annual tax credit of $14,463. This is added to the tax return based on depreciation. For ROI #2, the annual return is now 17.5 percent instead of the previously calculated 4.7 percent return without the historic tax credit. You can easily see the direct and significant financial gain possible through the use of the rehab tax credit.

APPRECIATION (ROI #3)

The greatest return on investment is typically from the continuing appreciation of the property's value. If properly maintained and regularly updated, properties increase significantly in value over time. This assumption initially seems contradictory, given the explanation that tax law assumes a decrease in the value of property over time, but such depreciation is a theoretical assumption, while the true market instead shows appreciation over time.

The amount of increase based on appreciation varies with local and regional market conditions. The case study example assumes an annual increase in the total value of the property of 3 percent. Thus, if the project is worth $536,576 upon completion, its value one year later will be $552,673, or a 3 percent increase of $16,097. Although the appreciation increase is based on the total value of the property, the ROI #3 compares this increase in value only to the cash investment made by the investor ($16,097/$107,315), showing ROI #3 to be 15 percent annually. In other words, the investor makes ROI #3 not only on his or her own money (the initial $107,315) but on the bank's money (the $429,261 mortgage) as well. Certainly this is a wonderful situation!

This relatively high ROI due to appreciation represents one of the primary reasons for investing in real estate. However, this return is realized only on the sale of the property and is dependent on an investor's willingness to tie up the money for an extended period. Real estate investment is not for those who need a regular, predictable return, but it can be rewarding for those who can invest relatively large amounts and wait for favorable market conditions.

Federal Funding Sources for Preservation

A historic project may benefit financially by taking advantage of external sources of funding. A variety of sources at the federal level may be considered for funding preservation projects. Among them are:

U.S. DEPARTMENT OF THE INTERIOR

Historic Preservation Fund: The Department of the Interior's Historic Preservation Fund (HPF) was established as part of the 1966 National Historic Preservation Act. Its purpose is to support the acquisition, stabilization, and development of historic resources and the identification and protection of historic and archeological properties.

Land and Water Conservation Fund: Under this program, funds are distributed for parks, trails, and other recreation sites. Occasionally, these sites tie in with historic resources.

Bureau of Land Management (BLM): Challenge Cost Share Funds provide matching funds to local communities for projects on or adjacent to BLM land.

U.S. DEPARTMENT OF COMMERCE

Economic Development Administration (EDA): The EDA provides funds for technical assistance, planning, and development of projects resulting in the creation of new employment. This may include projects using historic resources.

U.S. DEPARTMENT OF HOUSING AND URBAN DEVELOPMENT (HUD)

Community Development Block Grants (CDBG): Block grants make many millions of dollars available for housing, infrastructure improvements, and economic development. Projects associated with historic properties typically must be reviewed by the SHPO.

Low-Income Housing Tax Credit: This program can be used in conjunction with the RITC to create affordable housing in historic districts.

U.S. DEPARTMENT OF TRANSPORTATION

Intermodal Surface Transportation Efficiency Act (ISTEA) and *Transportation Equity Act for the 21st Century (TEA-21)*: Since 1991, the well-funded

Transportation Fund has diverted considerable money from highway construction and maintenance into its Enhancements Fund, established to provide flexible funding for transportation-related projects. Many historic preservation projects receive funding by showing a historical tie to transportation (e.g., historic railway stations, rails-to-trails, roadside inns, highway commercial buildings, bridges, etc.).

INSTITUTE OF MUSEUM SERVICES (IMS)

IMS is an independent agency within the executive branch that provides operating funding to historical museums. Funds are used to conserve American cultural, historic, and scientific heritage.

Chapter 11

Other Preservation Issues

Rural Preservation
—————————————

Some special aspects of historic preservation are important to represent the full spectrum of the field. This chapter briefly describes the unique relationship to rural preservation, urban growth and transportation, ethnic minority groups, landscape preservation, and maritime preservation.

Historic preservation has focused primarily on cities and their historic landmark buildings and districts. Recently, however, increasing attention has been paid to protecting our rural heritage, including hamlets, individual farms and their structures, and, especially, the conservation and protection of agricultural land. Under current market conditions, agricultural land is often worth much more to its owners when sold for suburban development than when kept and farmed. It is difficult to expect a farmer to ignore this economic reality and, as a result, large areas of prime agricultural farmland, especially farmland close to urban centers, are lost each year to speculative development.

Communities now recognize that such a changeover in land use not only takes farmland out of productive use but also leads to both sprawl of urbanized areas and degeneration of city centers and the urban core. Over the years, a variety of programs have been tried to protect rural areas. In the 1950s, programs of differential taxation were established, with farmland taxed based on its value as agricultural land rather than on its "highest and best" use for development. Later studies revealed that such programs enhanced the income of farmers who intended to keep farming anyway but did not significantly discourage the sale of farms that were opportunistically situated for development, because the income from the sale would be so much greater than possible tax savings.

Maine enacted a Farm and Open Space Tax Law in the 1970s. This gave farmers a tax incentive for preserving open space, farms, and forests by allowing for lower property taxes for such uses. Because tax assessors were unsure how much property taxes should be reduced, in 1993 the state legislature issued guidelines as follows:

OPEN SPACE RATES

	WITHOUT PUBLIC ACCESS	WITH PUBLIC ACCESS
Ordinary open space	–20%	–45%
Land used for forestry or farming but protected from future development by permanent easement restrictions	–50%	–75%
"Forever wild" open space (land protected by a permanent easement and used for no commercial purpose whatsoever)	–70%	–95%

Many communities have tried to deal with the problem of sprawl through a land use regulations approach. When farmland is zoned for agricultural conservation, it cannot be sold for intense development. This also reassures farmers that they will not be subject to nuisance suits from irate suburban homeowners who move in next to a farm and then complain about the noise and smell of farm operations. In New York, over three hundred conservation districts have been formed, controlling approximately six million acres or well over one third of the state's farmland.[1]

Some programs included a provision whereby owners can sell potential development rights for use in a different part of the township or county (see chapter 10). In Purchase of Development Rights (PDR) programs, the cost of obtaining development rights can vary considerably based on the location of the land. "For example, in 1984, the average per acre cost of the rights purchased was $807 in Maryland, $2,802 in New Hampshire, and $4,209 in Suffolk County, New York. Since participation in all PDR programs is voluntary, these figures represent a free-market exchange between the landowner and the government."[2]

CASE STUDY: CHERRY HILL, MICHIGAN

Cherry Hill is a small, historic hamlet (generally defined as a village without a commercial district) located in Canton Township in southeastern Michigan. It is just beyond the current edge of development in the western suburbs of Detroit. The residents of Cherry Hill recognized the imminent threat of development overtaking their rural character

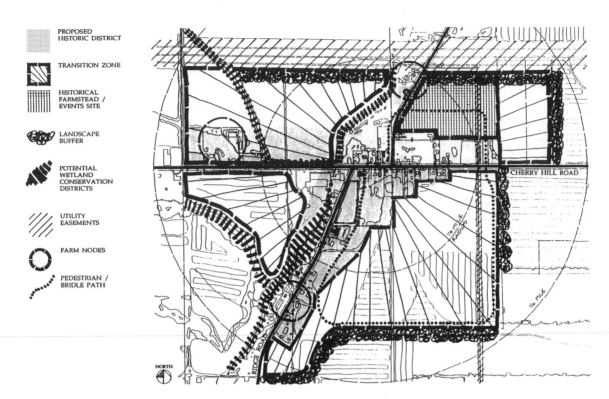

PROPOSED
HISTORIC DISTRICT

TRANSITION ZONE

HISTORICAL
FARMSTEAD /
EVENTS SITE

LANDSCAPE
BUFFER

POTENTIAL
WETLAND
CONSERVATION
DISTRICTS

UTILITY
EASEMENTS

FARM NODES

PEDESTRIAN /
BRIDLE PATH

NORTH

CHERRY HILL ROAD

RIDGE ROAD

*Context plan, Cherry Hill
Historic District, Cherry
Hill, Michigan*

and commissioned a study of how the character of their hamlet and the surrounding farmland could be protected.[3]

The project proposal presented to township authorities dealt with community concerns at three levels. The first was that the buildings that make up the hamlet itself be grouped in a historic district. Although the buildings individually are not especially significant, the district is justified on the ground that, as an assemblage of structures from various periods, they represent a historic community type that is rapidly disappearing. Cherry Hill is an excellent example of a rural hamlet with most of its architectural and cultural history still intact.

At the second level, a farmland conservation area was established covering the area surrounding Cherry Hill and large enough to provide a visual barrier against future suburban development. This farmland area was screened visually with rows of trees at the edge of existing farms.

The third proposal was to subject the development areas beyond the farmland conservation district to cluster development, which means that single homes may not be placed on larger lots in row upon row; new homes must be clustered more tightly, leaving more open space around the clusters.

This three-level approach was one of the most innovative proposals yet developed for dealing with the needs of rural preservation. Similar protective ordinances will likely become more common.

URBAN GROWTH BOUNDARIES

One way to preserve rural areas is to contain urban sprawl. The concern with encroaching sprawl has led some communities and states to adopt the concept of urban growth boundaries. In Oregon, growth boundaries define the limits of urban area growth and allow only very low-density land uses beyond them. This prevents the creeping urban sprawl found at the edges of most American cities. The technique accomplishes three things: "[I]t contains the cost of infrastructure, it protects the environment, and it helps prevent piecemeal destruction of the exurban landscape."[4]

Many of a community's poorer residents can afford to live only in areas of a city where rents are low. If these areas are designated as historic districts, often they become more desirable to others. As properties are improved, values go up, rents go up, and more affluent residents are attracted to the area. Former residents may be forced out by market conditions and look elsewhere for affordable housing. This migration of (primarily white) middle-class homesteaders into poor (mainly black and Hispanic) urban neighborhoods is known as gentrification, for it displaces its residents and makes the neighborhood more upscale in character. As described by one writer, "Restored carriage houses and pressed-tin ceilings have seduced more children of the suburbs back to the city than mean, shiny apartment towers."[5]

Gentrification

Preservationists should be conscious of this unintended side effect of establishing historic districts and encourage their local government to develop policies that allow low- and moderate-income residents to remain in an established neighborhood. Programs should be created to encourage lower-income residents to purchase and rehabilitate their residences.

The preservation movement recently has made serious strides toward identifying structures that are meaningful to minority and cultural groups. The Washington, D.C., home of Frederick Douglass, the nineteenth-century civil rights leader and orator, was the first major African American site to become part of the National Park Service system when it was acquired in 1962. This gave it increased recognition as well as sufficient funds for its restoration and continued maintenance.

Preservation and Minorities

Other cultural landmarks are also gradually receiving the recognition they deserve. In New York City in 1999, the federal General Services Administration funded the construction of an interpretive center on Broadway to memorialize the location of 415 colonial-era graves at the eighteenth-century African Burial Ground. The memorial on the National Historic Landmark site will be complemented by archeological research and an education and public information program.

Historic preservation is often seen in a negative light by members of minority groups whose heritage is not only manifested in buildings and land but through oral traditions—the stories of the families. To African Americans and Native Americans, this type of preservation may be more meaningful and appropriate. The buildings revered by white individuals as important emblems of their heritage may represent oppression and slavery to the African American community. As one black resident of Cincinnati bitterly observed, in speaking at the 1988 annual conference of the National Trust for Historic Preservation, "The only thing that historic theater was good for was putting me in the balcony." It is important for the preservation movement increasingly to recognize the significance of all sectors of our society and find appropriate ways to preserve their heritage.

New attention is also being given to concerns of Native Americans. For many decades the U.S. government had a policy of encouraging the assimilation of Native Americans into mainstream American culture, and systematically discouraging the preservation of traditional tribal culture and way of life, which resulted in the loss of many Native American traditions. That policy has changed in recent decades and is reflected in revisions to the National Historic Preservation Act. Tribes have been given authority to designate Tribal Historic Preservation Officers (THPOs), who have largely the same recognition and powers as State Historic Preservation Officers. This policy has reestablished a sense of pride and a greater degree of control for Native Americans in reasserting the importance of their cultural heritage.

Landscape Preservation

Historic landscapes present one of the most intriguing and difficult types of preservation, since buildings remain relatively static in their form, while trees and shrubs change with each growing season. Significant historic gardens, such as George Washington's garden around Mount Vernon and, on a bigger scale, Central Park in New York City, should be preserved largely in their original states. But this is a process of continual research, renewal, and replanting. The protection of scenic features such as Niagara Falls and historic battlefields such as Gettysburg have a different set of concerns and problems from those found with landmark buildings.

Perhaps the most common, though difficult, type of landscape preservation project is the reconstruction of historic gardens. Although gardens are often referred to in writings, seldom are accurate drawings or other documentation available. Other than for palatial structures, the tradition of recording garden plans does not generally exist; gardens were most often in the care of gardeners or caretakers who transferred their knowledge through oral apprenticeship traditions rather than on paper.

One of the greatest legacies of historic landscapes is that of Frederick Law Olmsted. Among the significant projects with which he was involved were the Chicago Columbian Exposition off 1893, the "emerald necklace" parks of Boston, Detroit's thousand-acre Belle Isle, and the most well known, New York City's Central Park. As beautiful as these landscape designs were, and as important as they have been to city planning, they are increasingly threatened by an American lifestyle that is not compatible with the sense of purpose Olmsted gave them. Olmsted wrote, "We want a ground to which people may easily go after their day's work is done, and where they may stroll for an hours, seeing, hearing, and feeling nothing of the bustle and jar of the streets, where they shall, in effect, find the city put far away from them."[6] Preservationists recognize that preserving the physical park is not sufficient, for such a property's true significance lies in how it is used and respected as a community amenity.

Maritime Preservation

A growing movement in the field of preservation, especially in coastal areas, is maritime preservation. The great loss of the country's maritime heritage and its need for attention has been recognized only recently.

To encourage these efforts, the National Trust for Historic Preservation established an Office of Maritime Preservation. This office provides technical assistance to groups and individuals involved in such work. Activities include the preservation, restoration, and reuse of lighthouses and other maritime structures as well as the designation and protection of historic ships and even undersea shipwrecks. Maritime preservation also includes efforts to preserve entire waterfront districts, which often have opposing threats—abandonment and development pressures. On another level, the need to preserve some of the older maritime skills, from knot-tying and scrimshaw to sailing techniques and wooden boat-building, is now recognized.

Cape Hatteras Lighthouse, located on North Carolina's Outer Banks, is the tallest brick lighthouse in the United States. When originally con-

Cape Hatteras lighthouse

structed in 1870, it was 1,500 feet from the shore. Soil erosion along the Atlantic coast has brought the ocean very close to the lighthouse, and the structure is in imminent danger. The National Park Service has studied the case and has had to weigh their mandate of preserving historical structures with that of preserving natural processes along the Atlantic seaboard. The three main options considered were (1) stabilizing the beach in front of the lighthouse with the construction of concrete groins; (2) constructing a seawall; and (3) relocation of the lighthouse farther inland. A report from the Ad Hoc Committee of Faculty of North Carolina State University concluded that the moving of the lighthouse was the only choice that was "technically feasible and consistent with both current knowledge of the shoreline and with existing public policy."[7] During the summer of 1999, the lighthouse was painstakingly moved.

Arthur Frommer articulated the important link between preservation and tourism, recognizing three major reasons people become tourists: rest and recreation, to view great natural sights, and because of an interest in achievements of the past.

Historic preservation is great for tourism, which brings with it economic benefits to a community. Tourism advocates throughout the world recognize that history, and historic preservation, pays. It attracts people, and income from them helps fund further preservation. Local advocates concerned about drawbacks of historic districts need not fear. Frommer notes, "There is no evidence, not a single indication, of any city that has declined commercially from historic preservation policies."[8]

Heritage interpretation is a term increasingly used to represent a new approach to preservation; it encourages travelers to appreciate heritage sites and local cultures in new and richer ways. Frommer describes the need for this multidimensional approach:

> After 30 years of writing standard guidebooks, I began to see that most of the vacation journeys undertaken by Americans were trivial and bland, devoid of important content, cheaply commercial, and unworthy of our better instincts and ideals . . .
>
> Those travels, for most Americans, consist almost entirely of "sightseeing"—an activity as vapid as the words imply. We rove the world, in most cases, to look at lifeless physical structures of the sort already familiar from a thousand picture books and films. We gaze at the Eiffel Tower or the Golden Gate Bridge, enjoy a brief thrill of recognition, return home, and think we have traveled.[9]

Heritage interpretation draws together formerly separated activities: historic preservation, tourism, and the "experience industries." It interprets local culture and history and makes it accessible to the public by providing interpretative experiences for visitors and tourists. The growth in this type of alternative tourism is an indicator that people have a sincere interest in understanding the true culture of places rather than the sameness inherent in more traditional tourism experiences of the past.

Some examples of these activities include:

• On the Amtrak train between Gallup and Albuquerque, New Mexico, a native Navajo interprets Native American culture, religion, history, and geology to passengers as they pass through this magical landscape.

- In Fort Myers, Florida, the former winter home of Thomas Edison, a "surprise hitchhiker" meets and boards motor coach tours. The hitchhiker is a living portrayal of Thomas Edison; the living history is accomplished by a local amateur actor.
- In India, the U.S. National Park Service is aiding the government in developing a national cultural park near the Taj Mahal as a first step toward India's encouragement of tourism at its major heritage sites.[10]

In the best presentations of cultural heritage, local cultures play an active role in determining what activities are appropriate, with either outright control of the programs or an equal voice in their planning. According to Marshall McLennan, professor emeritus of the historic preservation program at Eastern Michigan University, "The use of heritage should be as a conservation tool; it should not be exploitative or demeaning of the residents. Indigenous planners and participants can serve as the custodians of their culture, presenting authentic 'heritage experiences' to guests, and training their youth to pridefully carry on these interpretive programs in the future."[11]

One outgrowth of heritage interpretation is the recognition that the natural and cultural stories of a community should be interpreted not only for visitors but also for natives, who often have little knowledge of their own heritage. In communities like Rochester, New York, and Honolulu, Hawaii, community interpretation plans are used as tools for heightening a community's awareness of its own local resources. Such cultural storytelling is a process "as old as time, and is just as much the province of emotionally-invested and knowledgeable local residents as it is the province of trained professionals."[12]

Preservation and the Highway Program

Senator Joseph S. Clark said, in 1966, "It is time that Congress took a look at the highway program, because it is presently being operated by barbarians, and we ought to have some civilized understanding of just what we do to spots of historic interest and great beauty by the building of eight-lane highways through the middle of our cities."[13]

This response to the excesses of the urban renewal period of the 1960s challenged the prevalent attitude that the old was obsolete and blighted and should be removed to make way for the new. During the following decades, many historic buildings fell to the god of "progress," and there were no more heavy-handed aggressors than the bulldozers of the highway programs. Center cities, and their rich historic fabric of businesses and neighborhoods, were destroyed in the attempt to make them accessible to the new and powerful suburban commuter.

This approach of running roughshod over historic neighborhoods and structures finally changed significantly with the 1991 passage of a landmark bill, the Intermodal Surface Transportation Efficiency Act (ISTEA [pronounced "iced tea"], revised in 1997 as the Transportation Equity Act for the twenty-first century, or TEA-21). ISTEA recognized the U.S. Department of Transportation's Transportation Fund had a huge reservoir of money collected from user taxes, primarily the gas tax. Since the 1950s, this money had been used to pay for construction of the interstate highway system. But the network of new highways was being completed and pressure to make some portion of these funds available for other uses increased.

ISTEA and TEA-21 both included a provision that 10 percent of the funding in the bills was to go toward a program to enhance many types of transportation projects. Historic preservationists have seen this as an opportunity to redress some of the damage done during the decades of unstoppable construction and requested funding for the restoration and preservation of historic sites and structures linked to transportation. Since 1991, the Transportation Fund has provided substantial support for historic properties across the country.

The updated Transportation Equity Act has continued the enhancements program with only minor modifications and an expansion of eligible activities. To be eligible, a project must relate in some way to surface transportation.

Does the historic significance of a building decline if it is moved from one site to another? Yes, there is always some loss; the significance of a historic building is connected to its original location. Therefore, moving a historic structure from its original location should always be carefully evaluated.

Moving a Historic Building to a New Site

The tradition of moving buildings is long, but creating a neighborhood out of moved buildings because a developer likes it creates a false sense of history and how a neighborhood developed. Even if the setting and landscaping are recreated, some of those buildings were never meant to be seen next to each other.

In some situations, moving a building is appropriate, or at least acceptable. For instance, if moving is the only alternative to demolition, then relocation may be necessary. However, the National Park Service and its technical preservation services encourage moving only as a last resort. To stay on the National Register, the owner must convince the Park Service the new site is compatible with the historic structure.

*Moving a
Queen Anne house*

Sign Ordinances

Sign ordinances are an important element in any commercial historic district. Signs are a salient feature of the urban environment; they should be compatible with the historic area and reinforce its general character. When developing an ordinance to control signs, attention should be paid to two issues: (1) how to get rid of unsightly or inappropriate signs and keep historically important signs, and (2) design requirements for appropriate new signage.

To avoid the unintentional loss of significant cultural or historic resources, a community should survey and prepare an inventory of signs worthy of protection, including an evaluation of their historic significance. What determines whether a sign is significant enough for historic protection? Culver City, California, established three criteria, any one of which is sufficient for designation.

1. The sign must be of exemplary technology, craftsmanship, or design of the period in which it was constructed.

Sign on side of historic building

2. The sign is integrated into the architecture of a significant building or structure.
3. It demonstrates extraordinary aesthetic quality, creativity, or innovation, as determined by the historic commission.[14]

Other Issues

The field of historic preservation is broad. Among the interesting issues not addressed in this book are archeology, the use of new computer technologies, preservation and travel, international preservation, and more. Preservation is not an exclusive, but an inclusive, activity, and it can be seen from many perspectives.

The National Trust for Historic Preservation refers to the role of preservation simply as a responsibility to preserve our heritage and "protect the irreplaceable." It is for all of us to continue to explore the relevance of its role to our society and to become more aware of the importance of historic preservation in our everyday life.

Notes

CHAPTER I

1. Clem Labine, "Preservationists Are Un-American," *Historic Preservation* (March 1979): 18.
2. John W. Lawrence, Dean of the School of Architecture, Tulane University, 24 April 1970.
3. Adele Chatfield-Taylor, "From Ruskin to Rouse," in *Historic Preservation: Forging a Discipline*, ed. Beth Sullebarger (New York: Preservation Alumni, 1985), 27–28.
4. I. L. Peretz, "On History," in *Stories by Peretz*, trans. Sol Liptzin (New York: Hebrew Publishing Company, 1947), 202.
5. Harold Henderson, review of *Man Made the Town,* by Michael Middleton, *Planning* (February 1988): 35.
6. Eugène Emanuel Viollet-le-Duc, *Dictionnaire raisonné*, 1854–1868.
7. Norman Williams Jr., Edmund H. Kellogg, and Frank B. Gilbert, *Readings in Historic Preservation* (New Brunswick, N.J.: Center for Urban Policy Research, 1983), 16.
8. John Ruskin, "The Lamp of Memory," *The Seven Lamps of Architecture* (London: Hazell, Watson, and Viney: 1891), 353, 339.
9. Adele Chatfield-Taylor, "From Ruskin to Rouse," 30.
10. Ruskin, "The Lamp of Memory," 185.
11. David Lowenthal, "A Global Perspective on American Heritage," in *Past Meets Future: Saving America's Historic Environments*, ed. Antoinette J. Lee (Washington, D.C.: Preservation Press, 1992), 162.
12. *The Secretary of the Interior's Standards for Rehabilitation and Guidelines for Rehabilitating Historic Buildings*, rev. ed. (Washington, D.C.: U.S. Department of the Interior, National Park Service, Heritage Preservation Services, 1990), 5.
13. For a description of the controversy this project raised, see Tim Appelo, "Rescue in Seattle," *Historic Preservation* (October 1985): 34–39
14. *The Secretary of the Interior's Standards*, 6.

220 • Historic Preservation

15. From "The Future of Preservation," a roundtable symposium, quoted in *Architecture* (February 1998): 80.

16. Vincent Scully, 1996 Raoul Wallenberg lecture, College of Architecture and Urban Planning, The University of Michigan.

17. Carleton Knight III, "Philip Johnson Sounds Off," *Historic Preservation* (Sept./Oct. 1986), 34.

18. Robert Venturi, *Complexity and Contradiction in Architecture*, 2nd ed. (New York: Museum of Modern Art, 1990).

19. "The Temple of Love and Other Musings: A Conversation with Robert A. M. Stern," *Historic Preservation* (September-October 1982): 28.

20. Summarized in Brent Brolin, *Architecture in Context* (New York: Van Nostrand Reinhold, 1980), 15.

21. Peter Neill, "Personal Dialogues With Ghosts," in *Past Meets Future: Saving America's Historic Environments*, ed. Antoinette J. Lee (Washington, D.C.: Preservation Press, 1992), 45.

CHAPTER 2

1. Ann Pamela Cunningham. Farewell address recorded in minutes of the Mount Vernon Ladies' Association of the Union, June 1874, 5.

2. George Humphey Yetter, *Williamsburg Before and After: The Rebirth of Virginia's Colonial Capital* (Williamsburg, Virginia: The Colonial Williamsburg Foundation, 1996), 51.

3. Norman Williams Jr., Edmund H. Kellogg, and Frank B Gilbert, eds., *Readings in Historic Preservation: Why? What? How?* (New Brunswick, N.J.: Center for Urban Policy Research, 1983), 40.

4. From the HABS Web site, www.cr.nps.gov/habshaer/habs/habshist. htm, May 1999.

5. For more information on HABS, see "Racing against Oblivion," *Historic Preservation* (January-February 1983, 38–39, 45.

6. William J. Murtagh, *Keeping Time: The History and Theory of Preservation in America* (New York: Sterling, 1990), 47.

7. Albert Rains and Laurance G. Henderson, *With Heritage So Rich*. Rev. ed. (United States Conference of Mayors. Washington, D.C.: Preservation Press, 1983), 208.

8. Correspondence with Jerry Martin of the National Trust for Historic Preservation, May 7, 1999.

9. *Report to the President and Congress of the United States* (Washington, D.C.: Advisory Council on Historic Preservation, 1990), 70.

10. Antoinette J. Lee, *Past Meets Future: Saving America's Historic Environments* (Washington, D.C.: Preservation Press, 1992), 74.

11. *How to Appeal a Commission Decision*, Michigan Department of State Hearings Division, HD-96 (Lansing, September 1993).

12. Antoinette J. Lee, *Past Meets Future*, 16.

CHAPTER 3

1. Roberta Brandes Gratz, *The Living City* (New York: Simon and Schuster, 1989), 287.
2. Roberta Brandes Gratz, *The Living City*, 288.
3. Linda Wheeler, "Study: Property Values in Historic Districts," *Washington Post*, 23 September 1989.
4. Michigan Local Historic Districts Act, House Bill No. 5504, 1992, to amend Public Act No. 169, 1970, Sec. 2.
5. Michigan Local Historic Districts Act, House Bill No. 5504, Sec. 3.
6. Michigan Local Historic Districts Act, House Bill No. 5504, Sec. 4.
7. See Russell Wright, *A Guide to Delineating Edges of Historic Districts* (Washington, D.C.: Preservation Press, 1976).
8. The chart was prepared by Denis Schmiedeke, an Ypsilanti architect and preservationist. Some provisions of the Ypsilanti ordinance were amended under Michigan's 1992 amended Public Act.
9. Chong W. Pyen, "Historic District Dilemmas," *Ann Arbor News*, 12 January 1992.
10. Christopher Duerksen, *A Handbook of Historic Preservation Law* (Washington, D.C.: Conservation Foundation), 70.
11. *Texas Antiquities Commission* v. *Dallas County Community College District*, 554 S.W. 2d 924 (Texas 1977), and *Historic Green Springs, Inc.* v. *Bergland*, 497 F. Supp. 839 (E.D.Va. 1980).
12. *Reusing Old Buildings: Preservation Law and the Development Process*, Conference Proceedings of the Conservation Foundation, the National Trust for Historic Preservation, and the American Bar Association, Section of Urban, State, and Local Government Law, Fort Worth, Texas, 23–30 November 1984.
13. *Maher* v. *City of New Orleans,* 516 F2d 1051.
14. Alaska Statutes 29-55-010 through 29-55-020. From www.ncsl.org/programs/arts/gethistrec.cfm?record=822.
15. Arkansas Code Annotated 214-172-201 through 214-172-212. From www.ncsl.org/programs/arts/gethistrec.cfm?record=1030.
16. District of Columbia Code 5-1001 through 5-1015. From www.ncsl.org/programs/arts/gethistrec.cfm?record=786.
17. Indiana Statutes Annotated 36-7-11.2-1 through 36-7-11.2-67. From www.ncsl.org/programs/arts/gethistrec.cfm?record=1361._
18. *Virginia Historic Landmarks Commission* v. *Board of Supervisors of Louisa County*, 21 Va. 468, 230 S.E. 2d 229 (1976).
19. Based on information from Connie Malone, *United States Preservation Commission Identification Project* (August 1994), National Alliance of Preservation Commissions.

CHAPTER 4

1. *Berman* v. *Parker*, 348 U.S. 26, 33 (1954).

2. *Figarsky* v. *Historic District Commission*, 171 Conn. 198, 368 A.2d 163 (1976).

3. *Maher* v. *City of New Orleans*, 371 F. Supp. 653, 663 (E.D. La. 1974).

4. *Penn Central Transportation Company* v. *City of New York*, 438 U.S. 104, 98 S.Ct. 2646 (1978).

5. Charles M. Haar and Michael Allan Wolk, *Land Use Planning: A Casebook on the Use, Misuse, and Reuse of Urban Land*, 4th ed. (Boston: Little, Brown, 1989), 543.

6. *Penn Central Transportation Company* v. *City of New York*, Appeal from the Court of Appeals of New York, No. 77-444, 42 N.Y. 2d 324, 366 N.E. 2d 324, affirmed.

7. *Penn Central Transportation Company* v. *City of New York*, Appeal from the Court of Appeals of New York, No. 77-444, 42 N.Y. 2d 324, 366 N.E. 2d 324, affirmed.

8. See Charles M. Haar and Jerold S. Kayden, *Landmark Justice: The Influence of William J. Brennan on America's Communities* (Washington, D.C.: The Preservation Press, 1989), 154–68.

9. This was shown in *Society for Ethical Culture* v. *Spatt*, 416 N.Y.S. 2d, affirmed, 415 N.E. 2d 922 (N.Y. 1980), which upheld the designation of a meeting house structure.

10. Jane Brown Gillette, "Judgment Day," *Historic Preservation* (September-October 1991): 57. Note: The case was resolved in 1991 when the U.S. Supreme Court refused to review the decision of the U.S. Court of Appeals for the Second Circuit.

11 Jane Brown Gillette, "Judgment Day," 57.

12. Jane Brown Gillette, "Judgment Day," 60.

13. Amy Worden, "Court Denies St. Bart's Plea," *Preservation News* (February 1990): 22.

14. Amy Worden, "Court Denies St. Bart's Plea," 22.

15. Kim Kelster, "Supreme Court Rules for Preservation," *Preservation News* (April 1991): 2.

16. Brent Brolin, *The Battle of St. Bart's: A Tale of the Material and the Spiritual* (New York: William Morrow & Co., 1988), 194.

CHAPTER 5

1. *National Register Criteria for Evaluation* (Washington, D.C.: U.S. Department of the Interior), from www.cr.nos.gov/nr/criteria/criteria.html (May 1999).

2. The Henry Ford Museum has a 1946 diner, a 1941 Texaco gas station, and a 1960 Holiday Inn room in its collection, but displaying historic buildings in a museum is less desirable than preserving them at their original site.

3. Lecture by Professor Leonard Eaton at University of Michigan, 1984.

4. John Reps, *Views and Viewmakers of Urban America* (Columbia: University of Missouri Press, 1984) and *Bird's Eye Views: Historic Lithographs of North America* (New York: Princeton Architectural Press, 1998).

5. Sales literature (University Publications of America, 1994).

6. See Perry E. Borchers, *Photogrammetric Recording of Cultural Resources* (Washington, D.C.: U.S. Department of the Interior, Technical Preservation Services, 1977).

7. From www2.cr.nps.gov/nhl/nhl_p.htm.

CHAPTER 6

1. John Maass, *The Gingerbread Age* (New York: Bramhall House, 1957), 32–33.

2. Bertram Grosvenor Goodhue, *The Craftsman*, 1916.

3. James C. Massey and Shirley Maxwell, "Pre-Cut Houses," *Old House Journal* (November–December 1990): 41.

4. Robert Venturi, *Complexity and Contradiction in Architecture*, 2nd ed., 22–23.

CHAPTER 7

1. Brent Brolin, *Architecture in Context* (New York: Van Nostrand Reinhold, 1980), 7.

2. Kurt Anderson, "Spiffing Up the Urban Heritage," *Time*, 23 November 1987, 76.

3. *The Secretary of the Interior's Standards for Rehabilitation and Guidelines for Rehabilitating Historic Buildings*, rev. ed. (Washington, D.C.: U.S. Department of the Interior, National Park Service, Heritage Preservation Services, 1995), Standard No. 9.

4. Quoted in "The Future of Preservation," *Architecture* (February 1998): 80.

5. "Voluntary Design Guidelines Take Effect in Boulder, Colorado." From an unidentified newspaper article.

6. *Development Guide* (Scottsdale, Arizona, 1993), 9.

7. Antoinette J. Lee, *Past Meets Future: Saving America's Historic Environments*, 18.

8. Carl Abbott, "The Facadism Fad: Is It Preservation?," *Historic Preservation* (October 1984): 42.

CHAPTER 8

1. Bernard M. Feilden, *Conservation of Historic Buildings* (London: Butterworth Architecture, 1995), 6.
2. *The Secretary of the Interior's Standards*, Standard No. 7.

CHAPTER 9

1. E. F. Schumacher, *Small Is Beautiful: Economics As if People Mattered* (New York: Harper and Row, 1973), 148.
2. Tim Richmond and David Goldsmith, "The End of the High-Rise Jobs Myth," *Planning* (April 1986): 19.
3. Tersh Boasberg, "A New Paradigm for Preservation," in *Past Meets Future: Saving America's Historic Environments*, ed. Antoinette J. Lee (Washington, D.C.: Preservation Press, 1992), 150.
4. David Burch, "The Job Creation Process," MIT, cited in Ypsilanti Industrial Survey, prepared by Michigan Bell, 1988, 2.
5. Norman Tyler, *An Evaluation of the Health of the Downtowns in Eight Michigan Cities* (Ann Arbor, Mich.: University Microfilms, 1987), and *Evaluation Factors Associated with Perceived Downtown Health in Sixteen Michigan Cities* (East Lansing: Michigan State University, 1998).
6. Norman Tyler, "Evaluating the Health of Downtowns: A Survey of Small Michigan Cities," *Small Town* (September-October 1989): 199–200.
7. Information from http://www.mainst.org/about/approach.htm, May 1999.
8. Information from http://www.mainst.org/about/approach.htm, May 1999.
9. Dan L. Morrill, "Keeping History in Historic Preservation," *Small Town* (July-August 1983): 25.
10. Editorial, "The World from Main Street," *Small Town* (July-August 1991): 3.
11. Arthur Frommer, "The Link Between Tourism and Preservation," speech delivered at the Art Institute of Chicago, 5 Nov. 1992.

CHAPTER 10

1. Adele Chatfield-Taylor, "From Ruskin to Rouse," 29.
2. Reprinted from Thomas D. Bever, "Economic Benefits of Historic Preservation," in Norman Williams, Edmund H. Kellogg, and Frank B. Gilbert (eds.), *Readings in Historic Preservation: Why? What? How?* (New Brunswick, N.J.: Center for Urban Policy Research, 1983), pp. 79–81, with permission.
3. Thomas D. Bever, "Economic Benefits of Historic Preservation," 81.
4. Thomas D. Bever, "Economic Benefits of Historic Preservation," 79.

5. Thomas D. Bever, "Economic Benefits of Historic Preservation," 80.

6. Donovan D. Rypkema, *The Economics of Historic Preservation: A Community Leader's Guide* (Washington, D.C.: National Trust for Historic Preservation, 1994).

7. *1827 M Street v. District of Columbia*, No. 85-688, D.C. Court of Appeals, decided 29 January 1988.

8. North Carolina allows a 50 percent reduction of property taxes for landmarked buildings.

9. Thomas Coughlin, *Easements and Other Legal Techniques to Protect Historic Houses in Private Ownership* (Washington, D.C.: Historic House Association of America, 1981).

10. See National Trust for Historic Preservation and Land Trust Exchange, *Appraising Easements: Guidelines for Valuation of Historic Preservation and Land Conservation Easements* (Washington, D.C.: National Trust for Historic Preservation, 1984).

11. GAO study on abuses of tax incentives and appraisals.

12. Donna Ann Harris, "Philadelphia's Preservation Incentive," *Historic Preservation Forum* (Washington, D.C.: National Trust for Historic Preservation, September-October 1992): 10.

13. Prepared by John M. Sanger Associates, Inc., for the Foundation for San Francisco's Architectural Heritage.

14. Tax Reform Act of 1976 (P.L. 94-455).

15. Revenue Act of 1978 (P.L. 95-600).

16. Robert E. Stipe and Antoinette J. Lee, *The American Mosaic,* 24.

17. William MacRostie, "What Price Success?" *Progressive Architecture* (August 1985): 107.

18. Kim Kelster and Arnold Berke, "If Not Now, When?" *Historic Preservation News* (December 1993–January 1994): 22.

19. Nellie Longsworth, comments at a symposium sponsored by *Progressive Architecture* and the AIA, "What Price Success," quoted in *Progressive Architecture* (August 1985): 110.

20. Economic Recovery Tax Act of 1981 (P.L. 97-34).

21. Thomas J. Colin, "A Historic Anniversary," *Historic Preservation* (May/June 1986): 25.

22. See *Preserving America's Heritage: The Rehabilitation Investment Tax Credit*, published by Touche Ross & Company and the Ohio Historic Preservation Office, 1987.

23. *Preserving America's Heritage*, 3–4.

24. This information is from the Internal Revenue Service Rehabilitation Tax Credit Audit Guide (July 1998). The full text can be found at the Athena Information Management, Inc., Web page at www.greenepa.net/~aim/frehab.html.

CHAPTER 11

1. Jo An Kwong, "Farmland Preservation," *Urban Land* (January 1987): 21.

2. Jo An Kwong, "Farmland Preservation," 22.

3. Cherry Hill proposal by Quinn Evans Architects, Ann Arbor, Michigan; Norman Tyler, historical consultant.

4. Kristine M. Williams, "Preservation with Growth," *Planning and Zoning News* (May 1990): 10.

5. Kurt Anderson, "Spiffing Up the Urban Heritage," *Time*, 23 November 1987, p. 79.

6. Quoted in Jonathan Walters, "The un-greening of America," *Historic Preservation* (May/June 1981): 37–38.

7. From "Saving the Cape Hatteras Lighthouse From the Sea," North Carolina State University and the National Academy of Sciences, from www.nps.gov/htdocsl/caha/lighthouse reports.ntm, April 1999.

8. Arthur Frommer, "The Link between Tourism and Preservation," speech delivered at the Art Institute of Chicago, 5 November 1992.

9. Used by permission of Macmillan General Reference, a wholly owned subsidiary of IDG Books Worldwide, Inc. From *Arthur Frommer's New World of Travel, 5th ed.* by Arthur Frommer. Copyright © 1986, 1989, 1990, 1991, 1996 by Arthur B. Frommer.

10. From the course description of a heritage interpretation class given by Professor Gabe Cherem, Eastern Michigan University, 1993.

11. Marshall S. McLennan, "Heritage Interpretation Education at Eastern Michigan University: Evolving Conceptual Parameters," presented at the Second World Congress on Heritage Presentation and Interpretation, Warwick, England, August-September 1988.

12. Gabe Cherem, "Shamans, Stories, and 'Sis-ciplines': Part I," *Interpretation Central Clearinghouse Newsletter* (July-August 1993): 1-2.

13. Quoted in J. Barry Cullingworth, *The Political Culture of Planning: American Land Use Planning in Comparative Perspective* (New York: Routledge, 1993), 112.

14. Peter H. Phillips, "Sign Controls for Historic Signs," *Planning Advisory Service Memo*, American Planning Association (November 1988).

Further Reading

Periodicals

Cultural Resource Management: U.S. Department of the Interior, National Park Service. Washington, D.C. (www.cr.nps.gov/crm/)

The Old House Journal. Brooklyn, New York. (www.oldhousejournal.com)

This Old House. Time Publishing Ventures, Inc. New York, New York. (www.pbs.org/wgbh/thisoldhouse/magazine/index.html)

Preservation. National Trust for Historic Preservation. Washington, D.C. (www.nationaltrust.org/main/magazine/magazine.htm)

Historic Preservation Forum. National Trust for Historic Preservation. Washington, D.C. (www.nthp.org/main/abouttrust/pljoin1.htm)

Journal of the Association for Preservation Technology. Association for Preservation Technology. Williamsburg, Virginia. (www.apti.org/publish.html)

Journal of the Society of Architectural Historians. Society of Architectural Historians. Chicago, IL. (www.sah.org/journal.html)

Small Town. Small Towns Institute. Ellensburg, Washington 98926.

Traditional Building: The Professional's Source for Historical Products. Brooklyn, New York. (www.traditional-building.com/)

Style Identification References

Baker, John Milnes. *American House Styles: A Concise Guide.* New York: W. W. Norton, 1993.

Blumenson, John J.-G. *Identifying American Architecture: A Pictorial Guide to Styles and Terms 1600–1945.* 3rd ed. Nashville, Tenn.: American Association for State and Local History, 1981.

Borchers, Perry E. *Photogrammetric Recording of Cultural Resources.* U.S. Department of the Interior, Technical Preservation Services. Washington, D.C.: GPO, 1977.

Harris, Cyrl M. *Illustrated Dictionary of Historic Architecture.* New York: Dover Publications, 1977.

Longstreth, Richard. *The Buildings of Main Street: A Guide to American Commercial Architecture.* Washington, D.C.: The Preservation Press, 1987.

McAlester, Virginia, and Lee McAlester. *A Field Guide to American Houses.* New York: Alfred A. Knopf, 1984.

Poppeliers, John S., Allen Chambers, and Nancy B. Schwartz. *What Style Is It?* Rev. ed. Washington, D.C.: Preservation Press, 1984.

Rifkind, Carole. *A Field Guide to American Architecture.* New York: New American Library, 1980.

Whiffen, Marcus, and Frederick Koeper. *American Architecture, 1607–1976.* Cambridge, Mass.: MIT Press, 1981.

General Books

Advisory Council on Historic Preservation. *Annual Report to the President and the Congress of the United States.* Washington, D.C.: GPO, 1968–present.

Advisory Council on Historic Preservation. *The National Historic Preservation Act of 1966: An Assessment of Its Implementation over Twenty Years.* Washington, D.C.: Advisory Council on Historic Preservation, September 1986.

Americans with Disabilities Act (ADA): Accessibility Guidelines for Buildings and Facilities. Washington, D.C.: U.S. Architectural and Transportation Barriers Compliance Board, 1991.

Arendt, Randall. *Rural by Design: Maintaining Small Town Character.* Chicago: Planners Press, 1994.

"Bringing the City Back to Life," *Time,* 23 November 1987.

Brolin, Brent. *Architecture in Context.* New York: Van Nostrand Reinhold, 1980.

Byard, Paul Spencer. *The Architecture of Additions.* New York: W. W. Norton, 1998

Curtis, John O. *Moving Historic Buildings.* U.S. Department of the Interior, Technical Preservation Services Branch. Washington, D.C.: GPO, 1979.

Duerksen, Christopher, *A Handbook on Preservation Law.* Washington, D.C.: Conservation Foundation, 1983.

Duerksen, Christopher, and Richard J. Roddewig. *Takings Law in Plain English.* 3rd ed. Washington, D.C.: American Resources Information Network, 1998.

Feilden, Bernard M. *Conservation of Historic Buildings, Revised Ed..* London: Butterworth Architecture, 1995.

Fitch, James Marston. *American Building 1: The Historical Forces That Shaped It.* New York: Houghton Mifflin, 1972.

Fitch, James Marston. *American Building 2: The Environmental Forces That Shaped It.* 2nd ed. New York: Schocken, 1973.

Fitch, James Marston, *Historic Preservation: Curatorial Management of the Built World.* New York: McGraw-Hill, 1982.

Grieff, Constance, ed. *Lost America: From the Atlantic to the Mississippi.* Vol. 1. Princeton, N.J.: Pyne Press, 1971.

Grieff, Constance, ed. *Lost America: From the Mississippi to the Pacific.* Vol. 2. Princeton, N.J.: Pyne Press, 1972.

Guidelines for Completing National Register of Historic Places Forms. U.S. Department of the Interior, National Park Service, Interagency Resources, 1991.

Hammett, Ralph W. *Architecture in the United States: A Survey of Architectural Styles since 1776.* New York: John Wiley & Sons, 1976.

Harris, Cyril M. *Illustrated Dictionary of Historic Architecture.* New York: Dover Publications, 1977.

———. *American Architecture: An Illustrated Encyclopedia.* New York: W. W. Norton, 1998.

Hitchcock, Henry-Russell. *Architecture: Nineteenth and Twentieth Centuries.* Baltimore: Penguin, 1971.

Hosmer, Charles B., Jr. *Presence of the Past: A History of the Preservation Movement in the United States before Williamsburg.* New York: Putnam, 1965.

Hosmer, Charles B., Jr. Preservation Comes of Age: *From Williamsburg to the National Trust, 1926–1949.* Charlottesville: University Press of Virginia, 1981.

Jacobs, Jane. *The Death and Life of Great American Cities.* New York: Random House, 1961.

Lee, Antoinette J., ed. *Past Meets Future: Saving America's Historic Environments.* Washington, D.C.: Preservation Press, 1992.

Lowenthal, David. *The Past is a Foreign Country.* Cambridge, England: Cambridge University Press, 1988.

Lynch, Kevin. *What Time Is This Place?* Cambridge, Mass.: MIT Press. 1972.

National Park Service. *Respectful Rehab: Answers to Your Questions about Old Buildings.* Technical Preservation Services, U.S. Department of the Interior, Washington, D.C.: Preservation Press, 1982.

National Trust for Historic Preservation, Tony P. Wrenn, and Elizabeth D. Mulloy. *America's Forgotten Architecture.* Washington, D.C.: National Trust for Historic Preservation, 1976.

National Trust for Historic Preservation and Land Trust Exchange. *Appraising Easements: Guidelines for Valuation of Historic Preservation and Land Conservation Easements.* Washington, D.C.: National Trust for Historic Preservation, 1984.

Rains, Albert, and Laurance G. Henderson. *With Heritage So Rich.* Rev. ed. United States Conference of Mayors. Washington, D.C.: Preservation Press, 1983.

Reps, John. *Bird's Eye Views: Historic Lithographs of North American Cities.* New York: Princeton Architectural Press, 1998.

———. *Views and Viewmakers of Urban America.* Columbia: University of Missouri Press, 1984.

Revitalizing Downtowns, 1976–1986. Washington, D.C.: National Trust for Historic Preservation, 1988.

Roddewig, Richard J., and Cheryl A. Inghram. *Transferable Development Rights Programs: TDR and the Real Estate Marketplace.* Chicago: American Planning Association Report, May 1987.

Roddewig, Richard J. *Preparing a Historic Preservation Ordinance.* Chicago: American Planning Association Planning Advisory Service Report Number 374, 1983.

Ruskin, John. *The Seven Lamps of Architecture.* Mineola, New York: Dover Publications, 1990.

Rypkema, Donovan D. *The Economics of Historic Preservation: A Community Leader's Guide.* Washington, D.C.: National Trust for Historic Preservation, 1994.

Smith, E. Kidder. *Architecture in America: A Pictorial History.* Ed. Marshall Davidson. New York: W.W. Norton, 1976.

Stipe, Robert E., and Antoinette J. Lee. *The American Mosaic: Preserving a Nation's Heritage.* Washington, D.C.: Preservation Press, 1987.

Stokes, Samuel N. *Saving America's Countryside: A Guide to Rural Conservation.* Baltimore: Johns Hopkins University Press, 1997.

Sullebarger, Beth, ed. *Historic Preservation: Forging a Discipline.* New York: Preservation Alumni, 1985.

Svenson, Peter. *Preservation.* Boston: Faber and Faber, 1994.

Thurber, Pamela, ed. *Controversies in Historic Preservation: Understanding the Preservation Movement Today.* Washington, D.C.: National Trust for Historic Preservation, 1985.

U.S. Department of the Interior, National Park Service, Preservation Assistance Division. *The Secretary of the Interior's Standards for Rehabilitation and Guidelines for Rehabilitating Historic Buildings.* Rev. ed. Washington, D.C.: U.S. Department of the Interior, 1992.

Venturi, Robert. *Complexity and Contradiction in Architecture.* New York: Museum of Modern Art, 1966.

Weaver, Martin E. *Conserving Buildings: Guides to Techniques and Materials.* New York: John Wiley & Sons, 1993.

Williams, Norman, Jr., Edmund H. Kellogg, and Frank B. Gilbert, eds. *Readings in Historic Preservation: Why? What? How?* New Brunswick, N.J.: Center for Urban Policy Research, 1983.

Wright, Russell. *A Guide to Delineating Edges of Historic Districts.* Washington, D.C.: Preservation Press, 1976.

Yetter, George Humphrey. *Williamsburg Before and After: The Rebirth of Virginia's Colonial Capital.* Williamsburg, Virginia: The Colonial Williamsburg Foundation, 1996.

Appendix 1

Preservation Resources

Preservation Organizations

AMERICAN ASSOCIATION FOR STATE AND LOCAL HISTORY

Although a multinational organization (United States and Canada), the intent of the ASLH is to promote knowledge, understanding, and activities in history at the local level. This nonprofit, educational organization relies on memberships for funding.

Contact:
American Association for State and Local History
1717 Church Street
Nashville, Tennessee 37203-2991
www.aaslh.ord/index.html

AMERICAN CULTURAL RESOURCES ASSOCIATION

The membership of ACRA, formed in 1995, is made up of interdisciplinary professionals; the largest percentage are archeologists, but other architecture and planning disciplines are represented. The organization supports a number of preservation issues.

Contact:
American Cultural Resources Association
c/o Thomas R. Wheaton, Executive Director
6150 East Ponce de Leon Avenue
Stone Mountain, Georgia 30083
www.acra-crm.org/

AMERICAN INSTITUTE OF ARCHITECTS

The AIA has 58,000 members in more than thirty local, state, and international chapters, and a national headquarters in Washington, D.C. Through its public outreach, education, and government affairs activities, the AIA provides technical bulletins to its members regarding issues of preservation.

Contact:
American Institute of Architects
1735 New York Avenue NW
Washington, D.C. 20006
www.aiaonline.com/

AMERICAN PLANNING ASSOCIATION

The APA is a professional organization dedicated to advancing the art and
science of physical, economic, and social planning at the federal, state, and
local levels. Its objectives include "encouraging planning that will contribute to public well-being by developing communities and environments
that meet the needs of people and of society more effectively." The Planners Book Service makes available a variety of publications on historic
preservation planning.
Contact:
American Planning Association
122 South Michigan Avenue, Suite 1600
Chicago, Illinois 60603
www.planning.org/

ASSOCIATION FOR PRESERVATION TECHNOLOGY

The international APT was formed in 1968 to provide a central source and
network for the preservation disciplines. It offers a forum for the exchange
of information on conservation problems and techniques. It provides contact with top professionals and other international preservation organizations through its publications, courses, and an annual conference.
 Contact:
Association for Preservation Technology
P.O. Box 3511
Williamsburg, Virginia 23187
www.apti.org/

CAMPBELL CENTER FOR HISTORIC PRESERVATION STUDIES

The Campbell Center is one of a number of centers for the study of preservation technology. Summer workshops and laboratories cover a variety of
topics. The program is geared to those in midcareer in the fields of historic
preservation, collection care, and conservation. Located in Mount Carroll,
Illinois, on the site of a former seminary, the campus was purchased by the
Campbell Center in 1979. Courses in preservation technology typically
include Identification and Analysis of Historic Paint, Exposing Decorative

Paint Schemes, Deterioration and Conservation of Wood, Workshop on Masonry Preservation, and Preservation of Historic Landscapes.
Contact:
Campbell Center for Historic Preservation Studies
P.O. Box 66
Mount Carroll, Illinois 61053
www.campbellcenter.org/

C.H.I.N.

The Canadian Heritage Information Network (CHIN) is an agency within the federal Department of Canadian Heritage. CHIN provides information on Canadian museum collections, sponsors computer list-servs on topics of Canadian heritage, and gives training in collections management.
Contact:
Department of Canadian Heritage
Les Terrasses de la Chaudière
15 Eddy Street, 15-4-A
Hull, Quebec, Canada K1A OM5
www.chin.gc.ca

DOCOMOMO

This international organization was founded in 1990 to press for the documentation and conservation of the best examples of architecture from The Modern Movement. The name DOCOMOMO comes from the phrase Documentation and COnservation of the MOdern MOvement.
Contact:
DOCOMOMO International
Delft University of Technology, Faculty of Architecture
Berlageweg 1
2628CR Delft, The Netherlands
www.ooo.nl/docomomo/start.htm

INTERNATIONAL COUNCIL OF MONUMENTS AND SITES

ICOMOS encourages preservation activities at the national and international levels through education and training, international exchange of people and information, technical assistance, documentation, and advocacy. The U.S. Committee of ICOMOS includes professionals, practitioners, supporters, and organizations committed to conservation of the world's cultural heritage. The committee publishes a monthly newsletter, has ten specialized subcommittees, and administers an electronic mailing list called *usicomos*.

Contact:
International Council on Monuments and Sites
401 F Street NW, Room 331
Washington, D.C. 20001
www.unesco.org/whc/ab_icomo.htm

NATIONAL ALLIANCE OF PRESERVATION COMMISSIONS

The NAPC forms a network of over 2,000 landmark and historic district commissions and boards of architectural review in the United States. It provides a forum for the exchange of views among active preservationists and gives local commissioners a national voice.
Contact:
National Alliance of Preservation Commissions
P.O. Box 1605
Athens, Georgia 30603
www.arcat.com/search/profile.cfm?id=8371

NATIONAL CENTER FOR PRESERVATION TECHNOLOGY AND TRAINING, NATIONAL PARK SERVICE

The NCPTT was created through amendments to the National Historic Preservation Act of 1966 and is supported through appropriations given to the National Park Service. Located in Natchitoches, Louisiana, the center is an interdisciplinary effort to enhance the art, craft, and science of preservation and conservation of the built environment. Its activities comprise research, training, and information management. Each year it supports these activities through Preservation Technology and Training grants. Through its Internet online service, NCPTT provides information about current research and educational opportunities.
Contact:
National Center for Preservation Technology and Training
Northwestern State University, Box 5682
Natchitoches, Louisiana 71497
www. ncptt.nps.gov/

NATIONAL COUNCIL FOR PRESERVATION EDUCATION

The National Council connects preservation educators across the country. The organization works with federal agencies to set up a program of summer internships for preservation students.
Contact:
National Council for Preservation Education

c/o Michael Tomlan (E-mail: mat4@cornell.edu)
Department of City and Regional Planning, 210 West Sibley Hall
Cornell University
Ithaca, New York 14853-6701

NATIONAL MAIN STREET CENTER

The Main Street Program is administered through the National Main Street Center, established in 1980 and part of the National Trust for Historic Preservation. The center works with communities across the nation to revitalize their historic or traditional commercial areas. The center provides side services related to downtown revitalization, including training programs, technical assistance, an online business card service for professionals, a newsletter, a regular National Town Meeting conference, a certification program, and an awards program for successful revitalization efforts.
Contact:
National Main Street Center of the National Trust for Historic Preservation
1785 Massachusetts Avenue NW
Washington, D.C. 20036
www.mainst.org/

NATIONAL PARK SERVICE, DEPARTMENT OF THE INTERIOR

The Heritage Preservation Services Division of the National Park Service provides federal support to preservation activities across the country. Its four general areas of activities are planning and preservation, grants and tax credits, geographic information systems (computerized mapping), and training and internships.
Contact:
Heritage Preservation Services
National Center for Cultural Resources Stewardship and Partnership Programs
National Park Service
1849 C Street NW, NC330
Washington, D.C. 20240
www2.cr.nps.gov/

NATIONAL PRESERVATION INSTITUTE

The NPI is a nonprofit organization offering specialized information on education and training in preservation. It conducts seminars and workshops for sponsoring organizations, and provides technical assistance to owners of historic properties.

Contact:
National Preservation Institute
P. O. Box 1702
Alexandria VA 22313
www.npi.org/about.html

NATIONAL TRUST FOR HISTORIC PRESERVATION

The National Trust for Historic Preservation was established in 1949 as the umbrella organization for preservation activities at federal, state, and local levels across the country. Although established by Congress, it has a quasi-public/private status, relying primarily on memberships and donations to cover expenses. The Trust has a wide range of activities, including stewardship of nineteen historic properties across the country. Other significant activities include sponsorship of an annual national preservation conference, publication of *Preservation* magazine, and support for its National Main Street Center.
Contact:
National Trust for Historic Preservation
1785 Massachusetts Avenue NW
Washington, D.C. 20036
www.nationaltrust.org

PARTNERS FOR SACRED PLACES

This nondenominational, nonprofit organization was founded in 1989 to promote the preservation of historic religious properties. It provides assistance through free information and advice about property maintenance, fundraising, and professional references. It also coordinates conferences and training programs, publishes reference books on property maintenance, and generally advocates for religious properties.
Contact:
Partners for Sacred Places
1616 Walnut Street, Suite 2310
Philadelphia, Pennsylvania 19103
www.sacredplaces.org/

PLANNING AND ARCHITECTURE INTERNET RESOURCE CENTER

This website provides some of the best links to web sites relating to architecture and planning and has a significant listing on historic preservation. The site is sponsored by the State University of New York at Buffalo.
www.arch.buffalo.edu/pairc

PRESERVATION ACTION

Since its founding in 1974, Preservation Action has lobbied for stronger legislation at the federal, state, and local levels. The organization's goals are to elevate historic preservation as a national priority through legislative actions; monitor federal agency actions that affect the preservation of the nation's historic and cultural resources; participate directly in policy development; and create an environment for others to succeed with their preservation initiatives.

Contact:

Preservation Action
1350 Connecticut Avenue NW
Washington, D.C. 20036
www.preservenet.cornell.edu/pa.htm

PRESERVE/NET

Preserve/Net is an Internet site, administered by Cornell University, featuring a wealth of information on preservation across the country as well as links to other Web sites. Included at the Preserve/Net site is the Preservation Education Directory, a state-by-state listing of preservation programs at universities in the United States.

Contact:

Preserve/Net
www.preservenet.cornell.edu/preserve.html

RESTORE

This educational corporation offers the opportunity for training in state-of-the-art architectural conservation and preservation maintenance techniques. Workshop students include a cross section of architects, engineers, craftworkers, contractors, cultural resource managers, architectural conservators, preservationists, and others involved in the building industry.

Contact:

RESTORE
152 Madison Avenue, Suite 1603
New York, New York 10016

SOCIETY FOR AMERICAN ARCHEOLOGY, UNIVERSITY OF CONNECTICUT

The SAA is the largest archeological organization in the country. Begun in 1934, the Society's goal is to stimulate interest in archeology. It encourages public access to archeological sites and works to protect sites against looting and damage.

Contact:
SAA
900 Second Street, NE # 12
Washington, D.C.
20002-3557
www.saa.org

SOCIETY OF ARCHITECTURAL HISTORIANS

SAH encourages interest in architecture and architectural history and pro-
motes the preservation of significant structures and sites. It has thousands of
members throughout the United States and no membership requirements.
Its primary activities are an annual conference, support for local chapters,
and publication of the *Journal of the Society of Architectural Historians*.
Contact:
The Society of Architectural Historians
Charnley-Persky House
1365 North Astor Street
Chicago, Illinois 60610-2144
www.sah.org

SOCIETY FOR COMMERCIAL ARCHEOLOGY

Established in 1977, The Society is dedicated to preserving significant elements of the 20th century commercial landscape. Its primary focus is road
side architecture, including signs, symbols, and artifacts.
Contact:
Society for Commercial Archeology
P.O. Box 235
Geneseo, NY
14454-0235
www.sca-roadside.org/

Appendix 2

Degree Programs in Historic Preservation

In 1978, *Preservation News* listed fifteen programs in preservation at universities in the United States. The list has since grown to fifty undergraduate and graduate programs that are member institutions of the National Council for Preservation Education, together enrolling some 1,200 students, many from foreign countries. This is the largest group of preservation students to be found anywhere in the world.

In addition to the programs listed here, a number of concentration or certificate programs can be found within the architecture curriculum at various universities; offerings in this field are changing rapidly.

SCHOOL	DEGREE	PROGRAM EMPHASIS
Art Institute of Chicago	MS in H.P.	Construction, Documentation, Restoration, Site Management
Ball State University	MS in H.P.	Built Environment, Community Relations
Boston University	MA in H.P.	Management, Conservation, MA/JD, Documentation
Columbia University	MS in H.P.	Conservation, Design, Planning, History
Cornell University	MA, PhD in H.P. Planning	Planning, Conservation, Research, Documentation
Eastern Michigan University	MS in H.P., Certificate	Preservation Planning, Administration, Heritage Interpretation
University of Georgia	MA in H.P., Certificate, JD/MHP	Preservation Planning, Technology, Research, Conservation

Georgia State University	MA in Heri.P.	History, Folklore, Building Materials, Interiors
Middle Tennessee State University	MA/DA H.P.	Administration, History, Cultural Resources, Museums
Savannah College of Art and Design	BFA, MFA	Technology, Interpretation, Law, Economics, Design
University of Hawaii at Manoa	Graduate Certificate in H.P., MS in H.P.	Technology, Documentation, Landscapes, Administration
University of Pennsylvania	MS in H.P., PhD Architecture/ Planning	Documentation, Management, Materials, Technology, Planning
University of South Carolina	MA, Applied History	History, Research, Museums
University of Utah	MS Architecture Studies	Documentation, Administration
University of Vermont	MS in H.P.	Planning, Materials, Cultural Resources
University of Virginia	Interdisciplinary Master Certificate	Architecture, Landscape, Planning
University of Washington	Graduate Certificate	Architecture, Planning, Preservation Planning
Youngstown State University	Cert. H.P. (Bachelors/Masters)	History, Cultural

Bucks County Community College	H.P. Certificate	Documentation, Building Analysis	**Undergraduate Programs in Preservation**
Goucher College	BA in H.P.	Urban Preservation	
Mary Washington College	BA in H.P.	Theory, Construction, Planning, Documentation	
Michigan State University	BA, H.P. Special	History, Philosophy, Planning, Field Work	
Roger Williams University	BS in H.P.	Planning, Construction, Documentation, Research	
Southeast Missouri State University	BS in H.P.	Administration, Restoration, Archival Management	

Architectural Terms

To understand architectural styles, one must understand the architectural vocabulary. The terms listed below are commonly used to describe architectural components and elements.

ARCHITRAVE: The main beam that sets on column capitals and forms the lowest part of an entablature.

BALUSTRADE: A railing composed of a series of upright members, often in a vase shape, with a top rail and often a bottom rail.

balustrade

BARGEBOARD: A decorative board running along the edge of a gable (often called *vergeboard*).

bargeboard (vergeboard)

BATTLEMENT: A parapet wall at the edge of a roof with alternating slots and raised portions.

BAY: A unit of a building facade, defined by a regular spacing of windows, columns, or piers.

BAY WINDOW: An exterior wall projection filled with windows; if curved, called a *bow window*; if on an upper floor, called an *oriel window*.

bay

BOND: The pattern of overlapping brick joints that binds them together to form a wall (e.g., common bond, Flemish bond, English bond).

buttress

BRACKET: A decorative element supporting a wall projection, cornice, or other exterior feature.

BUTTRESS: A mass of masonry or brickwork projecting from or built against a wall to strengthen it.

CANTILEVER: A projecting structural member, the end of which is supported on a fulcrum and held by a downward force behind the fulcrum.

CAPITAL: The top portion of a column or pilaster.

CARRARA GLASS: Pigmented structural glass (commonly black) with a reflective finish, used commonly in the 1930s and 1940s.

CASEMENT WINDOW: Window with hinges at one side.

casement window

CINQUEFOIL: Decorative element representing a five-leafed form.

CLAPBOARD SIDING: Tapered wood boards lapped one over another to form horizontal siding.

CLERESTORY: Windows located at the highest point of an exterior wall, usually for sunlighting of the interior.

clapboard siding

COLUMN ELEMENTS:

CAPITAL: The top, crowning feature of a column.

PLINTH: The lower square form at the base of a column.

FLUTING: Concave grooves running vertically up a column.

CORBEL: An incremented wall projection used to support additional weight, most commonly constructed of brick.

CORNICE: The decorative projecting element at the top of an exterior wall.

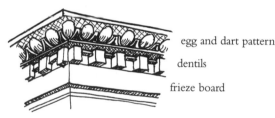

egg and dart pattern

dentils

frieze board

cornice

CRESTING: An ornamental ridging at the top of a wall or the peak of a roof.

CUPOLA: A small dome rising above a roof, usually with a band of small windows or openings.

DENTILS: Rectangular toothlike elements forming a decorative horizontal band in a cornice.

DORMER WINDOW: A window and window structure that project from the slope of a roof.

DOUBLE-HUNG WINDOW: Window with two sashes, one above the other, each of which slides vertically.

EAVE: Lower edge of a roof extending beyond the exterior wall.

ENGAGED COLUMN: A column integral with a wall surface, usually half round in form.

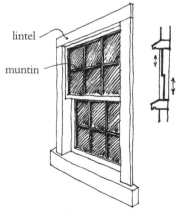

lintel

muntin

double-hung window

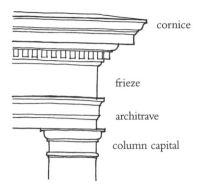

entablature

ENTABLATURE: The larger horizontal form setting on and spanning column capitals; it includes the architrave, the frieze, and the cornice.

ENTASIS: The subtle bulge in the vertical form of a classical column.

FACADE: Usually the front exterior elevation or face of a building.

FANLIGHT: Fan-shaped window, usually located over an entrance door.

FASCIA BOARD: A flat, horizontal board between moldings, typically used with classical styles.

FINIAL: A decorative ornament placed at the peak of a roof.

finial

FRIEZE: A decorative horizontal band located just below a cornice or gable.

GABLE: The triangular section of exterior wall just under the eaves of a double-sloped roof.

GAMBREL ROOF: A double-sloped barnlike roof, often associated with Dutch colonial architecture.

gambrel roof

HIP ROOF: A roof with slopes in the direction of each elevation, commonly in four directions.

KEYSTONE: Center stone in a masonry arch.

keystone

LABEL: A molding over a door or window.

LANTERN: A small turret with openings or windows all around, crowning a roof peak or dome.

hip roof

LINTEL: The horizontal support over a door or window.

MANSARD ROOF: A steeply sloped roof covering the exterior wall of the top floor of a building, named after the French architect Mansart and commonly associated with the Second Empire style.

lantern

mansard roof

MODILLIONS: A series of simple brackets usually found in a cornice.

MULLION: The vertical member separating windows, doors, or other panels set in a series.

MUNTIN: Wood pieces separating panes of glass in a window sash.

NEWEL POST: Wooden post located at the top or bottom of a stairway balustrade.

OCULUS: A round window.

ORIEL WINDOW: A projection from an upper floor of an exterior wall surface that contains one or more windows.

PALLADIAN WINDOW: Large window unit with an arched window in the center and smaller windows on each side.

PARAPET: An extension of an exterior wall projecting above the roof plane, commonly used to hide the plane of a low-sloped roof.

PEDIMENT: The gable form at the top of the facade of a classical style structure; also used over windows and doors.

PILASTER: A flat, rectangular partial column attached to a wall surface.

PITCH OF ROOF: The angle of a roof slope, expressed in a ratio of vertical to horizontal (e.g., 6:12).

PORTE COCHERE: A covered entrance for coaches or vehicles, usually attached to the side elevation of a building.

PORTICO: A covered porch attached to the main facade of a building, supported by classical order columns.

QUATREFOIL: A decorative element representing a four-leafed form.

QUOINS: Decorative stones at the corner of a building.

RAKE: The extension at the end of a gable or sloped roof.

RUSTICATION: Large stone blocks or stone forms with deep reveal masonry joints.

newel post

oculus

oriel window

palladian window

pediment

portico

quoins

segmental arch

SEGMENTAL ARCH: A partial arch form, usually made of brick and located over window or door openings.

SHAKE: Split wood shingle.

SHED ROOF: A single-pitched roof, often over a room attached to the main structure.

SIDELIGHT: Narrow window located immediately adjacent to an entrance door.

SINGLE-HUNG WINDOW: Window with two sashes, one above the other, the lower of which slides vertically.

SOFFIT: The underside of an architectural element.

TERRA-COTTA: Clay blocks or tiles, usually glazed, used for roof tiles or decorative surfaces.

TRACERY: Traditional intersecting ornamental work found in windows.

TRANSOM: A small window located immediately above a door.

TREFOIL: Decorative element representing a three-leafed form.

TURRET: A small tower located at the corner of a building, often containing a staircase.

VERGEBOARD: See *bargeboard*.

turret

Index

(Page numbers in italic refer to illustrations not otherwise referenced in text. Specific locales or structures are listed under U.S. state name heading.)